MALCOLM ANDREWS is a respected Australian author and journalist. In his 46-year career, he has worked for such media organisations as *The Australian*, the *Daily Telegraph* (Sydney), the *Daily Express* (London) and the Nine Network's current affairs program *Today*. In the early 1970s, he spent five years in Munich working for the US State Department at Radio Free Europe, which broadcast news behind the Iron Curtain.

As a freelance writer and broadcaster based on the New South Wales north coast, Andrews writes extensively on a wide variety of subjects for a whole spectrum of newspapers and magazines.

There is hardly a rugby league publication in the world for which he hasn't written at some stage during his career. He is currently Australian correspondent for the British weekly, *Rugby Leaguer & League Express*. And for two decades he wrote a page of trivia ('Footy Facts') in *Big League* magazine.

Andrews has written 28 books, many of them on rugby league, including the encyclopaedic *ABC of Rugby League*. He is a long-serving judge of the Golden Boot, awarded annually to the best rugby league player in the world.

GW00567354

MALCOLM ANDREWS

HARDMEN

RUGBY LEAGUE'S ROUGHEST, TOUGHEST AND MOST COURAGEOUS PLAYERS

ALLEN&UNWIN

SYDNEY·MELBOURNE·AUCKLAND·LONDON

Front cover, top: St George five-eighth Brian 'Poppa' Clay charges under a tackle by Balmain forward George Piper during a 1962 encounter at the Sydney Cricket Ground. *(Author's collection)*

Front cover, bottom: State of Origin hardmen . . . New South Wales captain Paul Gallen looks for support as he is seized by Queenslander Sam Thaiday. *(Copyright © Action Photographics)*

Back cover: Newtown Test second-rower Dick Townsend collars Western Suburbs centre Peter Burns in the 1918 City Cup final. It was the forerunner of the 'grapple tackle' that plagued the game in the early 21st century. *(Author's collection)*

Page ii: Sometimes players trying to be 'hardmen' come off second best . . . as Cronulla's Rick Bourke found out in 1978. When trying to tackle Wests Magpies fullback John Dorahy, Bourke found himself plunging head-first into the turf. *(Author's collection)*

First published in 2012

Allen & Unwin
Sydney, Melbourne, Auckland, London
83 Alexander Street
Crows Nest NSW 2065
Australia

Phone: (61 2) 8425 0100
Email: info@allenandunwin.com
Web: www.allenandunwin.com

Cataloguing-in-Publication details are available
from the National Library of Australia
www.trove.nla.gov.au

ISBN 978 1 74237 502 1

Internal design and typesetting by Voss Design

Cartoons by Pete Player
Caricatures by Ulf Kaiser

Printed and bound in Australia by Griffin Press

10 9 8 7 6 5 4 3

The paper in this book is FSC® certified. FSC® promotes environmentally responsible, socially beneficial and economically viable management of the world's forests.

To Ray Fletcher

A good mate and trusted Yorkshire colleague who keeps fighting with a courage greater than that shown by any of the rugby league players on whom he has reported for decades.

Contents

'I always enjoyed the game more when there was a body or two lying about. It made the job a bit more interesting.'

Vince Karalius on his rugged approach to rugby league

Acknowledgements

THIS BOOK would never have appeared without a lot of help from friends.

I am proud to say that I followed that respected sports writer Ian Heads OAM into journalism, a year behind him as a cadet with the *Daily Telegraph* and learning from his efforts. He gave me a few good ideas about hardmen. Louis Bonnery, the former coach of the French Test side, and Colin Hutton, the mentor of the Great Britain touring side that came to Australia in 1958 and taught our blokes a thing or two, related some wonderful anecdotes. Terry Liberopoulos of *Rugby League Review* delved into his records as did Sean Fagan from www.rl1908.com.au. Colleagues such as Tim Butcher, Graham Clay, Andy Wilson and Phil Caplan in England were very helpful. I suspect they wanted a good coverage of eras in which the Poms used to beat us at both football and fisticuffs. And Ray Fletcher was of immense help, not only with some wonderful anecdotes, but with the statistics from the series of Rothmans Year Books he and David Howes used to publish.

Keith Heap, a retired Port Macquarie teacher, sporting tragic, former bookmaker, golfing fanatic and good mate, gave me some great ideas and read most of the yarns after my hours at the computer keyboard—and offered a few suggestions.

Then there were the artists. Pete Player is one of the funniest cartoonists in the world. He has had me chuckling with several of my books which he helped illustrate. But he always asked, 'Is this one okay?' You betcha, Pete! And Ulf Kaiser was the finest caricaturist I have known. For a decade or so, after we worked together on *The Australian*, we used to collaborate on a series of profile pieces about famous people which we syndicated around Australia's major provincial newspapers. I wish we were still weekly partners in print.

'It was a real bloodbath. John O'Neill got 16 stitches in one of his shins. It was a huge gaping wound with blood everywhere. But he still couldn't keep the grin off his face.'

Father John Cootes on 'The Battle of Headingley' in 1970

Introduction

WHENEVER RUGBY LEAGUE FANS get to talking about their favourite game in the local pub or club, the conversation will invariably turn to 'the good old days'. Or maybe that should be 'the bad old days', when violence on the football pitch largely went unchecked. Stiff-arm tackles delivered with the sole aim of maiming the opposition player. Head-butts designed to smash noses and fracture cheekbones. Spear tackles that drove players headfirst into the turf with never a thought that the consequence could be a broken neck. And more fisticuffs than on a Monday night at the old Sydney Stadium at Rushcutters Bay.

When the going got tough, the tough got tougher. The ranks of rugby league around the world were peppered with hardmen—blokes who refused to take a backward step. If they were badly hurt they never showed it because that would encourage the opposition to single them out for extra treatment. As there were no replacements in 'the bad old days' players stayed on the pitch, ignoring the pain of broken jaws, shoulders, arms and . . . yes . . . occasionally broken legs!

Hardmen is the story of some of these players and many of the matches that have achieved iconic status in the sport—because of either the brutality dished out by the two sides or the courage of injured players who refused to leave their mates short-handed.

Then there were the famous matches—or to describe them more accurately, the infamous matches—where it was a case of every man for himself.

But this book is not just about thuggery. What about the courage of pint-sized Gold Coast star Preston Campbell, who played more than half a match in 2008 with a broken jaw but didn't tell any of his team-mates? A little bloke with a big heart! Other tiny fellows with big hearts, thrown around like rag dolls but bouncing up with a bravado that suggested they were ready for more . . . much more.

This book is not meant to be the definitive survey of rough, tough and courageous men. I have looked for the interesting anecdotes, rather than plough through the career records of the sport's hardmen. Ruben Wiki's penchant for drinking kava. Jack Harrison's Victoria Cross in the Great War, and Newtown's 'Nutsy' Bolt, whose body was not discovered until almost 70 years after that awful conflict. Herb Narvo getting knocked out one night to lose the Australian heavyweight boxing championship but turning up to play for St George the next afternoon. Lolo Mazon's refusal to be imprisoned by the Nazis during World War II. And Shane Webcke, for whom pain was never a problem.

Hardmen? They were definitely that!

Malcolm Andrews
Port Macquarie, New South Wales
June 2012

They didn't Massa with Johnston

RUGBY LEAGUE'S ROUGHEST AND TOUGHEST far too often plead innocence when sent for an early shower by referees. The tackle wasn't really high. The coathanger was only a reflex action. He was going down and that's why I connected with his melon. And, in the old days . . . it wasn't me. Once television arrived on the scene, the culprits were never again able to use that excuse.

In the case of William 'Massa' Johnston, a rugged ironworker in his day job, it was a legitimate legal defence. Massa—no one is quite sure how he got the nickname—was the first player sent off in a rugby league Test match in Australia. He was a member of New Zealand's professional All Blacks, who were derisively dubbed the All Golds by a blinkered *Sydney Morning Herald* journalist loyal to the rugby union code from which Massa and his team-mates defected. But they wore the description with pride.

In 1908, the All Golds were returning to New Zealand from Britain, where they had beaten the Northern Union (England) in their three-Test series, with Johnston scoring the winning try in the third (and deciding) encounter at Cheltenham. They stopped off in Australia to help out the fledgling professional code.

Johnston was dismissed by referee Tom Costello for smashing Australian captain Arthur 'Ash' Hennessy to the ground a few minutes after the start of the First Test at Sydney's Agricultural Ground, on 9 May. Costello did not see the incident, but was convinced Johnston was the fellow who felled Hennessy. However, the New Zealander was subsequently exonerated after one of the touch judges revealed Massa was the victim of mistaken identity and that another Kiwi was to blame.

One could readily understand why referee Costello jumped to the conclusion that Johnston was responsible. The former rugby union international had already made history in his homeland during 1904 as the first player to be sent off in the Ranfurly Shield provincial competition, when playing for the Otago side that lost 15–13 to Wellington. Even today the All Blacks Rugby Union website obliquely refers to Johnston's love of the biff, describing the 1.83 metre forward as a 'relatively big man for the era, who had a liking for the game's robust, physical aspects'. The biography goes on: 'His only appearances in representative rugby were six matches for Otago. That was sufficient for him to make an impact, both good and bad.'

Johnston was one of nine All Blacks from the 15-a-side code who were in the All Golds side. He has a special place in the annals of the then allegedly amateur code, having toured Great Britain in 1905 with the team known to this day in New Zealand as 'The Originals'. Indeed, he was one of the instigators in the breakaway movement and on the All Golds tour served as one of the management panel.

More than a century later, Massa Johnston is remembered for much more than his 'robust' play. The William 'Massa' Johnston Award is conferred on the Man of the Tournament at the annual Cheltenham Nines in England, the scene of his greatest triumph.

Such was his impact in Old Blighty that Wigan lured him back to England for two seasons before he had a final season with near-neighbours Warrington. He finally settled in Sydney and worked as the doorman at the Royal Agricultural Society's Members Pavilion at the ground where he was sent off in 1908. He had come the full circle!

Opposite: *A contemporary English caricature of the New Zealand All Golds enforcer Massa Johnston*

"Massa" Johnston

Stirred not shaken

HIS CONTEMPORARIES WERE IN AWE of the strength of rugby league pioneer Sid 'Sandy' Pearce. They also knew opposition players could not cope with him when he was on fire. But Pearce was a gentle man at heart. So often it needed a sly punch from a team-mate in a scrum to stir him up. Then there would be no stopping him.

His talents were best summed up in a speech by another great forward of that era, Frank Burge. Speaking at a memorial dinner in 1940, Burge explained:

> Football has never had a gamer, rougher, tougher nor more loyal team player. Old Sandy, a hooker, was easily the best I have ever seen in his position. The fact that [he was] thirty-eight when he toured England in 1921 is sufficient testimony to his skill. In the scrums Sandy would have those English hookers eating out of his hand. He would pack in with one arm loose, and as the ball came in he would whack the opposing hooker on the ear, then he would give them a twist, always getting the ball as it came in each time. Pearce had the strength of ten men. He neither drank nor smoked to any extent, and seldom swore. As part of his training he would spar two or three rounds with six or seven of us in succession, finishing each spar by allowing us to whale into his body with punches he made no attempt to block.

Burge also told of an example of Pearce's prodigious strength. Sandy once carried a 45-kilogram bag of oysters from Sussex Street on the western side of the Sydney CBD to Double Bay, more than 5 kilometres away, hardly breaking into a sweat as first he climbed the steep hill into Kings Cross and then the second incline out of Rushcutters Bay.

Pearce came from one of Australia's most famous sporting families,

Opposite: *Sandy Pearce was a great all-rounder.*

which provided great rowers, swimmers and rugby league players. They included Henry 'Bobby' Pearce, twice Olympic champion (1928 and 1932), unbeatable as a professional and regarded by most experts as the greatest sculler the world has ever known.

Sandy Pearce left school early to join the Double Bay family business established by his English-born father, a fisherman and ship's captain

as well as being a well-known sportsman in his own right. Sandy was a great all-rounder, excelling as a sculler, sailor, swimmer and boxer who sparred with the legendary Les Darcy. But his real forte was football, first in rugby union with Eastern Suburbs before being a leading light in the 1907 breakaway movement that formed rugby league. With his close friend from school days Dally Messenger, he turned out for New South Wales against A.H. Baskerville's touring New Zealand All Golds, who stopped over in Sydney en route to England. He played a full Test series against the tourists when they returned to Australia on their way home after their trail-blazing trip.

Pearce also made two Kangaroo tours of Britain. He went with the first side, in 1908–09. He declined a second Kangaroo visit three years later because he had been married for less than a year, but made the 1921–22 side, playing his final Test, at The Boulevard ground in Hull, when he was 38 years and 158 days old, a record that is unlikely ever to be beaten.

On that last visit, Pearce suffered a broken leg in the match against Dewsbury on the famous (but now extinct) Crown Flatt ground. The injury brought his splendid career to an end. But such was his popularity that, as he lay in hospital with a leg in plaster, hundreds of English fans went to visit him, many of them taking expensive presents. The visitors included one of the local players, who had promised him a Dewsbury jumper. Back in Sydney Sandy toyed with the idea of maybe having one last season but sanity prevailed. 'A man must retire from the hurly burly sometime,' he told a reporter from *The Referee* newspaper. 'Don't you think my time has come?'

After his playing days were over, Sandy Pearce turned to coaching the Sydney University side, an enthusiastic group of youngsters who often found the going tough against the seasoned professionals of the Sydney Premiership competition.

Pearce died suddenly at Double Bay in November 1930, nine years after his last Kangaroo tour. The cause of death was given as 'a strained heart'. He was just 47 years old and did not live to see his son Sid 'Joe' Pearce become a Test player, too.

The India rubber demon

FRANK BURGE WAS ONE OF THE GREATEST PLAYERS in the history of the game Down Under, earning a place in Australia's Team of the Century when the sport celebrated its 100th anniversary in 2008. He was arguably an even greater coach. And for many years he was a judge in the *Sun-Herald* Best and Fairest Player competition, at the time the definitive adjudication of the finest player in a Premiership season. So his comments on the merits of a contemporary had to be respected.

Burge admitted that Eastern Suburbs forward Jack 'Bluey' Watkins was the only tackler he ever feared. Burge's comments were echoed by a host of their peers. In every published description of Watkins, they expressed glowing admiration of his cover defence.

With his shock of curly red hair, Watkins was one of the real personalities of the early days of the code. He was a fiery individual noted for his footballing knowledge as well as his outstanding copybook tackling. Watkins played mainly as a lock, but was equally at home anywhere in the pack. Indeed, he began his 14-year stint with Eastern Suburbs during 1913 in the front row, even though at the time he weighed only 63 kilograms. That's 13 kilograms lighter than one of the smallest players of recent years in the National Rugby League, Preston Campbell, and 40 per cent less than Australia's Test lock Paul Gallen. But Watkins had no fear of anyone.

He made his Test debut against the touring British Lions in 1914, but then had his international career interrupted by World War I. He was back in the limelight soon after the Armistice. Watkins toured New Zealand in 1919, playing in all four Tests. And, despite having his Kangaroo tour in 1921 brought to a premature end by surgery on a cartilage injury, he managed to make another two Test appearances.

That was the year when *The Referee* newspaper in Sydney described him in colourful terms: 'Jack Watkins, a type apart as a forward, is a back and forward rolled up in one compact India-rubber man.'

Watkins last played for New South Wales against Queensland in 1924, but he remained a force in club football even after that, captaining Easts in 1926, at the age of 35. He played 137 first-grade games for the club and was a member of two of their Premiership-winning combinations (in 1913 and 1923).

His status in the game was ably summed up in the 1935 *Rugby League Annual*: 'A demon tackler, it is said of him that he grassed more wing-three-quarters than any other lock man.' British newspaper *The Sporting Chronicle*, not known for its hyperbole, commented after he toured with the Kangaroos: 'The best loose forward [lock] we have seen for some time.' In 1953, the respected Australian sporting magazine *Sports Novels* chose him as the best lock to have played in the first 45 years of the game in Australia. And there have been few better in the intervening years.

Ken McMorrow, a leading light in the administration of Sydney's Eastern Suburbs club, told *Rugby League Week* magazine of a conversation when the great will-o'-the-wisp half-back of the 1920s Duncan Thompson was at a Roosters home match during the early 1970s. Thompson entered the dressing room and was introduced to the players and officials. McMorrow recalled how an elderly man drew him aside and with a wistful look quietly noted: 'I made my name tackling him!' It was Bluey Watkins!

Giants among giants

IT WAS NO WONDER they called Ben Gronow 'Big Ben'. He was a huge man, standing tall like the clock tower on London's Houses of Parliament to which he was compared. A stonemason by trade, he was more than 1.8 metres tall and wore size 10 shoes. One of the most vivid memories his grandson David had of him was his huge hands—'great for the perfect hand-off and picking up small children like me!'

One of Gronow's team-mates in the forward pack for the Huddersfield club and the Northern Union (England) was another giant, Doug 'Duggie' Clark, later to become a professional wrestler. David Gronow explains that before every match Ben and Doug would contact the opposing pack and ask the question: 'What's it going to be today, rough or smooth?' Tactics were decided according to the reply. In many matches when their opponents failed to give an answer, they were glad to do so after a few minutes of action, pleading: 'Let's have it smooth!' Or that's the way they tell it around Huddersfield.

It took a superb side to win all four Cups in Britain during the same season. All told, only three ever managed it. Huddersfield was the second in 1914–15 (seven seasons after Hunslet became the first and 13 years before Swinton became the only other). It will never happen again as these days they don't have county competitions, just the Challenge Cup and the Super League Premiership.

They dubbed the 1914–15 Huddersfield side 'The Team of All Talents'. And so it was! It was crammed with internationals and others who were unlucky not to have worn their country's colours. The legendary centre Harold Wagstaff was captain. Aussie try-scoring freak Alby Rosenfeld was one wing, with another Test man Stan Moorehouse on the other. Welsh wizard Johnny Rogers was at five-eighth. Fred Longstaff was the lock-forward. Jack Chilcott played either at prop or in the back row. And, of course, there were Gronow and Clark. While they weren't internationals, the goalkicking whiz Major Holland was at full-back and Tommy Gleeson, from the Glebe club in Sydney's inner-west, who had

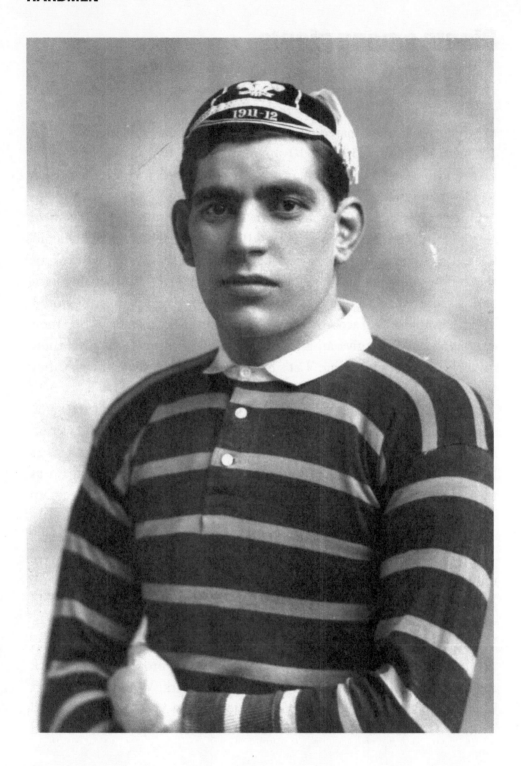

played opposite Dally Messenger in the 1911 grand final, was Wagstaff's centre partner.

It was a great era in which Huddersfield reigned supreme—and but for World War I, when the Challenge Cup was suspended, the club may have had an even more impressive record. As it was they won the Cup three times—beating Wakefield Trinity 6–nil at Thrum Hall (Halifax) in 1913, St Helens 37–3 two years later at Watersheddings (Oldham), and Wigan 21–10 at Headingley (Leeds) in 1920 after the Cup tussles returned. They figured in four straight Championship Finals between 1912 and 1915 and again in 1923—winning three times (1912, 1913 and 1915). In 1913 Clark scored a hat-trick of tries as Huddersfield beat Wigan 29–2. And in 1915 Gronow scored two tries and kicked seven goals when beating Leeds 35–2.

Wagstaff, Gronow and Clark all made their Test debuts against the 1911–12 Kangaroos and were to play vital roles for the Northern Union in clashes with the Australians over the next decade.

Gronow was a goalkicking ex–Welsh rugby union international from Brigend, who was capped four times in 1910 and had the honour of being the player who kicked off in the first ever Test held on the famous Twickenham ground, on 15 January. Later that year he signed for Huddersfield for £120. He made two tours to Australia with the Lions, in 1920 and 1924. On the first he was in fine form, scoring two tries and kicking 65 goals (for 136 points) in just 16 appearances. He was 35 years of age when he returned in 1924, one of the oldest players ever to make a Lions tour.

It seems that while on that final tour Gronow was scouting around for an Australian club with which to play. The following year he and his young family emigrated. Research by historian Sean Fagan revealed his decision was based on the need to improve the health of his eldest son, who suffered from bronchitis and needed a drier climate. It is believed

Opposite: Ben Gronow, wearing the cap he won when Huddersfield, the so-called Team of All Talents, won the English Championship during the 1911–12 season

the family originally stayed with Gronow's former Huddersfield team-mate Tommy Gleeson, and he planned to play for Gleeson's old club, Glebe. Instead he ended up playing for Grenfell, in the central-west of New South Wales, cementing his place as the only British Test star to have played for an Australian club in the first 50 years of the game Down Under.

Fagan's research disclosed that Gronow played his first game for Grenfell (wearing royal blue jerseys) against Caragabal in a friendly match on 30 May 1926. Grenfell won 37–3. A local newspaper reported:

> Gronou [sic] was the man on whom all interest was centred. The big fellow showed great form with the boot, landing five goals in conditions much against goal-kicking. In view of big matches ahead he was content to watch his men, and to instruct them, and never really looked a trier. It looks as though Gronou will find a team of our chaps.

Fagan explained how homesickness took hold among the Gronow family members and the decision was soon made to return to England. But, before leaving, Gronow convinced Grenfell's winger, Ernie Mills, to travel with them back to England with the offer of a contract with Huddersfield. Mills went on to be one of Huddersfield's most prolific try-scorers between 1927 and 1935.

Although he neither asked for nor gave any favours on the football field, Gronow was a real pin-up figure, with his own fan club—a rarity among rugby league players even today. And off the pitch he was anything but the hardman who frightened opponents on both sides of the globe. His grandson David recalled:

> He was a quiet, gentle man and a teetotaller all his life. Nothing seemed to faze him, although my father said he was a strict

Opposite: Duggie Clark (pictured) and Ben Gronow made a fearsome combination in Great Britain's Test side

disciplinarian when the boys were growing up at home. Granddad Ben used to chase them upstairs when they annoyed him. Yet my dad maintained he never caught them!

DUGGIE CLARK was signed from Brookland Rovers in 1909 for £30 and was to spend the next 16 seasons playing at Huddersfield's famous Fartown ground. He toured Australasia with the Lions in both 1914 and 1920. The second visit was quite remarkable as he had been discharged after World War I with a 95 per cent disability certificate after being gassed twice on the Western Front, where he also won the Military Medal for heroism. His most dramatic effort on the football field was in the so-called Rorke's Drift Test, the decider at the Sydney Cricket Ground in 1914 (see 'England Expects').

In total Clark played 11 Tests, against Australia and New Zealand. He later—disability and all—turned out for many years on the professional wrestling circuit. He was wrestling in Australia in 1936, at the same time as the Lions were making a rugby league tour. The British players were on hand to cheer him on at Leichhardt Stadium in Sydney when he defended his British Empire Heavyweight Championship against Australian champ, the Russian-born Tom Lurich. The newspaper advertisement for the bout trumpeted:

> Despite Clark's prowess when an English Rugby League International, he ranks even higher as a WRESTLER. The English Rugby League Tourists will OFFICIALLY be present at tonight's match. Hear them render from the ring their "SONG OF ENGLAND".

Their rousing chorus was no help. Clark lost his title to Lurich.

Opposite: Duggie Clark poses next to his wrestling and rugby league trophies. Don't you just love the carving set in the foreground?

England expects...

Arguably, more people learned about the Zulu wars from the 1964 movie *Zulu* than from any well-meaning schoolteacher. You remember, don't you? Michael Caine's character, in his unmistakable accent, uttering the immortal words: 'Zulus. Thousands of them!' Actually, it was Nigel Green's character and that wasn't the exact quote. But who are we to expose ourselves as pedants.

After all, the heroic stand by 139 British soldiers against a 4000-strong Zulu horde at the South African mission station of Rorke's Drift in January 1879 has become part of British folklore, with 11 soldiers honoured with the Victoria Cross, the most ever in one military encounter.

And, journalists being what they are, it was inevitable that one of their craft would eventually dub a battle on the rugby league field after that famous battle with the Zulus. What is surprising is that it took 35 years for that anonymous journalist's creativity to come to the fore.

It referred to the deciding conflict in the 1914 Ashes series. No team in the history of international rugby league has shown the courage and determination to overcome all odds to equal that of England's Third Test combination. Ten exhausted men (there were no replacements allowed in those days) held off 13 eager Australians for most of the second half to score a 14–6 victory and clinch the Ashes.

The match was a controversial one even before the kick-off, with England* only taking the field under protest.

The tourists had gone into the First Test at the Agricultural Ground in Sydney the previous Saturday under-strength, having lost both full-backs, Oldham's Alf Wood and Wigan's Gwyn Thomas, through injury. In desperation they played Leeds prop-forward Billy Jarman in his Test debut as 'custodian'. It mattered not! The visitors outclassed the Australians 23–5, scoring five tries to a lone touchdown by the home side in the closing minutes of the game.

---

* The side was officially known as the Northern Union, but, despite there being Welshmen in the touring squad, newspaper reporters from both Britain and Australia referred to the Test side as representing England.

The Second Test was held only two days later, on the King's Birthday Holiday. It was the first Test to be played on the Sydney Cricket Ground and attracted a record-breaking 55,000 spectators. Three of the England stars—the Huddersfield pair of Stan Moorhouse and Jack Chilcott and Wigan's Bert Jenkins—had suffered injuries in the opening Test and were unable to play, but Thomas was back. The tourists led 7–nil early in the action but soon after half-time they lost winger Jack Robinson (Rochdale Hornets) with a fractured collarbone. The Australians capitalised and went on to win 12–7 and level the series.

Despite a mounting injury toll, the tourists were unperturbed as the Third Test was not supposed to be played until they returned from a visit to New Zealand. Then the Australian authorities dropped a bombshell. They rescheduled the decider for the following Saturday, when the tourists had been due to take on New South Wales. The British were livid. Three Tests in eight days with a limited squad carrying a long list of injuries! They would not agree.

The Australians, not to be dissuaded, cabled the English authorities in Leeds to explain that the event would lose much of its crowd appeal if left until after the New Zealand section of the tour. And the English hierarchy agreed, ordering tour manager John Clifford to go ahead with the game. The cable from Britain concluded with the famous quote from Admiral Horatio Nelson before the Battle of Trafalgar: 'England expects that every man will do his duty.'

In a stirring dressing-room speech before the clash, Clifford told his charges they were 'playing for England's honour, playing for right versus wrong!' And what an honourable display they turned in.

Full-back Wood, back after missing the first two encounters, took to the field with a broken nose. Winger Frank Williams injured a leg in the second minute of the game. He stayed on but was a virtual passenger. Soon after, Huddersfield forward Duggie Clark broke a thumb, but he, too, battled on.

Britain led 9–nil at the interval. The second half had been underway for only a few minutes when Clark broke clear and headed for the tryline. The great Aussie half-back Arthur 'Pony' Halloway raced across to tackle him. Clark went to palm him off but, wary of his injured thumb, decided to smash Halloway out of his path instead. Halloway ducked and Clark, off balance, crashed heavily to the ground and badly fractured a collarbone. He had it strapped, but eventually could not continue. Minutes later, Williams was again injured and forced off the field. Oldham centre Billy Hall followed soon after, with concussion.

Ten men and 30 minutes to go! Captain Harold Wagstaff and his courageous cohorts rose to the occasion. Magnificent defence repeatedly kept the 13 Australians at bay. Then, with 20 minutes remaining, Wagstaff cut through and sent the ball to forward Chick Johnson, who was playing as a makeshift winger. Just inside the Australians' half, Johnson dropped the ball to the turf and began dribbling it soccer-style. Halloway stood rooted to the ground, seemingly mesmerised. Winger Wally Messenger (brother of the great Dally Messenger) did not know how to counter Johnson's tactics. Johnson finally kicked past full-back Howard Hallett, regathered and, fending off South Sydney back-rower Billy Cann, fell across the tryline to score. Wood booted the conversion and the tourists had an unlikely 14–nil lead.

The Australians began to panic but a try to Messenger gave them a slim hope. However, 'catch-up football' resulted in error after error, including one in which Tedda Courtney spilled the ball when over the tryline. Hall came back for the final few minutes, but by then the British had the game in their keeping and even a late try to Australia's captain and centre, Sid Deane, couldn't bridge the gap.

The visitors had covered themselves in glory and, just like the soldiers at the original Rorke's Drift encounter, had earned themselves a place in British folklore. But they never got to dine out on their success. Just over three weeks later the world was plunged into the Great War, the most devastating military conflict in history, in which more than nine million soldiers lost their lives.

The awful day Nutsy Bolt died

ONE OF THE TOUGHEST of all the tens of thousands of blokes who have pulled on a rugby league jumper over the century and a bit of the game's existence is a player virtually unknown except to historians. He was a centre called Herbert Bolt, better known by his nickname, 'Nutsy'.

Nutsy lived in the Sydney suburb of Bexley, these days in Dragons territory but back then part of the catchment area for the Newtown side. He worked as a brickmaker, which fitted in well with the working-class roots of the famous Newtown Bluebags. Bolt played 52 matches for the Bluebags from 1912 to 1915 and was usually first into the melee when a brawl broke out. He was not the biggest of men but he had plenty of ticker and always gave as good as he got, even when standing toe-to-toe with the largest of front-row forwards.

Twice in 1913 Nutsy pulled on the light blue jersey for New South Wales, playing alongside the legendary Dally Messenger when the state side went to Queensland. In the second of the encounters, Nutsy was sent off for brawling. He didn't quibble with the Queensland referee's decision, with a contemporary newspaper report revealing the action of the referee received 'general endorsement'.

At the end of the 1915 season Nutsy Bolt prepared for a fight of a different kind. The day after the Bluebags were eliminated from the Premiership, he headed for the Agricultural Ground next to the Sydney Cricket Ground and began training with the 55th Battalion of the Australian Imperial Forces (AIF). Within a year Corporal Bolt would be fighting one of the bloodiest battles of World War I, at Fromelles on the Western Front.

It was there that the Australians were virtually used as cannon fodder by the leadership of the British Army. A miscalculation by Lieutenant-General Richard Haking, commander of the British Corps, and one of his colleagues, General Sir Charles Monro, resulted in the worst day in the history of the AIF. At dusk on 19 July the pair ordered an attack on German positions even though those taking part would be sitting ducks. The carnage continued until the next day.

Nutsy Bolt was one of 5533 Australians who were killed or injured in that awful 24 hours. Some 1547 British troops were also gunned down as German machine-gun fire tore through their ranks. The Germans lost fewer than 1000. A contemporary report described the horror:

> Men were cut in two by streams of bullets that swept like whirling knives. It was the charge of the Light Brigade once more, but more terrible, more hopeless.

A statement by Private Frank Johnston of the 55th Battalion, who survived the Battle of Fromelles, described Bolt's death:

> On the morning of 20 July 1916 at about 5 am at Fleurbaix, Nutsy and I were close to one another when we were attacked by the Germans. He got more than six of them with his bayonet and the butt of his rifle, when he got a bullet through the head. He fell instantly being killed outright. He was as game as any man.

Nutsy's body was buried in a mass grave that was lost in the mists of time.

The 22-year-old left a widow, Jennie, and a baby daughter, Monica. His fellow Bluebags pulled out all stops to raise money for them. There was a parade through Newtown to Erskineville Oval, where a series of unique events were held, including chopping up an effigy of the Kaiser. The winner was the bloke who got the biggest piece of the German ruler. There was enough money raised to look after Jennie and Monica for years to come.

In 2008 the mass grave was discovered and the following year the bodies exhumed. Nutsy's remains were identified by DNA. In 2010, on the 90th anniversary of the battle, he was formally laid to rest in his own grave in a new military cemetery at Fromelles. Baby Monica's daughter, Josephine Shelley, by then 60 years old, was on hand with several other descendants to honour Nutsy Bolt.

And at Henson Park two days earlier they remembered Nutsy and a lower-grade Bluebags player, Alex Clingan, who was also killed in the battle, before the Jets, as they are now known, took on Wentworthville in the New South Wales Cup. A bugler played the 'Last Post' and there was a minute's silence.

Lest we forget.

Nutsy Bolt and his wife, Jennie, and daughter, Monica

World's bravest footballer

AUSTRALIANS NEVER GOT TO SEE JACK HARRISON, the bravest rugby league player in history. But they nearly did. The Hull winger—some critics suggest he was one of the greatest the sport has ever known—was chosen to tour Australia in 1914. But Kaiser Wilhelm II of Germany had other ideas. The sabre-rattling of the Kaiser and his allies helped bring on World War I, the rugby league tour was cancelled and Jack Harrison never made it through the so-called war to end all wars.

But his bravery in the battlefields of the Somme was exceptionable—winning a Military Cross before earning a posthumous Victoria Cross. Many other footballers died, but none in such exceptional circumstances. Few soldiers have ever won a Military Cross. Few have won a Victoria Cross. Even fewer have won both.

His father, a boilermaker on the Hull shipyards, worked hard to give Jack Harrison a good education that earned him a job as a schoolteacher. But it was on the football field that he excelled. During the 1914–15 football season he scored 52 tries, a club record that still stands almost 100 years later. Indeed, in two seasons with the Humberside club he touched down for 106 tries in 116 matches.

Soon after the birth of his son, Jack Junior, Harrison volunteered to fight against Germany.

On 25 March 1917, Lieutenant Harrison displayed conspicuous gallantry leading a patrol into no-man's-land and in this action he was awarded the Military Cross. The citation noted:

He handled his platoon with great courage and skill, reached his objective under the most trying conditions and captured a prisoner. He set a splendid example throughout.

Less than six weeks later, on 3 May, his brigade attacked the German lines at Oppy Wood, a well-defended locale that was considered a vital area in the battle. Harrison's platoon was pinned down by heavy machine-gun fire. Harrison, armed with only a pistol and several hand grenades, threw himself at the enemy. Members of his platoon looked on as he dodged between shell holes, weaving in and out of the barbed wire towards several German machine-gun posts. His platoon watched as he fell after tossing a grenade that blew up one of the machine-gun posts. Harrison was never seen again. He had been killed by the machine gunners he had silenced.

'His self-sacrifice and absolute disregard of danger was an inspiring example to all,' said the citation for his Victoria Cross. A fund was set up in Hull to provide for his son's education. Jack Junior went on to serve in World War II and was also killed, during the evacuation of Dunkirk.

A memorial plinth for Jack Harrison VC MC was unveiled at KC Stadium, the home ground of Hull FC, on VE (Victory in Europe) Day, 8 May 2003.

A rare photograph of Jack Harrison VC in his Hull football gear

In the early twenty-first century, the media zeroed in on what they claimed was a defensive innovation that should be immediately outlawed. The so-called grapple tackle! But was it so new?

Terry Williams, the rugby league historian who has more facts about the famous Newtown club at his fingertips than you can poke a stick at, unearthed this photo for his 2008 book *Through Blue Eyes*. It shows an incident in the final of the City Cup in 1918 when Newtown's future Australian Test second-rower Dick Townsend grabbed Western Suburbs centre Peter Burns in what looks suspiciously like a grapple tackle. And it didn't earn a penalty from the famous referee Tom McMahon. Williams reckoned one could only wonder at the incident, as Burns had played with Townsend for Newtown in 1915 and 1916 before joining Wests.

THE BIRTH OF THE
GRAPPLE TACKLE

Filling opponents with fear

AUB KELLY WAS HARDLY A BIG FELLOW. That's probably why his St George team-mates called him 'Jockey'. But he was a fearsome tackler, so brutal in defence that in 1928 a sportswriter dubbed him 'The Terror'. Both names remained with Kelly for the rest of his life; which name you used depended on how you felt about him. During that same season in a June match against Western Suburbs he was one of four players—three from St George and one from Wests—sent off by referee J. Miller after an ugly confrontation described by *The Bulletin* as 'one of the roughest and foulest exhibitions of football that has ever disgraced that historic arena, the Sydney Cricket Ground'. The Terror stomped on the face of the Wests full-back Frank 'Skinny' McMillan and was suspended for the rest of the season.

The official report by the New South Wales Rugby League noted:

> The Match of the Day was marked by a few episodes that turned the match into a farce, more or less, through the actions of several of the players losing self-possession that should have been part of the equipment of very true sportsmen.

Well, that's one way of saying it!

Nevertheless there was no denying Jockey Kelly was a tough competitor. The official history of the St George club published a description of him written by an unnamed journalist in 1928:

> He was last year considered almost universally the greatest forward in Australia, and one of the greatest the League code has produced. He filled many an opponent with genuine fear. He was greatest as a destroyer and some of his diving tackles will never be forgotten by those who were thrilled by them.

The St George history also had team-mate Ernie McCormack years later telling a story about Kelly's courage.

McCormack said:

I played with him one day when he dislocated his shoulder. He didn't worry about first-aid, but raced to the goal posts and bumped the shoulder back into position. He finished the game.

No ordinary men

STORIES ABOUT THE STRENGTH AND COURAGE of Mick Madsen read like something out of a 'Boys' Own Annual'. The Toowoomba prop of the 1920s and 1930s (baptised Peter, but known to everyone as Mick) was one of the most feared in the history of the game . . . both in Australia and Britain. The great half-back and even greater coach, Duncan Thompson, who played with him in Queensland, recalled one of those anecdotes:

> The powerful torso all but bursting his jersey, the craggy features, one could believe the legends that grew around him—such stories as standing with a 300-pound bale of wool on his shoulders while directing a passing motorist to Toowoomba.

Most stories claim that Madsen balanced the bale on his left shoulder while waving directions with his right hand. Think of it this way: many of the modern-day fitness freaks of rugby league who spend hours upon hours in the gym can but dream about bench-pressing 300 pounds [140 kilograms], let alone nonchalantly hoisting it on one or even both of their shoulders.

Then there was the amazed sporting journalist in England who reported on Madsen's performance against St Helens Recreation on the 1929–30 Kangaroo tour:

> A big, stocky Australian prop, [Madsen] barged through in typical style to block the opposition pack, giving his backs room to move with the ball. Suddenly, out of the clouds, he collected a smash in the face that would have hospitalised an ordinary man. But Madsen was no ordinary man. He did not fall down, but grimaced, spat out a tooth and kept playing. And his jaw felt heavy. The following day English doctors confirmed that the Australian prop had broken his jaw in two places.

Years later Madsen was to explain: 'We played it tough in those days. But that's the way I liked it.'

Mick Madsen tries to break the defence in the Kangaroos match against the Oldham Roughyreds at the latter's home ground Watersheddings in Manchester on the 1933 tour of Britain.

Madsen was never one of those players who made the headlines, despite those colourful stories about his sturdy resilience. And when, in 1982, the respected *Rugby League Week* magazine got eight experts to pick the greatest Australian side of all time, many critics were surprised by his inclusion. Except those who played with and against him!

He was a big man compared with other players of his era, standing 186 centimetres tall and weighing 96 kilograms. He had monstrous 'Popeye' arms that no one could miss seeing because, unlike most of his contemporaries, he played with the sleeves of his jumper rolled up well above the elbow.

Madsen made his Test debut in 1929, on the first of his two Kangaroo tours to Britain, turning out in the first two encounters, at Craven Park in Hull and Headingley, Leeds, before breaking his jaw. He played all three Tests when Britain toured Australia in 1932. And he was a dominant figure in all three Tests on the 1933–34 Kangaroo tour, captaining Australia in the second encounter, at Headingley, when the tour skipper Frank 'Skinny' McMillan was out injured.

The big fellow made his final appearance in the international arena in the deciding Test of the 1936 series, in Sydney. Intriguingly, he was chosen as hooker, even though he had never played in that position in the past. He refused to play until he was convinced that his good mate Arthur Folwell, who was expected to fill the hooker's role, was suffering from influenza. Folwell, a fine sport, was bitterly disappointed at not being chosen, but lied to Madsen about his alleged flu to avoid any embarrassing incident. Ray Stehr, one of the props with Madsen that day, relied on a fishing cliché in a scathing remark about the selectors' stupidity: 'Teak-tough Mick was one of the greatest forwards in the game's history. But he couldn't hook a yellowtail.'

PLAYING ON THE OTHER SIDE OF THE WORLD during this era was a man just as tough as Mick Madsen. Joe Thompson had an incredible strength acquired as a coalminer toiling in the pits of south-west Wales, backbreaking work begun when he was just 13 years old.

He had come to the attention of the Leeds club when playing a 1923 rugby union Test against England at the famous Twickenham Stadium just outside London. A contemporary newspaper reported how, at one stage, the Welsh back-rower walked to the touchline, spat out a few broken teeth, and then went back into the game 'as though it was nothing at all out of the ordinary'. Forwards didn't keep their front teeth for long in those days. It seemed a wasted effort as Wales lost the match 7–3. However, it was to be Thompson's only international appearance in the so-called amateur code. The Leeds scouts swooped quickly and within weeks he was playing rugby league.

At first Thompson wondered whether he had made a big mistake in switching codes. Late in life he recalled: 'So fast was my first game, against Huddersfield, that I thought I was playing in a seven-a-side match.' He soon adapted—much to the dismay of opponents in both hemispheres. To this day he remains the only forward to play in three different British touring sides that won the Ashes in Australia (in 1924, 1928 and 1932).

Unlike many forwards of that era he used his boots legally. He was an expert at dribbling the ball soccer-fashion—at times for at least half the length of the field. And there were few who could match him when kicking for goal. It was only the fact that he toured Australia with the record-breaking legend Jim Sullivan that he did not get to show Aussie spectators just how accurate he was. In fact, on the club scene he outscored Sullivan in both the 1927–28 and 1929–30 seasons and kicked a total of 921 goals during his ten years in rugby league.

Thompson was also acclaimed for his ability at lock-forward to wheel the scrum when the ball was being lost so it would emerge into the hands of his half-back.

THOMPSON AND MADSEN were to figure prominently in one of the most brutal rugby league matches in history—the Second Test of the 1932 Ashes series, remembered as 'The Battle of Brisbane' (see following story).

The Battle of Brisbane

Anglo–Australian Test matches are always tough encounters. At times they become so tough they border on atrociously brutal. Such was the case in the Second Test of the 1932 series, a clash dubbed 'The Battle of Brisbane'.

The First Test, played before 70,204 people at the Sydney Cricket Ground on the Monday of the King's Birthday Holiday weekend in June, indicated Britain and Australia were evenly matched in football ability (the tourists scraped home 8–6). The Battle of Brisbane, 12 days later, showed they were just as close in thuggery. The Australians' team manager, the legendary Harry Sunderland, described it as 'the hardest, fiercest and most rugged' of matches and obliquely referred to some 'disgusting incidents'.

J.C. Davis, editor of *The Referee* sporting newspaper, writing under the pen-name of 'The Cynic', summed it up:

> The forward battle developed on tornadic lines, players being flattened by the cyclonic tackling of heavy, powerful, well-trained men with the full rigor of give-all, take-all tactics. It became the most desperate and rugged game imaginable. Players were strewn like dead men on the field, or were carried off to touch-lines to recover. They were chiefly Australians.

His description was echoed by Sunderland: 'Trainers stood on the sidelines with buckets of water, reviving men as they were knocked out.'

The Australians certainly came off much worse than their opponents. Their scoreboard of injuries read:
- second-rower Dan Dempsey, a broken wrist
- half-back Hec Gee, knocked out, with a badly gashed mouth
- centre Eric Norman, severe concussion
- prop Frank O'Connor, split eye
- full-back Frank McMillan, knocked out
- five-eighth Eric Weissel, torn ligaments in an ankle.

The violence was undoubtedly provoked by some astonishing gamesmanship by Sunderland. Before the match he visited the England dressing room and insulted the tourists with a curt dressing-down on how they should approach each play-the-ball. He used two-shilling coins to represent the Australians and pennies for the British and pointed out what they had been doing 'illegally' in the First Test. The visitors were livid and their captain, Jim Sullivan, told Sunderland in no uncertain terms where he could shove his pennies and two-bob bits. And the British carried their anger onto the field.

The Australians got off to a wonderful start, with a try to Gee (converted by Weissel) in the opening seconds of the game. In the 12th minute, Gee darted from the base of the scrum, some 20 metres from the visitors' line, and sent winger Joe Wilson (from Ipswich Brothers) over for Australia's second try. The conversion was missed, but Australia had a handy 8–nil lead.

Moments later the fighting erupted when referee Joe Simpson disallowed what seemed to be a legitimate try by Alf Ellaby. It was a spectacular effort by the great British winger. But Simpson ruled there had been obstruction on Ellaby's opposite number Cliff Pearce. From then on almost every tackle produced a foul . . . a punch, a kick, a high stiff-arm tackle or a combination of all three.

A penalty goal to Weissel stretched the Aussies' lead, but early in the second half the tourists hit back with tries to Leeds winger Stan Smith and Wakefield Trinity five-eighth Ernie Pollard, reducing the lead to 10–6. With the Australian ranks being decimated it seemed only a matter of time before the British took the lead—and, with victory, the Ashes.

But the Aussies, battered and bloodied, refused to throw in the towel.

As Smith looked likely to score his second try, the Australian defenders smashed him into the corner post. The famous Huddersfield centre Stanley Brogden was about to touch down when Australia's lock Frank O'Connor unbelievably managed to punch the ball out of his hands.

Then, as the seconds ticked down to full-time, came the defining moment of the afternoon. Weissel, Dempsey and Gee were all on the sideline being treated for injuries when a bomb (in those days called an up-and-under) was spilled by Sullivan well inside Australia's half. Weissel and Gee abandoned their treatment and returned to the fray. Weissel got to the loose ball first and, ignoring his injured ankle, half ran, half hobbled 70 metres down the field only to be caught 10 metres from the line. From the ensuing play-the-ball, Gee was able to score.

Against all the odds, the depleted Australian line-up had won the Test 15–6. But, as one critic wrote, 'It wasn't clear who won the fight.'

When men were beasts

RAY STEHR never let facts get in the way of a good quote. In the late 1970s this wild man of rugby league approached me to ghost-write his autobiography. 'I'll tell you my story. You think up the quotes to embellish it and I'll put my name to them,' he said to me in all sincerity. But I would not have needed to do so. Stehr was without peer as far as classic one-liners were concerned. We need hardly wonder how he would have fared in this modern age where television relies so heavily on such pithy, whimsical throwaway lines. He would have been a megastar.

Sadly, in the 1970s, publishers had not yet discovered how well rugby league books could sell—so we never got a book shaped by the fertile mind of Ray Stehr. Instead, we have to rely on snippets of his newspaper musings published under such headlines as 'When Men Were Beasts' and a brief personal outline of his career penned for a book self-published by prolific sports journalist Jack Pollard, *Rugby League the Australian Way*.

But Stehr is not remembered for his fertile mind. He honed a place in rugby league history with his no-nonsense approach to life. To suggest Ray Stehr was a rebel is like saying Julia Roberts was a pretty woman. One of the finest prop-forwards the game has known, he gave no quarter on or off the field. He locked horns with some of the most brutal players in both hemispheres—and usually came out on top in the melees. And both as a player and later as a media figure, he had running verbal battles with referees, tour managers and officials.

Yet as a kid Stehr looked destined to spend his entire life in a wheelchair. He'd had a few games of junior football with the Warialda Bantams in the New England area of northern New South Wales. But at the age of eight, a blood clot formed at the base of his spine and he couldn't move his legs. Doctors put his lower body in a plaster cast and strapped him to a bed. And that's the way he stayed—completely immobilised—for around 12 months, with no cure in sight. Friends suggested to his parents that maybe they should look beyond accepted medical procedures. And, as a last resort, they did.

Stehr explained:

A Chinese herbalist [R.J. Sing] in Oxford Street, Sydney, went to work on me with all sorts of foul-tasting exotic brews and potions. To the delight of my mum and dad, this ancient treatment worked and the clot was dissolved. I still had to wear a corset for a while, but I could walk again . . . and then run . . . and then eventually play footy. Many years later, in 1933, I was walking in King Street near Hyde Park with some Eastern Suburbs team-mates after we had been chosen in the Kangaroo team to tour Britain. If I remember correctly, [second-rower] big Joe Pearce was one and [half-back] Vic Thicknesse was another. I suddenly noticed the old Chinese bloke who had cured me walking on the other side of the road. My mates thought I had lost it . . . gone crazy . . . when I let out a yell, sprinted across the street and started pumping the old man's hand. They had no idea how much I owed him.

Stehr was in the headlines almost from the day he pulled on his first Eastern Suburbs jumper. After a few games in reserve grade in 1928, he was called into the top side for a trial match against Newcastle. He was only 15 years old, the youngest player ever to appear in a Sydney first-grade rugby league side. A story is told about that selection. It may have been apocryphal but it is too good not to repeat. Stehr was playing marbles with schoolmates in a back lane near his home in the suburb of Paddington on the day the Easts officials found themselves a man short for the encounter. An official discovered where he was playing marbles, took the youngster home to get his gear and then drove him up to Newcastle. Stehr went well and, from the following season until his retirement 17 years later, he was a permanent first-grader.

It was a vintage era for Easts—especially from 1935 to 1937, three seasons in which they lost only one game. Stehr was only 20 when

Opposite: *An iconic photograph of Ray Stehr showing his rugged tackling style in a club game for Eastern Suburbs*

chosen for the 1933–34 Kangaroo tour—and a cocky 20-year-old at that. Needless to say, the English forwards were keen to knock that cockiness out of him. Just 15 minutes into his first appearance on tour, against St Helens Recreation, he was creamed by a stiff-arm tackle that left him unconscious.

'It was the first time I had been laid out on a football field, an event that made me more than a bit cranky about English methods [of tackling],' he noted. A dose of smelling salts quickly brought him back to reality but he remained dazed for the rest of the afternoon and later could not remember much about what happened during the match. That's why we can take a story he wrote years later for *The Sun* newspaper in Sydney with a grain of salt. Dan Dempsey, who had played hooker in the same game, was carried off with blood spurting from a cut over one eye, the result of a kick in the face in what Stehr claimed was 'as vicious and foul an incident as I have ever seen'. Stehr went on to relate how Dempsey suddenly sat up and held the edges of the gash together. 'Put a f***ing safety pin in it and let me get back out there,' he demanded. Nice yarn, Ray!

The young Aussie firebrand was soon matching the hard-headed old English forwards at their own game. Against Warrington he was sent off for flattening Test forward Jack 'Cod' Miller, who was later to go on to make a then-record 526 appearances for the Lancashire club in his 20-year career. 'By the time I got home to Australia I was well and truly versed in the mayhem that can occur in the name of football,' Stehr said. And heaven help anyone who stood in his way. There are no official statistics concerning send-offs in Australian Premiership and representative games but Stehr must have gone very close to setting a record—and often feigned injury in order to have an opposition player dismissed.

He resumed his running battle with the British when the Lions toured Australasia in 1936. Stehr's old antagonist 'Cod' Miller was in the touring side and the pair came face to face in the First Test at the Sydney Cricket Ground. There was plenty of niggle, with Swinton's

> ## 'I enjoyed every moment of it, stiff-arms and punches in the mouth, and kicks in the shins included.'
>
> ### Ray Stehr

Martin Hodgson twice being cautioned in the first half and other warnings handed to his second-row partner Harry Woods (Liverpool Stanley) and—dare we say it—Stehr. The patience of referee Lal Deane eventually wore out and just before the interval, with Australia ahead 4–3, he despatched Stehr and Lions prop Nat Silcock Snr for early showers. Silcock was a veritable 'man mountain' but had a reputation for being clean and fair. One English newspaper report noted: 'They shook hands as they crossed the touchline and later disported themselves as though they were best of pals.'

What the newspaper did not explain was that, as the pair walked from the field, an amazed Silcock had turned to Stehr and mumbled: 'I can't believe it. I've never been sent off before today.'

Stehr just grinned and replied: 'Don't worry, mate, you'll soon get used to it.'

Australia won the Test 24–8 but the tourists squared up the series with a 12–7 victory at the Gabba (Brisbane Cricket Ground) in a dour match marred by an incredible 71 scrums—almost one every minute—with Tommy Armitt winning them 49–22 for the Lions.

The Australians realised that the decider back in Sydney was going to be a rough-house affair and went in without a hooker, preferring instead three props—Stehr, South Sydney's Frank Curran and Queenslander Mick Madsen (see 'No Ordinary Men').

Strangely enough this makeshift front row was winning lots of ball from the scrums, but as Stehr explained, 'We were stamping on Armitt's feet.' Midway through the half, the game exploded:

We won a scrum and the ball was moving along our back line towards the English left wing when Jack Arkwright came through the scrum as it broke up and gave me a face full of knuckles. [See 'Arkie Had the Last Laugh'.] I went after him, blasting away when I caught up with him.

Referee Lal Deane, who had halted play for a knock-on, headed back to break it up and I tried my Lionel Barrymore act,* diving for the ground, clutching my face. There was enough blood on my face to make it look convincing. But I had forgotten how I had tried the same trick in an Easts–Souths match earlier in the season, also refereed by Deane. He had been left with egg on his face when he had sent off Curran and had been lampooned in the newspapers for falling for the three-card trick. This time Deane sent both Arkwright and me off. With my dismissal, I became the only player ever to be sent off in two Tests of an Ashes series. We lost the match 12–7 and I copped a three-match suspension. But I never had any regrets for what I did on that July afternoon.

After he retired with a club best of 174 appearances in Easts colours, as well as 97 representative games, including 11 Tests and a then-record 33 for New South Wales, Stehr remained just as controversial. Television came to Australia in 1956, and he soon made a name for himself as an outspoken critic of the game's administrators. Some of his most vehement clashes were with Jersey Flegg, the chairman of the Board of Control. Stehr dubbed it the Board of No Control.

---

* Lionel Barrymore was a renowned American stage and movie actor who won an Academy Award in 1931.

Until the day he died, in 1983, aged 70, he never made excuses for his conduct. He told Pollard:

Rugby league has been an important part of my life. It is one of the greatest games invented by man. A game of infinite skill which, like all contact sports, can become very wild. A game in which tempers flare and punches fly. A game for ham actors and a game for heroes. I enjoyed every moment of it, stiff-arms and punches in the mouth, and kicks in the shins included. I've found that the bruises help make a man out of you.

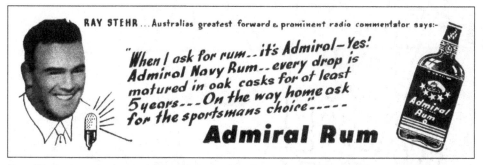

Ray Stehr regularly endorsed 'masculine' products in advertisements that appeared in Rugby League News, the official premiership program.

Arkie had the last laugh

Jack Arkwright holds a unique record in rugby league. He is the only player to have been sent off twice in the one game while representing his country. The giant Warrington prop had a fearsome reputation when he toured Australia with the 1936 Lions. And hard heads in opposition teams were keen to light the 25-year-old's fuse. This was especially the case with the notorious Ray Stehr, who locked horns with him when the Englishman made his Test debut in the second encounter of the Ashes series at the Gabba in Brisbane. But despite several skirmishes the pair managed to remain on the field, with Queensland referee F.L. Moynihan turning a blind eye to their running on-field battle.

It was very different matter when the Great Britain side met New South Wales Northern Districts at Rugby League Park, Armidale, three days before the Third Test, which would decide the Ashes series. It was a case of 'anything goes' with a succession of all-in brawls and Arkwright was in the thick of it. The *Sydney Morning Herald* correspondent clearly understated the mayhem that had the full-house of 6980 fans baying for blood:

> Early in the game it was apparent that solid tackling was affecting the temper of players on both sides, and the linesmen repeatedly ran in to report illegal play. On many occasions a number of players used their fists, and referee B. Garrahy should have done more than award penalties.

Eventually he did. As the clock wound down the home side led 15–14. But then Great Britain winger Barney Hudson scored an unconverted try to snatch back the lead. Moments later the violence erupted again and Arkwright was sent off. As he walked from the field, the Northern Districts skipper Jack Kingston, a 1929–30 Kangaroo tourist who was at that time the captain–coach of the Werris Creek club, asked the referee to allow Arkwright to return to the fray.

Arkwright was to later explain:

I tackled a player a little hard and another player [believed to have been Kingston] raced across to argue with me over the tackle. I thumped him and, although I was sent off by the referee, their captain persuaded him to bring me back again. I think they wanted to take their revenge on me.

Instead, Arkwright continued from where he had left off and four minutes from full-time he tackled the Northern Districts five-eighth Tommy Ezart. The pair hit the turf and Arkwright rained blows on his smaller opponent as they wrestled on the ground. For a second time, Garrahy gave the Englishman his marching orders. Once again the local players pleaded that he be allowed to finish the game—but this time the referee was unmoved.

No further action was taken against Arkwright, clearing the way for him to play in the deciding Test, where once more he was sent off (together with Stehr).

Ironically, Arkwright had started his football career with a junior rugby union side in St Helens named the Sutton Comics. But his professional career with St Helens and Warrington (from 1929 to 1945), during which he played 11 internationals for England and Great Britain, was anything but comical.

Bravo, Narvo

JACK JOHNSON WAS A FAMOUS NAME in Australian boxing history. The first to draw the crowds was the African–American behemoth who fought Canadian Tommy Burns for the world heavyweight championship in 1908. They slugged it out in the famous Sydney Stadium specially built at Rushcutters Bay for that fight and an earlier world championship bout, also involving Burns. Johnson so creamed the title-holder that police eventually moved in and ordered the referee to stop the fight in the 14th round.

Since then there have been at least half-a-dozen homegrown boxers named Jack Johnson fighting in Australia, including one heavyweight who won 64 of his 84 bouts in the 1930s and 1940s. Two of the successes were against Newtown and St George footballer Herb Narvo for the Australian heavyweight title. The second, at Sydney Stadium on Saturday 6 April 1946, was a torrid affair, with both fighters going at each other hammer and tongs. After five brawling rounds, Johnson put Narvo down for the count.

Narvo took such a pounding that night he decided to end his boxing career after 29 fights in which he won 21 and drew another. But he wasn't going to let a beating in the ring interfere with his other sporting career— and less than 24 hours later he shook the cobwebs from his head and was back on the footy field. Talk about tough!

Frank Hyde, arguably the greatest rugby league broadcaster in Australian history and before that a fine player with Newtown, Balmain and North Sydney, said in the 1990s: 'He was the best second-rower I ever saw.' Hyde may have been a little biased, as he played with Narvo at Newtown in the late 1930s and the forward's no-nonsense play helped give many a try-scoring break to the Bluebags back line, of which Hyde was an integral part. But there is no doubt Narvo was a daunting figure on the football field. Contemporary reports use a wide variety of adjectives to describe his efforts—resilient, hard-hitting, robust, durable, challenging and just plain hard.

He was born Herman Nawo. But, like many immigrants, his European parents decided to Anglicise their names during World War I to avoid people thinking they were Germans. Although a Sydneysider by birth, he grew up in a challenging environment in Newcastle. As a schoolkid he soon showed exceptional ability in several sports, especially cricket, cycling, football and boxing. Because of Narvo's physical stature, his upbringing and eventual backbreaking work as a waterside worker unloading ships at the Newcastle dockyards, it was to be football and boxing in which he was to make a name for himself. However, he admitted later in life that he never really enjoyed boxing because of the shonks and criminals involved, although he was clever with his words when talking about them. 'They weren't fair dinkum,' he would say. As the adage says—a nod is as good as a wink to a blind horse!

Narvo joined Newcastle Norths as a 20-year-old and 12 months later, in 1934, was chosen for the New South Wales Country side that took on the best players in the Sydney Premiership in their annual clash. It was a preview of things to come. Two years later he had his first taste of international football as a member of the first Newcastle representative side to beat a touring Lions squad. The Novocastrians defeated England 21–16 at Newcastle No 1 Sportsground in front of 10,000 screaming fans. It was by all accounts a brutal display by both sides, but Narvo gave as good as he got. This whetted Narvo's appetite for more clashes with the 'Chooms' and he moved to the big smoke to join Newtown in hope of gaining selection on the 1937–38 Kangaroo tour, the first that would visit France as well as Britain.

He was regarded as a certainty—but his hopes were shattered when he missed out on the squad of 28. The English club Huddersfield had made him an offer and he was just about to accept when news reached Australia of the fate that had befallen Eastern Suburbs forward Joe Pearce. He had broken a leg during a match played in New Zealand while the Kangaroos were en route to England via the Panama Canal. The Australian Board of Control (the forerunner to the Australian Rugby League) hurriedly

Opposite: Herb Narvo, the pugilist

organised a berth for Narvo on a ship travelling in the opposite direction, through the Suez Canal, and Huddersfield missed out on one of the signings of the decade. Narvo was to play 22 matches, missing only three after his belated arrival in the Old Dart. One was the First Test at Headingley, Leeds. But he appeared in the other five Tests on tour. And after the match on the French leg, in which the Kangaroos whipped Racing Club de Albi 47–3 in ankle-deep mud, the correspondent for *The Sun* newspaper in Sydney cabled: 'Narvo continues as the greatest forward of the tour.'

There are a couple of wonderful stories told about Narvo. In the last match in England, against Broughton Rovers on Boxing Day, the conditions at Manchester's Belle Vue Stadium were foul—below zero temperatures, thick fog and patches of ice across the pitch. None of the Australians wanted to play, least of all Narvo. And he expressed his opinion in no uncertain words to Harry Pierce, the captain of the Kangaroos on that miserable afternoon.

'Tough luck, mate,' said Pierce. 'We're all in the same boat.'

'Well, we'd need a boat if all this ice melted,' was Narvo's reply.

A few minutes into the game, Narvo laid out one of the Broughton players and was immediately sent off. He headed for the dressing room, but not before winking at Pierce.

After the match in Toulouse against the South of France, against a virtual Test side and the only match the Kangaroos lost in that country (largely thanks to the fact that they had a four-hour trip to get to the ground, arriving with just enough time to get changed before kick-off), Narvo kept telling team-mates he must have been Australia's Player of the Match because the crowd, estimated between 10,000 and 15,000, kept calling out his name. He was deflated when it was explained they were in fact chanting 'Bravo, bravo, bravo' and not 'Narvo, Narvo, Narvo'.

Back home, with the winds of war blowing the world into inevitable conflict, Narvo went home to Newcastle, trying in vain to find a vocation that would provide him with a career after football. But when World War II actually broke out he enlisted in the Royal Australian Air Force as a physical fitness instructor. Based at Richmond airbase north-west of

Sydney, he still had the opportunity to play football and was a member of the Newtown side which thrashed North Sydney 34–7 to win the 1943 grand final, helping himself to a try in the bargain. But military duties meant he missed the final and grand finals the following year when Balmain took out the title.

The military always came first—even when it came to sport. On one occasion that year Narvo had played for Combined Services in a rugby union match before racing across town to join the Bluebags for a rugby league game an hour later.

After the war, Narvo signed a lucrative contract (by the standards of the day) as captain–coach of St George for the 1946 season. St George had finished second-last the previous season, but Narvo lifted the team, most of whom were youngsters, to the grand final. Once there they scored four tries to three but were still beaten 13–12 by Balmain. Two of the Tigers' tries were hotly disputed. And the St George players left the field muttering about the display by George Bishop, one of the most controversial referees in the sport's history.

Narvo, still searching for the elusive after-football career, had a couple more seasons in the bush before one more year with Newtown in 1949 and finishing his career back at Newcastle Norths.

Statisticians reckon his wandering ways made him the only footballer to twice play in a side that racked up a century of points—Newcastle Norths beating Morpeth–Maitland 127–16 in 1938, and Cootamundra smashing fellow-Riverina club Junee 121–4 in 1947.

There was no doubting Narvo's tough physique. But there was one fight he couldn't win. After returning to his job as a wharfie, he lost a battle with cancer in 1958. He was only 46. Just before his death he had signed himself out of hospital in Newcastle and travelled to the Sydney Cricket Ground to watch the Third Ashes Test, featuring some of the game's other hardmen such as Peter Dimond, Alan Prescott and Vince Karalius.

He would not have been out of place on the field that day!

Dave who?

MORE THAN 750 PLAYERS have pulled on green and gold jerseys for Australia since the breakaway from rugby union in 1907. And only the keenest of fans would recognise the names of each and every one of them. When it comes to full-backs, Clive Churchill, the man called 'The Little Master', stands supreme. But it is perhaps only elderly enthusiasts who will shout his praises. The middle-aged will speak in glowing terms about Graeme Langlands, while the kids of today cannot imagine anyone better than Billy Slater.

So what about Dave Parkinson? Dave who? That would be the usual reaction among the younger generations of fans. A check of the record books will show them how the Balmain full-back, who joined the Tigers from Cessnock in the Hunter Valley at the start of 1944, played three Tests against the touring British Lions in 1946 before he had even made an appearance in New South Wales colours. But, more importantly, when the Australian game was celebrating its first 100 years, the officials responsible for the centenary website named Parkinson as the man responsible for one of the ten gutsiest efforts in the sport's entire history.

It's a story of raw courage—for Parkinson played for almost the entire game in one of those Test appearances with a broken leg.

The 1946 Lions hold a special place in the annals of rugby league. The tour was organised in an effort to lift the spirits of the people of Britain, Australia and New Zealand after they had endured six awful years of World War II. There was one major problem that had to be overcome. There were no passenger ships sailing between England and Australia on which the British league stars could travel. The problem was solved by Australia's Minister for External Affairs Dr Herbert Evatt. He was also the patron of the game in Australia and persuaded his government counterpart in London to find bunks for the 26 players on the aircraft carrier HMS *Indomitable*, which was sailing Down Under to repatriate British troops who had been fighting in South-East Asia against the Japanese. The media in Australia quickly dubbed the Lions 'The Indomitables'. And so they were.

But if the spectators' spirits were lifted, it wasn't quite the case as far as the footballers were concerned. The British were plagued by transport and hotel problems and a badly organised itinerary. Under their inspirational captain, Gus Risman, they had drawn the First Test at the Sydney Cricket Ground (SCG) 8–all and won the second encounter at Brisbane's Exhibition Ground 14–5. For the Ashes decider it was back to the SCG, with the British forced to play three country matches in the nine days before the Third Test.

Tempers were frayed even before the players took the field, with many having scores to settle after clashes in the earlier Tests. Australia's most experienced referee Tom McMahon knew he was going to have his hands full trying to control the inevitable mayhem.

Just seven minutes into the action Parkinson was hammered in a legitimate tackle. He didn't know it at the time but the tackle had broken his left leg near the ankle. The pain was excruciating, but he had no intention of quitting. After all, in those days there were no replacements for injured players and it was hard enough winning a Test match against the old enemy with a full complement of players, let alone 12 men.

It didn't take long for the game to erupt, with almost all the players trading blows. McMahon reckoned Lions second-rower Les White was the man who started the brawl and penalised him accordingly. But it didn't halt the mayhem, with one fight following another for most of the game. Alf Drewry, covering the tour for the *Yorkshire Post* newspaper, noted: 'Much of the forward play . . . was more appropriate to the boxing ring.'

In the 63rd minute McMahon decided he had seen enough and sent off Aussie back-rower Arthur Clues. At a function after the match, Clues questioned the referee, claiming his punch aimed at Lions five-eighth Willie Horne had missed. 'That's why I sent you off,' came the tongue-in-cheek reply. 'I sent you off because you missed!' Taking advantage of the extra man, the British won the Test 20–7.

Australia's manager Harry Sunderland noted: 'There was more downright bad sportsmanship and disgusting bad temper than I have seen in thirty-six years of watching rugby league.'

To which the tough old English prop Ken Gee countered: 'We expect Test matches to be tough, otherwise why play them?'

Dave Parkinson, whose broken leg cost him a place in Balmain's team which beat St George 13–12 in that year's grand final seven weeks later, would most certainly have agreed with the sentiment.

Fewer daring deeds since interchange

For the first half-century of rugby league, teams were not allowed to replace any players, even if they were seriously injured. This is why there were so many wonderful stories of teams, sometimes down to just ten players instead of the usual 13, posting amazing victories. There was a substitute for Australia in the Second Test of the 1924 Ashes series but contemporary reports don't reveal why this was allowed. But, after the abolition of the 'no-yard' play-the-ball rule in 1951, with players forced to stand back 3 yards (2.7 metres), then 5 yards (4.5 metres), and eventually 10 metres, the game became so much faster that it was obvious replacements would have to be permitted. The first were in 1966, but only injured players were allowed to be substituted. Over the years the game's administrators settled on four players on the substitutes' bench with ten interchanges allowed, and two more if the game went into extra time. So these days footballers don't play on with broken legs and collarbones.

What's this ear?

HENSON PARK IN THE SYDNEY SUBURB OF MARRICKVILLE is one of the most famous of all rugby league grounds. It is like no other. There is the quaint but robust two-storey King George V Stand on one side, a landmark clearly visible from the planes landing and taking off from nearby Kingsford Smith Airport. On the other side is 'The Hill'. Now that the renowned Sydney Cricket Ground 'hill' has disappeared under several modern grandstands, the one at Marrickville remains the most celebrated in Australia. Nearly all the 30,510 who jammed Henson Park in 1959 to watch a match between the two giants of the era, St George and Western Suburbs, stood up on the Hill.

But Henson Park is best known as the home ground for the pioneer club Newtown. They were originally known as the Bluebags after their simple blue jersey. But in the 1980s, as a marketing exercise, they metamorphosed into the Newtown Jets. Tradition has it that these days when the Jets play a home game in the New South Wales Cup, the official attendance is always announced as 8972—the crowd who were at Newtown's last home game in the Premiership big league back in 1983. You see, Henson Park is steeped in tradition.

Stories abound about incidents both on and off the field. The most controversial of all occurred on Saturday 28 July 1945, when the Bluebags took on St George. Little was expected that afternoon. After all, Newtown was running second on the ladder—while the Dragons were second-last. But 15 minutes into the clash all hell broke loose. A scrum packed down near the Newtown 25-yard line. Opposite each other in the front row were St George prop Bill McRitchie and Newtown's footballing policeman Frank 'Bumper' Farrell, one of the roughest, toughest players ever to lace up a football boot.

Suddenly the two front-rowers were locked in fierce combat. McRitchie alleged Farrell was biting one of his ears. He clawed at Farrell's face in an attempt to force him to stop biting. 'For God's sake, let me go,' McRitchie roared. It was then that the referee George Bishop came around the scrum from the other side and pulled out the pair to issue a caution.

'Look what he's done to my ear,' McRitchie said to Bishop.

'Look what he's done to my face,' Farrell interjected.

Bishop just looked Bumper in the eye and noted: 'I know what was going on there. If I had managed to see you do it, you would have been banned for life.'

The St George captain Jim Hale later swore that he had seen Farrell spit out a piece of the ear.

McRitchie was about to pack down in the next scrum when another Newtown player, Herb Narvo, a tough but fair forward and Australian heavyweight boxing champion, said to him: 'Hey, Mac, you had better go and see about that ear. It's in bad shape.' McRitchie was rushed to nearby Lewisham Hospital where it was discovered that the bottom and part of the side of his ear had been bitten off. Over the next 22 weeks he was in and out of hospital as surgeons rebuilt the damaged ear with skin grafts from other parts of his body.

A month after the incident, when McRitchie had recovered enough to give evidence, the New South Wales Rugby League (NSWRL) opened an inquiry. He told the NSWRL general committee that he did not provoke Farrell:

> He was solely responsible for the injury I received on the day in question. That is the truth, the whole truth. I have been associated with a lot of sport—football, baseball and cricket—and I have never witnessed or felt such a thing as that done to me. You could never imagine a man could do such a thing.

In his defence Farrell told the committee he had seven false top teeth and ten on the jawbone and had left his dentures in the dressing room. This swayed sufficient members of the committee, who found Bumper not guilty by 15 votes to 12. But that was not the end for Farrell. As a policeman he also had to face a police inquiry. If found guilty, his career

Opposite: Bumper Farrell's face shows the ravages of a long, harsh career.

would be over. But that inquiry returned the same verdict. It is said that the investigating officer quipped: 'If you didn't bite the ear, you must have given it an almighty suck.'

Three decades later, when I was working for the *Daily Telegraph* in Sydney, Bumper was head of security, checking everyone who entered the offices of 'the Tele' and sister newspapers, the *Daily Mirror* and *The Australian*. I put the question straight to him. Bumper just laughed and said, 'It couldn't have been me, could it?'

Bumper Farrell on the rampage for Newtown

FARRELL MAY HAVE BECOME PART OF AUSTRALIAN FOLKLORE as a result of the ear-biting incident. But even without the controversy he was still one of the most terrifying opponents in the years immediately before and after World War II. The war robbed him of the chance to run up a long list of international appearances. But he did play in four Tests: two each against Great Britain and New Zealand. Farrell turned out in a record 223 first-grade matches for his club side, Newtown, between 1937 and 1951. And he captained the Premiership-winning team which thrashed North Sydney 34–7 in the 1943 grand final.

Clive Churchill, the man who became known as 'The Little Master', had a grudging admiration for the bloke he called 'Old Bumper'. Churchill was to write in his autobiography:

In my opinion, he was the forward most feared either in club or international football. During his imposing career I think he took more than he received. Farrell was never afraid to go into the hurly-burly of the rucks. Many times he took a terrific lacing of fists and boots. Admittedly he returned the assault in good measure. And he acquired a reputation for turning on the rough stuff. I often wonder how he survived so long on the football field.

Bumper was uncompromising off the field, too, as head of the Police Vice Squad. If opposition players felt he gave them a hard time, it was nothing compared with the treatment handed out to homosexuals by Sergeant Farrell. He made no secret of his contempt for them. It was heaven help those he met after dark on the streets of his inner-Sydney bailiwick. And there were no civil libertarians back then to look after their rights.

Farrell's influence as a policemen even reached the famous Snowy Mountains Scheme, where thousands of migrant workers were brought in from overseas to build the giant hydro-electric project. In the 1950s love-starved miners, after weeks up in the camps in the mountains, would descend on Cooma, the town where the scheme's headquarters was located, looking for girls. Sadly, there weren't any. So the police had to contend with an increasing number of sexual assaults and it was a case of 'lock up your daughters'.

Plainly, this had to stop. The local police called their mate Bumper in Sydney. He was eager to help the womenfolk of Cooma and had a simple solution. He headed down to Chapel Street, the centre of the red light district in the Sydney suburb of Darlinghurst.

'You, you and you,' he pointed to three ladies of the night. 'You're on tomorrow night's train to Cooma. It's for three weeks' work and you'll make a pretty packet. I'll send another team down for the next shift.'

The three recruits had no choice but to comply with Bumper's orders. When they staggered off the red-eye special at Cooma Railway Station, they were taken to their new quarters in a pleasant little cottage on the outskirts of town. The red light went up in the window, the miners made a beeline for the house and the attacks on the Cooma women ceased almost overnight.

And, yes, Bumper was right. The ladies did make a pretty packet and soon there was a waiting list of volunteers.

FORMER NEWTOWN SECRETARY Frank Farrington would tell a story about playing with Bumper Farrell in a trial match in 1949. A young winger from the country was hoping to snare a contract with the Bluebags. But he didn't do his chances any good by dropping a pass with the line wide open. Farrell, the Newtown captain–coach, was furious and shoved the youngster to hooker for the next scrum, where Bumper proceeded to rough him up, explaining the reason for his none-too-friendly attitude: 'This is where we have to bloody well win the ball so useless bastards like you out in the backs can knock it on!'

He didn't look the part

FOR THE BENEFIT of the younger generation of sporting fans, used to equating success with physique, it is important to introduce the name of rugby league's Brian Bevan. He had no rippling muscles. His puny physique was like those seen in contemporary newspaper advertisements showing eight-stone weaklings as the victims of bullies intent on kicking sand into their faces. In those days the steroids used illegally by so many modern young men to boost the size of their bodies were unknown.

But Bevan's looks were deceiving—oh, so deceiving. Few footballers have looked less athletic. He was thin and balding, and he would run onto the field with heavy strapping on his spindly legs. Indeed, estimates suggest that it took an hour or so to get the bandages on properly so he could make his way out of the dressing room and onto the pitch. But, even though he looked emaciated, he was as hard as nails. A freak? Certainly in ability! He had a freakish touch of genius that put him up among the greatest figures in world sporting history.

Football—any code of football—has never known a scoring machine like him. In 18 seasons in British rugby league, the expatriate Australian scored more tries than any other player in history. He notched a phenomenal 796 in club games and another 38 in representative and so-called friendly matches—some 300 more than his nearest rival, Welshman Billy Boston. Yes, almost a third more than the next best. And in the modern game no player comes remotely close to what Bevan achieved.

The great Australian forward Harry Bath, who played hundreds of games with Bevan for the English club Warrington, said of the freakish winger:

Brian never had any counterpart in Australia in my time. Maybe Dally Messenger had the same magical effect on crowds in the early days of rugby league. But no player ever provided sustained thrills for so many fans over such a long period as Bevan did. He always gave me the impression he had a radar built into the toes of his football boots and this steered him around everyone between him and the tryline.

Yet, surprisingly, no one in his home country ever recognised his greatness. Bevan had made little impact on rugby league before he joined Warrington in 1945, from the Sydney club Eastern Suburbs.

What was it that made Warrington recognise the talent of the Australian sailor who had arrived in Britain on the HMAS *Australia* during World War II? Your answer is as good as the next. But the British soon realised he had tremendous acceleration and a prodigious sidestep. In his autobiography, which respected Sydney journalist Ian Heads tried in vain to get published, Bevan explained:

> The long hours spent perfecting my sidestep in Australia stood me in good stead. It's one of the greatest attributes a player can possess, yet I rarely see it used today . . . in general players tend to begrudge the time necessary to master it. For my part it was a schoolboy phobia for racing the crowds out of the Sydney Cricket Ground. It all began with my desire to get home early after big games. The way out of the ground was down a long pathway with concrete posts set along each side of it. Awkwardly at first, I would try to weave my way between spectators and posts in a bid to get to the front. It became a habit, and with growing exuberance and proficiency I developed the knack of dodging all obstacles. My father helped me perfect the sidestep even further by taking me to the local park and encouraging me to run at top speed at posts placed five or six yards apart.

Bevan had a penchant for multiple try-scoring feats. Twice, in Britain, he went over for seven in one match. Yes, seven! Four times he scored six, seven times he notched five, and on 22 occasions he finished a match with four tries. And trebles were common as far as Bevan was concerned, with a career total of 69. Perhaps this should be pointed out to today's journalists when they begin to wax lyrical about players who manage two

Opposite: Brian Bevan in his Warrington jersey

or three hat-tricks during their careers. Or even to the players themselves, who far too often are legends in their own lunchtime.

One major record which did elude Bevan was that of scoring the most tries in a single season. In 1952–53 he scored 72 for Warrington, eight short of the tally set by fellow-Australian Alby Rosenfeld in the 1913–14 season. Bevan had three other seasons when he topped 60: 1950–51 (68), 1953–54 (67) and 1954–55 (63). Bevan was in Warrington sides which won two Challenge Cups (1950 and 1954) and three Championships (1948, 1954 and 1955).

This fellow who had the fans jumping to their feet every time the ball came his way looked as if he would break in two every time he was tackled. Yet he always bounced back on his feet within the twinkling of an eye. Was it all that strapping that made him look like an Egyptian mummy?

Heads found the answer in Bevan's unpublished autobiography:

It was a precaution that I made a ritual of and one which kept me free of any serious injuries during my playing days. I always made sure of both knees being padded as this part of the body is most vulnerable of all to injuries. The only bad knocks I sustained during my whole career were a knee ligament injury (absent for six weeks) and a broken jaw (off for two months).

One can only shake one's head.

And how did he manage to stay in the game for so long—he was 40 years old when he finally called it quits in 1964—and score so many tries? Bevan wrote:

I was often asked these questions. My answer always was that I loved the game. Fitness was my first priority, followed by a perseverance in speed and sprint training, a routine I adhered to doggedly through my career. I also had a kind of mania for running spikes—and the use of these in sprint training helped me retain my speed season after season. Stamina training and plenty of physical exercises played a major part too. I found that shadow boxing was second to none when it came to stamina building. I also developed some kind of killer instinct on the field . . . in plainer terms an attitude of almost hating the opposition, so much so I completely shut myself off from a lot of things.

Heads understands that. He relates a story told to him by Vince Karalius a couple of years before the 'Wild Bull of the Pampas' died. Karalius recalled playing in a charity game with Bevan, when the old wingman was 50 years of age. Whippet-thin and still fast, Bevan had run in four tries in a match featuring the best players in the land. Karalius explained how he was sitting in the bath with Bevan after the game, and patted him on the back, noting, 'You've not lost your touch, old pal.'

Bevan didn't smile. He just looked at Karalius and said, 'I should have had six.'

'He always gave me the impression he had a radar built into the toes of his football boots . . .'
Aussie great Harry Bath on his
Warrington team-mate Brian Bevan

Broken legs didn't stop Patton

ARTHUR PATTON WAS ONE OF THE MOST COURAGEOUS Australian wingers of all time. He played 15 seasons of top-flight rugby league. Even broken legs in 1945 and 1948 failed to force him off the field—although after the second fracture he did decide to ring down the curtain on his great career. Renowned *Sydney Morning Herald* sporting journalist Tom Goodman rated Patton as the fastest runner with the ball seen in Sydney football. An indication of the speed of this gutsy sportsman from the New South Wales south coast was his performance in the 1937 Stawell Gift footrace, the country's premier professional sprint. He was beaten into third place in the final, just 20 centimetres behind two athletes to whom he gave starts of more than a metre. But in an era in which pro athletics was incredibly popular, he took out a couple of the other major titles, the Deniliquin Gift and the Benalla Gift.

'Squib' Patton was robbed of a Test career by World War II. Several times he topped 50 tries in a season. In 117 first-grade games for Balmain he notched 95 tries, which remained a club record until the Tigers merged with Western Suburbs in 2000. He was also one of only four players to have scored a record five tries in a single game for Balmain.

His final appearance on the football field was in the 1948 Sydney preliminary final against St George. It was an heroic performance. Patton broke a leg in the first half when tackled 10 metres from the tryline after a 60-metre dash. Replacements were not allowed in those days and Patton refused to leave his team-mates, despite their urging him to go to the dressing room. He played the rest of the match in great pain, with his injured leg heavily strapped so he could stay on his feet. His courage was rewarded when Balmain scraped home winners 13–12. Sadly the Tigers lost the grand final a week later to the Western Suburbs Magpies.

Vive la résistance

NO ONE IS SURE whether French Test prop Louis 'Lolo' Mazon ever met Australian Test cricket larrikin Keith Miller. But their paths could well have crossed as they strode the world sporting stage at the same time in the late 1940s and early 1950s. And both had earlier faced fear and conquered it.

Mazon, arguably the toughest forward in the history of rugby league in France, had fought in southern France for the Maquis de Picaussel, an arm of the Resistance movement that conducted a guerilla campaign against the occupying Nazi troops during World War II, while Miller, cricket's great all-rounder, flew Royal Australian Air Force fighter planes over the skies of Britain in aerial dogfights with the Luftwaffe.

As a teenager, Mazon was twice imprisoned by the Nazis and twice escaped. On the first occasion, in September 1943, it was from Schweinfurt in Bavaria, where he had been forced to work as a labourer in a munitions factory for two years. Mazon made his way through hostile territory and back into his beloved southern France, where he witnessed the crucifixion of a 17-year-old colleague in the Resistance. This ignited a fierce hatred of the enemy which stayed with him for the rest of his life. No sooner had he seen the execution than he was captured again. But two days before Christmas he staged his second escape, evading a hail of bullets from his Gestapo guards. Mazon eventually played a role in the 1944 liberation of his home town of Carcassonne as well as nearby Quillan and Limoux.

It is because of his efforts in the Maquis that Mazon was dubbed 'Granddad Taillefer' after a French court jester who is part of his country's folklore. At the Battle of Hastings in 1066, the original Taillefer had grabbed the sword of a slain soldier and had killed several English knights before being cut down himself.

Back to Keith Miller: in one match on the Australian cricket team's 1948 Ashes tour of England, Miller was chided by the Aussie captain Don Bradman for his apparent lack of success. 'You can't handle pressure,' the great man is said to have suggested.

SURELY AN 'ESCAPE TUNNEL' FROM A SCRUM TO THE TRY-LINE IS AGAINST THE RULES ?!
I'M LOOKING.. I'M LOOKING..
RULES

The comment was like a red rag to a bull. 'Can't handle pressure?' Miller retaliated. 'This isn't pressure. Pressure is flying a Spitfire with a Messerschmitt up your arse!'

Mazon would have known exactly what Miller meant. And after his torture by the Gestapo, taking on the might of the rest of the rugby league world in 16 Tests and internationals, including the historic series success over Australia in 1951, was probably a piece of cake.

It didn't look like it at first. The Frenchmen's form in the early matches on the groundbreaking 1951 tour was so patchy Jersey Flegg, the chairman of the Australian Board of Control, threatened to send them home early if they did not show a rapid improvement. When I was writing the history of the famous Bondi Icebergs winter swimming club, to coincide with its 75th anniversary in 2004, I learned the reason for the poor early tour displays from veteran Icebergs swimmer Keith 'Lucky' Doran, then 87 years old. Doran recalled:

Everyone was writing them off as a team of duds when they visited the Icebergs on the Sunday before the First Test. They watched our swimming races and then joined us in the clubhouse for a snack and a few drinks. We drank beer, most of them drank wine. The Frenchman who was seated at my table—I think it may have been the forward Mazon—was admiring the Icebergs' pennant, which was the prize for winning the morning's race. He was particularly intrigued by the polar bear. He told me he would love to take a pennant back home to show his family and friends in the south of France. Well, I had a couple in my locker and gave them to him. He wanted to pay me, but I shook my head. I reckoned I could win a couple more to replace them. We had a few more drinks and then he pulled me across the table and whispered, 'Back us in the Test.' I laughed. Everyone reckoned the Frogs were hopeless and the Australians, who had beaten the Poms the previous year for the first time in 30 years, would give them a terrible hiding.

Mazon smiled and whispered to Doran again:

> My friend, you are never too old to learn something. We only had
> enough cash to pay for our fares and accommodation on this tour. So
> how do we pay for our drinks and entertainment? We make ourselves
> look bad and then back ourselves with the bookmakers at good odds.
> My friend, I tell you once again . . . back us to win the Test.

So Doran did, getting odds of around 5–1, with 10 points start, from his
local SP bookmaker. And the French won the Test 26–15. 'I bet all my
savings—around £100,' Doran told me. 'And I won £500. It was huge
money in those days. I had never bet on a football match before, and
I have never bet on one since.'

No wonder the French played like men possessed. They looked to have
the game firmly in their grasp with a half-time lead of 16–2. Mazon
had set up one of the tries, for winger Raymond Contrastin, nicknamed
'Tintin' after the famous European children's comic book character. But
in the second half, the French dropped the intensity of their defence and
allowed Australia to reduce the deficit to just one point.

Henri Garcia, the renowned French sports writer who was reporting
on the historic tour, explained a decade later:

> Lolo Mazon, good old Granddad Taillefer, was an angry man, furious
> that he'd allowed himself to slacken off, raging against a fate that was
> so kind in the first half but so cruel afterwards. He felt he had points
> to prove against these Australians who looked almost as tough as
> him. As a general rule Mazon isn't what you would call an Adonis.
> Moreover he was blunt with [fellow-forward] François Rinaldi, a
> Burt Lancaster look-alike, and said he was too pretty for the front

Opposite: *Renowned French sports writer Henri Garcia said that Mazon
'sported a nose which exemplified his whole career: expressive, tortured
and belligerent'.*

row. 'A pretty prop can never make a good prop,' he declared. 'For the front row you have to be ugly—as ugly as sin.' At that point a grimace of determination came over his face and Lolo was ugly, magnificently ugly. With strapping around his forehead, hair all over the place, nose dribbling blood and jersey hanging out over his shorts, he had all the savage beauty of Attila the Hun. Mazon was the scourge of the Kangaroos and they thought twice about tackling him (and closed their eyes) with two or three needed to subdue him.

The French pack began to overwhelm the Australians. Garcia continued:

As to how the match ended, people have spoken to me in Australia about it with every superlative in the English language—and there are plenty. For 15 minutes France produced super rugby. Slowly, as if building up the effect, France approached the coup de grâce. The beast was on its knees. The moment of truth had arrived.

Two more converted tries gave the Frenchmen that 11-point victory. The patron of the New South Wales Rugby League and former president of the United Nations, Dr H.V. 'Bert' Evatt (he was to become leader of the Labor opposition in Federal parliament ten days later, after the death of Ben Chifley), was amazed at the efforts of the French, especially Mazon, and told the victors: 'This exhibition of champagne rugby league has today achieved more for France than anything her ambassadors have done since the turn of the century.'

Australia won the Second Test, a savage encounter in Brisbane, 23–11, and then the tourists shocked everyone in the sport by thrashing Australia 35–11 in the decider at the Sydney Cricket Ground, with their forwards leading the way. What followed was an incredible rolling party. These days footballers have their Mad Monday celebrations. Imagine that for three straight days before the French team left for the New Zealand leg of the tour. The ill-named Ashes Cup, donated by City Tattersall's Club, was never without some type of alcohol, from champagne to pastis—and everyone was welcome to gulp down the contents. And the forwards such as Mazon made sure they got their fair share. 'We all have eyes like piss-holes in the snow,' coach Jean Duhau told Garcia on the morning they flew out.

It was Lolo's last visit to Australia. He continued playing at club level as a member of the AS Carcassonne sides that won the French Championship in 1952 and 1953 and tasted victory in the finals of Le Coupe de France in 1951 and 1952, to add to his 1950 Championship success. And when it came time for him to retire the famous club gave him a unique gift. They paid a plastic surgeon to reshape his nose, battered by years of stand-up, on-field slugging matches and more than a few head-butts and stray fists in scrums.

Back to Garcia:

Unfortunately, destiny decided to thumb her nose at him. One fine Sunday morning, the famous Carcassonne club found itself short of a big prop. The supporters went off in search of Lolo to see whether he'd do this little favour. Good grief, one game wouldn't make any difference to an old warrior, and anyway, the bugger was in good nick. On principle, he made them beg a bit, maybe a small consideration also in mind. So he returned to the front line, his [new] classical profile a rallying point. His comeback was going superbly, when a minor skirmish suddenly broke out. The Carcassonne trainer was called for, and Lolo left the field with a bloody nose.

And this is why, thanks to unkind fate and an opponent's fist, Mazon sported a nose which exemplified his whole career: expressive, tortured and belligerent. Nothing frightened him, player, crowd or referee, except the displeasure of his charming wife who led him, shall we say, by the nose.

The clues to scalping a Frenchman

IN SPORT IT IS SOMETIMES DIFFICULT to separate fact from fiction. The great cricket writer Neville Cardus admitted late in life that he regularly made up pithy quotes allegedly uttered by Test stars. 'And they dined out on them for decades,' Cardus explained, with not a hint of apology.

So what was the true reason Australian hardman Arthur Clues was banned from playing rugby union? Around the famous Headingley ground in the Yorkshire city of Leeds you will be told how when he was just 16 years old, Arthur was running touch in a game at Parramatta in Sydney's west. His sister's boyfriend was playing in the match and when the said boyfriend was laid out by an opposition player, young Arthur ran onto the pitch and rained blows on the miscreant's head with the wooden stick of his flag. The assault left the player with a face resembling a plate of spaghetti bolognaise. Arthur was then banned for life. Or so the story goes and Clues never denied it.

Around Parramatta they tell a different story. The teenage Arthur Clues and a couple of mates from the Parramatta rugby union club wanted to run themselves into some semblance of fitness before the start of the 1943 season. So they played in the trial matches at Pratten Park, in the suburb of Ashfield, for the Western Suburbs rugby league side. Clues played so well that the Wests officials listed him in their ranks for the coming season—and a week or so later when Clues turned up to play for Parramatta in the amateur code of rugby union he was shown the door. He was told he was a professional, even though he hadn't received a penny from Wests for those 'training runs'.

It was hardly a yarn of which folklore is made! Anyway, to cut a long story short, Clues began playing for the Wests Magpies. Wests weren't the best of sides in those days but Clues stood out.

'He was a magician when he had the ball in his hands,' recalled the legendary radio broadcaster Frank Hyde, who played against Clues and

Opposite: Few players ever managed to break a tackle by Arthur Clues.

later broadcast matches in which he appeared. 'He was tall, lean and mean. You only liked him if you were playing with him. But off the field he was the nicest bloke you'd ever want to meet.'

Mean? Meaner than a junkyard dog? Quite possibly!

A rangy back-rower whose day job was that of a motorbike policeman, Clues forced his way into the New South Wales side in 1945 and into the Test line-up a year later when the first British side to tour since World War II arrived for the Ashes series. He played in all three Tests, being sent off in the last for throwing a punch at Willie Horne during a skirmish. The blow missed by half a metre, for which the pint-sized five-eighth from the north-western English county of Cumberland should have been eternally grateful. At the very least, Clues was later to suggest, he deserved to have been sent off—for not connecting with his haymaker. Again, this story has two versions—the other being that referee Tom McMahon chastised him for missing his target.

In those days, which club you played for was decided by where you lived. The fledgling Parramatta side had hoped to have Clues, who was living in its area, in the suburb of Harris Park, as the star player when the Eels made their 1947 debut in the Sydney Premiership. The new club offered him £5 a match as an incentive to play. It seemed good money for a policeman earning just £8 a week. But the Parramatta officials were dismayed when they heard that the English side Leeds had trumped them with a £750 signing-on fee, a return fare to England, plus match payments of £7 a win and £5 a loss. It was a king's ransom in that era.

Clues left for England. And he was lost to the Australian game forever.

Arthur Clues was not just a great footballer—he was also a competent cricketer. He is believed to have been the only man to have hit a century and scored a try on two of the most famous sporting arenas in the world—the Sydney Cricket Ground and Headingley, Leeds.

ÉDOUARD PONSINET was France's equivalent to Clues. A draughtsman by trade, he was meticulous with the delicate lines he drew on architectural plans. But for one who relied so much on his hands, he had a callous disregard for their protection. He was a part-time boxer. He had a party trick that involved ripping a pack of playing cards in half with the ease of tearing a flimsy bus ticket in two. And when he packed down in the second row for the AS Carcassonne club, he had no compunction in burying a fist in the face of the opposition hooker or maybe, if Ponsinet was feeling particularly peeved about the way the game was progressing, the face of one of the big front-row forwards from the opposing team.

The man they called 'Pon Pon' seemingly knew no fear!

Neither did Élie Brousse, his giant partner in crime in the French national side. Brousse for several years was a policeman based in the maritime city of Marseille. If you were a copper in Marseille you had to be tough and rough to hold sway over the scum who controlled the importation of drugs and every other possible form of contraband through the city's Mediterranean waterfront. He was also a paradox— he had been involved in the silk-spinning industry before taking on the thugs of Marseille.

The pair of tough nuts are said to have had a particular dislike of Australian players and it was never more obvious than when France took on the Other Nationalities side in the International Championship staged each year in the northern hemisphere. Other Nationalities (or the Empire-Brittanique as the French called them) consisted almost exclusively of expatriate Aussies playing in England. The other two sides in the four-cornered tournament were England and Wales.

Brousse and Ponsinet singled out Clues for special treatment in a clash in December 1950 at Bordeaux's Stade Municipal. The record crowd of 28,000 roared their approval as the duo regularly hit Clues and his team-mates late and high. At least they did until the Aussie got his revenge.

Respected English sportswriter Raymond Fletcher remembers Clues explaining the encounter:

The way he told it was a great story, but in print and within the restrictions of good taste it loses much of the Clues vernacular. Briefly, it begins with Ponsinet laying about Other Nationalities forwards like nobody's business. Kiwi Bert Cooke suggested that Clues stop the French c***. So Arthur did—with a forearm smash. Arthur reckoned he meant to catch him across the chest, but Ponsinet ducked and Clues almost scalped him. Even tough fellow-Aussie forward Harry Bath was almost sick at the sight.

PONSINET AND BROUSSE INTRODUCED THEMSELVES to the Australian public on the 1951 French tour Down Under—the first by any side from the land of croissants, baguettes, pâté de foie gras, Cointreau and pastis. Befitting a French team there was plenty of champagne football—but there was also an abundance of violence that would not be out of place in one of those Marseille waterfront cafes that Brousse patrolled.

It all came to a head in the Second Test at the Gabba in Brisbane with Ponsinet and Brousse dishing it out to the Australians. As Henri Garcia, the renowned correspondent for the newspaper *L'Equipe*, reported:

The game fell into a rut of one-on-one battles. And exchanges turned pretty rough as players took it out on each other, with punches coming in without warning. Most didn't know who'd hit them in the tide of nastiness. First-aid men were kept busy on the sideline. Women had fits of hysterics in the stands. Élie Brousse, that giant of a second-row, had hands like shovels. He didn't tackle, he just laid a huge paw on an opponent's shoulder and the poor soul felt his knees give under the unbearable pressure. He would manage four or five yards then collapse at the Catalan's feet.

Opposite: *Frenchman Édouard Ponsinet had many a battle with Aussie hardman Arthur Clues.*

Brousse tried his not-so-gentle persuasion on rugged Australian centre Noel Hazzard. Garcia continued:

> Brousse's claw didn't bring him down at first, so the French superman seized him around the waist and smashed him to the ground, head-first. The Kangaroo linebreaker had never suffered such humiliation before and retaliated violently.

The pair were dispatched to the dressing rooms. Australia won the match.

Famous sportswriter Jim Mathers noted in his match report in *The Truth* newspaper: 'This was the dirtiest international since the famous Battle of Brisbane in 1922.'

The brutality was not finished. In the next tour match at Toowoomba, Ponsinet was rested but Brousse made up for his absence with a personal vendetta against Test prop and Toowoomba captain Duncan Hall, who in one melee split Brousse's top lip with a perfect right cross. Brousse replied with a solid left hook that laid Hall out. Both players were sent off.

The stage was now set for the Third (and deciding) Test, back at the Sydney Cricket Ground. Once again it was 'take no prisoners' with Ponsinet and Brousse leading the carnage. Just before the break, with France ahead 15–4, Brousse dived for the tryline, stretched out and touched down next to the right upright. Big Aussie second-rower Brian Davies slid across the turf, pushing him into the post and catching Brousse's head with both boots in the process.

When he woke up, Brousse could afford to smile, even though he remembered little of the second half. The Frenchmen had won 35–14. However, the conquerors were still angry. Heaven help any Aussie who crossed their paths in the future. And many would—including Arthur Clues.

Just over three months later Ponsinet and Brousse came up against Other Nationalities. The French had won the title the previous season and

Opposite: Program for the violent 1951 clash remembered as 'The Battle of the Boulevard'

The Rugby Football League

Hull's First
Jean Galia International Cup Game

France

VERSUS

Other Nationalities

AT

The Boulevard
Hull

ON

Saturday
Nov. 3rd

1951

Puig-Aubert, the French full-back, who beat the records of Dally Messenger and Jim Sullivan on an Australian tour.

OFFICIAL PROGRAMME - - Price 6d.

were keen to keep their crown. Although there were a New Zealander, a Scot and an Irishman in the Other Nationalities team, all of the side's other players who turned out at The Boulevard ground in Hull that afternoon—Saturday, November 3, 1951—were Australians, including former Test stars Clues, Pat Devery and Lionel Cooper, as well as the greatest winger in the history of the game, Brian Bevan. Another was wrestler and ex–rugby union Test prop Robert 'Wallaby Bob' McMaster, notorious for the deeds of his pet dog Kelly, who used to run onto the field and try to bite the referee.

The simmering hatred of the Aussies didn't take long to manifest itself in a match that has become part of rugby league legend as 'The Battle of The Boulevard'. The 18,000 fans roared as the Other Nationalities kicked off. Within two minutes Clues was lying prone on the pitch, smashed by Ponsinet from behind when he didn't have the ball. The Leeds star was carried off unconscious on a stretcher and taken to hospital. He wasn't the only casualty. At one stage Other Nationalities were down to 11 men. New Zealand five-eighth Peter Henderson finished with his head swathed in bandages and half-back Jeff Burke had his nose smashed to a pulp by a forearm jolt from Ponsinet. It was only then that referee George Phillips decided enough was enough and gave the Frenchman his marching orders.

Jack Murray, Hull's trainer, had the job of wielding the magic sponge on the wounded Other Nationalities players. He noted: 'I haven't seen anything like it since Jutland [the historic World War I naval battle].'

Scottish lock-forward Dave Valentine put it more succinctly: 'We won by four knock-outs to three.'

Other Nationalities won on the scoreboard, too, 17–14. The tough ex–Eastern Suburbs winger Cooper scored three tries and his Huddersfield team-mate Devery (formerly with Balmain) booted four goals.

The final encounter between Ponsinet and Clues took place back in Bordeaux in October 1953. Other Nationalities put up a high kick in the first minute. And, according to Clues, when Ponsinet saw his Australian nemesis charging down the pitch towards him, he ignored the ball and leaped over the fence into the crowd. He wasn't going to be scalped again.

Once he retired, Clues led a quiet life running a sports store in Leeds. He was also happy to talk about the good old days. The facts? Well, you were never really sure when listening to his colourful tales. But why spoil a good yarn?

Great Britain Test forward Geoff Gunney toured Australia with the 1954 Lions and later played with Clues at Hunslet. Gunney admired Clues greatly, saying he was 'brilliant—a dirty sod but brilliant', adding: 'One day when he kicked me all over the ground I think I earned a bit of respect because he couldn't get me off. When I was making my way in the game, I used to dream of being half as good as Arthur Clues. As a player he could do anything. He was quite pacy although people didn't realise that. He could fight . . . he had good hands . . . a good player.'

God save Whacka

IT'S DOUBTFUL IF THEY EVER BRED A FOOTBALLER tougher than Johnny 'Whacka' Graves. Whacka grew up on the coalfields west of Newcastle at a time when you had to be mean to survive. They may have dubbed his team the Maitland Pumpkin Pickers—but the players were known throughout the local mining town as being better at picking fights than picking the edible yellow cucurbits. Graves later played rugby league for South Sydney. And you didn't play for the Rabbitohs unless you could handle yourself both on the field and in the dark alleys around Redfern Oval. Hence the nickname of Whacka!

Nevertheless, Graves was a fine player. Flamboyant. That's one way of describing his characteristic never-take-a-backward-step style of defence and speed in attack. The South Sydney fans adored him. Not so those cheering for the opposition sides that came up against Whacka. But they respected this tough winger who had a penchant for scoring lots of tries and kicking more than the occasional goal. An indication of his ability is that he managed to play seven Tests for Australia at a time when there were few opportunities. His four tries in a grand final (for Souths against Manly in 1951) still stands as a record for a Premiership decider six decades later, as do the South Sydney club records of five tries in a match (against Eastern Suburbs in 1949) and 29 points in a game (also against Easts, in 1952, when he scored three tries and booted ten goals).

Whacka's ability was brought to the notice of the Rabbitohs when he starred for Newcastle in a fiery encounter with the 1946 British Lions. Their visit was aimed at lifting the spirits of the Australian people after the nightmares of World War II. But the Aussie fans rediscovered an old 'enemy'—the British footballers. Almost every game provided a display that would never have been acceptable under the Marquess of Queensberry rules of boxing. The match in Newcastle was no exception, with the 19-year-old Graves on his representative debut making it quite clear he was just as tough as the coalminers and mill workers from the north of England. Graves scored two tries that afternoon as Newcastle

Hard-hitting Rabbitohs discuss tactics at training (left to right: Clive Churchill, Les 'Chic' Cowie, Jack Rayner and Johnny 'Whacka' Graves).

beat the tourists 18–15. With memories of the war still strong, one newspaperman suggested that 'The game would have sent the late Dr Goebbels into ecstasies, thanks to the way the Novocastrians gave it to the Englishmen.' However, a proviso was added: Nazi Propaganda Minister Goebbels would have been 'bewildered to note the warmth of the reception accorded the visitors wherever they journeyed'. As the adage says, what happens on the field stays on the field.

One of the tourists, tough Welsh second-rower Doug Phillips, showed this to be the case in his diary, dismissing the furore in one brief sentence: 'Saturday: June 15—left Sydney 9 am, played and got sent off 20 minutes before the end.'

It was on the 1948–49 Kangaroo tour of Britain that Whacka Graves had his closest shave—and, rest assured, he had some close ones during his career. Some suggested he diced with death. Or was that just the hyperbole of some bored Aussie sporting journalist on a quiet Sunday in northern England?

His narrow escape came after the match against Huddersfield at the club's famous Fartown ground. During the encounter, Graves knocked out Johnny Hunter, an Australian who was the darling of the Huddersfield fans. (Hunter was to score 16 tries that season, a record for a full-back in the English game.) It was a high stiff-arm tackle that would have been thoroughly acceptable in Redfern . . . but not in Huddersfield, the birthplace of rugby league.

Hunter was carried off on a stretcher and the crowd was baying for Graves' blood. At the end of the match, they climbed over the fence and headed for the Kangaroo winger. Thankfully, the local secretary, in a stroke of genius, thought quickly and ordered the town band to strike up 'God Save the King'. As the fiercely patriotic English crowd stood to attention while the national anthem was played, Graves darted off the field to the sanctuary of the dressing room. And it was there that he stayed for a long, long time until the last of the fans headed for their own sanctuary—the local pub. At least that's the story still told to this day around the watering holes in Huddersfield.

Former Great Britain coach Colin Hutton recalled another side of Whacka:

I was playing for Widnes in 1948 and was full-back for the final club match played by the Kangaroos, who ended up winning 18–8. In the second half, we were attacking the Australians' tryline. Our half-back Tich Anderson put in a grubber kick which was fielded by Graves, who was playing on the left wing. In a few strides he was clear of the rest of the Widnes players with only me to beat. In classical style I showed him the touchline and moved in for the tackle. Then I felt a giant hand on the top of my head and down I went face first into the turf. When I looked up Whacka was striding away to score a 90-yard try. To rub salt into the wound, he then proceeded to convert the try from the touchline. The legendary Aussie Harry Sunderland described it as the most spectacular try of the tour.

There was a sequel. In 1962 I was in Australia as coach of the Lions and early in the tour we attended a function at South Sydney Leagues Club in Redfern. Whacka was there and I made the mistake of reminding him of the try. Subsequently, at every function at which our paths crossed, Whacka, surrounded by admirers, would call me over and laugh, 'Col, come here and tell them about my try.' It's 2010 and I'm now 84 years old—but the memory of that hand-off is as vivid as the day it happened 62 years ago.

Then there is the story about a club match at Redfern Oval. Graves was lining up a vital kick at goal from on the sideline. The crowd had encroached onto the field having spilled over the fence in front of 'The Hill' and Wacka had to clear a path for his run to the ball. One of the fans forced out of the way grinned at Graves: 'Bet you a tenner you miss!'

'You're on, sucker,' came Wacka's reply. And he calmly booted the goal.

At full-time Graves raced to the spot from where he had kicked the goal and collared the fan: 'You didn't think you would get away without paying, did you?' Knowing Whacka's reputation when the going got tough, the fan quickly handed over the £10 note.

Well, you would, wouldn't you!

'I felt a giant hand on the top of my head and down I went face first into the turf. When I looked up Whacka was striding away to score a 90-yard try.'

Former Great Britain coach Colin Hutton

A half-trained terrier

WHEN YOU ARE THE SMALLEST PLAYER ON THE FIELD but a genius whose wonderful talents can swing a game, you have to expect to be singled out for special attention from the opposition. So it was with Clive Churchill. The media dubbed him 'The Little Master'. That he was. Little, standing just 170 centimetres, and weighing only 76 kilograms. And he was a master of his craft.

He rates as arguably Australia's greatest rugby league full-back . . . maybe even the nation's finest player. Jersey Flegg, for three decades chairman of the Australian Board of Control (the forerunner of the Australian Rugby League), said of him:

> Churchill was the greatest all-round champion the rugby league code has known. Churchill excelled in both attack, where he had an uncanny knack of chiming into the back line to provide opportunities for his wingers, and in defence, where he was a devastating tackler and could relieve pressure on his side with long, accurate kicks for touch. He was the complete footballer.

That meant he was the target for suspect tackles, forearm jolts and wayward boots and knees. Churchill soon adopted the policy of 'get in first'. How shall we put it? There were many opposition players who were laid out by Churchill's unique style of tackling. Churchill himself admitted in his autobiography, *They Called Me the Little Master*, that over the years he had regularly heard people saying, 'He's a stiff-arm merchant.'

Alf Drewry, rugby league correspondent with the *Yorkshire Post*, was to the point: 'He has the temperament of a prima donna and the temper of a half-trained terrier.' And Alan Hulls, a sports reporter for *The Sun* newspaper in Sydney, explained:

> Nobody ever suggested Churchill is an angel. He has often shown temper and sometimes spite. But for years he has been subjected to

a lot of provocation, and would not be human if he did not actively resent some of the things that have been done to him. It is not suggested that opposing coaches urge their players to put Churchill out of action by any method possible. But there are obviously some warlike fellows in teams who consider it their mission or, perhaps, the smart thing to do.

Churchill never denied sailing close to the wind:

I must readily admit I was no angel, no tin god. At times I was even the villain and I confess I resorted sometimes to that vicious form of retaliation known as the stiff-arm tackle. But I have a clear conscience about any dirt that would be laid at my door.

My objective was to play clean, hard football, not to resort to any form of back-lane thuggery on the field. But being a marked man ... I felt I had to get in for my chop, so to speak, and by retaliation I stopped many players from seeking a return engagement with me. If I used my fists, I had reason to do so. And in the matter of assault on the field I am quite sure I was more sinned against than sinning.

He had his first taste of representative football in 1947, when chosen to play for Country Seconds in the annual clash with City. South Sydney scouts, who had already watched him play in the Newcastle competition, lured him to Sydney with an offer of £12 a win (and nothing for a loss). Churchill made his first international appearance against New Zealand in the Second Test of the 1948 series, displacing goalkicking star Noel Pidding. From that moment on, Churchill had a mortgage on the Test full-back spot and Pidding was forced to switch to the wing to regain a place in the Test line-up.

Opposite: *Clive Churchill, with his sleeves rolled up in typical fashion, taunts his opponents with a sidestepping run.*

At the end of that season Churchill made the first of six overseas tours as a player (he also made one as non-playing coach of the 1959–60 Australian Kangaroos). And by the time he had appeared in his last international, in 1956, Churchill had played a record 37 Tests—35 of them in succession. There were 14 against Great Britain, 13 versus France and 10 against New Zealand.

Churchill may never have made such an impact on the international scene had it not been for a ban on poaching players from other countries. In 1949 he was offered £10,000 to play for the British club Workington Town. It was a princely sum for a fellow who was earning just £9 a week as a sports goods salesman. But the Board of Control refused to give Churchill a clearance and he was forced to remain in Sydney, where he played in four Premiership-winning sides with Souths (1950, 1951, 1953 and 1954).

The Little Master became the first man to captain Australia in three series against archrival Britain. And, in 1950, he was also the first in 28 years to skipper an Australian Ashes-winning combination.

After he bowed out of the international arena as a player, he turned his talents to coaching, with considerable success. He coached Queensland and Australia and then steered his old club, South Sydney, to four Premierships in five seasons (1967, 1968, 1970 and 1971). The Rabbitohs were runners-up the other year (1969).

Just before his death from cancer in 1985, Churchill was honoured with an Order of Australia award and then heard that a new grandstand at the scene of some of his greatest triumphs, the Sydney Cricket Ground, was to be named after him.

Ian Heads, the doyen of Australia's rugby league journalists, saw another side to Churchill, as he explained in the Tom Brock Memorial Lecture, in 2000:

At my home in Sydney, one of the greatest of players—maybe the GREATEST of them all—Clive Churchill is remembered unusually.

At the time when my twin children were tiny, Clive had the bottle shop at Frenchmans Road, Randwick, and I would occasionally visit him there for a yarn or for some supplies . . . for medicinal purposes only, of course. There, Clive would entertain my kids with a brilliant Donald Duck impersonation. Sadly that same bottle shop which was his working life for a while contributed to Clive's early demise. He never seemed the same man after the brutal pistol-whipping he took from some villains there one night. But at my place he is remembered affectionately . . . as a funny little bloke in a grog shop who could impersonate Donald Duck to a tee.

Churchill's old sparring partner from 1951, Puig-Aubert of Carcassonne, remembered Clive with something approaching love, I suspect. I recall a highly enjoyable afternoon at Lang Park years ago when, over several games of pool and several glasses of port, Puig-Aubert talked of his battles with Churchill and of the '51 side, smoke issuing from the ever-present Gitane, arms and cue waving to illustrate: 'Ahhh Churcheel . . . he would be here and I would kick THERE . . . and he would be there . . . and I would kick HERE. Churcheel . . . he is my friend.' Although slightly more gruffly, Clive saw it that way, too. The mutual respect and affection between the two of them was very real.

Heads you win

George Hugo was part of rugby league folklore. But few of today's fans would know his name, let alone his exploits on the footy field.

Hugo was typical of those thousands of fine club footballers on whom our great game was built. It was an incident in 1955 that catapulted him into the limelight. It is remembered as the day Clive Churchill played with a broken arm—to help South Sydney on its way to a Premiership.

The Rabbitohs were in one of their vintage eras. They had won the Premiership four times in the previous five seasons (and had been robbed on the other occasion by a very, very strange refereeing performance in the grand final). Yet at the start of 1955 the Rabbitohs fell in a heap. After ten of the 18 rounds of the competition proper, they had won just three matches and were running last on the competition table. If they were to take out the Premiership again, they would have to win every remaining game, including three in the finals series. What followed was a remarkable winning streak.

After winning six straight, Souths came up against Manly at Redfern Oval in the penultimate round. It was Saturday 13 August, with another do-or-die effort needed. Five minutes into the game, Hugo, an unfashionable Sea Eagles winger who in the words of the cliché always gave 110 per cent, came bursting down the right wing in front of the grandstand like a runaway bull. A try was beckoning. He had beaten the first line of defence and only Churchill stood between him and the tryline.

Many years later, Hugo recalled:

I could see Churchill coming across. I was 14 and a half stone [93 kilograms]. He was less than 11 stone [70 kilograms]. I had up a good head of steam and decided I'd try to run over the top of him. Suddenly he came in high, swinging a stiff-arm at me. I saw it coming and ducked my head. The arm caught me on top of my skull. I heard a snap as I went down. I knew from the sound it made, he had broken the arm. But he had got me with a beauty, I was down but he'd saved the try. A few bells were ringing in my head.

Hugo has never been angry about Churchill's high tackle—something that would not be countenanced by today's referees. 'He often used methods that were questionable, but he was only a little bloke and they were tough times back then, when it was a case of anything goes,' Hugo explained.

It is history how Churchill played on. To get him through the 80 minutes, he had the broken arm strapped, using the cover of a school exercise book as a makeshift splint. Right on full-time, Test lock Les 'Chic' Cowie scored in the corner to level the scores 7–all. And Churchill kicked the conversion to give Souths an unlikely victory.

The Rabbitohs—without the injured Churchill—went on to beat St George in the final round, then Manly (14–12) in the minor semifinal, St George again (18–14) in the preliminary final, and Newtown (12–11) in the grand final, to retain their crown.

'It's interesting being part of history,' Hugo smiled as he remembered the incident. 'The story has kept cropping up regularly over the years.'

And he can boast about his own piece of courage. He once broke an ankle but didn't even know it:

I thought it was a sprain and carried on regardless. I had a couple of weeks off. It still hurt even after I returned, but that was the way it was in those days. There were no club doctors back then. No expert medical teams. I only found out it had been broken years later when I needed an X-ray. In the intervening years I would often feel a stab of pain when I stepped in a pothole or slipped on the footpath. I eventually realised why!'

Brawn *and* brains

UNTIL WALLY LEWIS ARRIVED ON THE SCENE, many critics regarded Duncan Hall as the greatest Queensland player in the history of the game. And with good reason! He was one of the toughest players of all time and capable of intimidating the roughest of opposition forwards. But Hall also had supreme ball skills that earned him 23 Test caps and 24 maroon jerseys for Queensland, as well as the honour of inclusion in Australia's Team of the Century. He would have played even more Tests for Australia but for a severe nasal problem which made breathing difficult for much of his career and a chronic knee injury that brought a premature end to his playing days.

Hall started in the senior ranks in 1945 in Rockhampton, on the Capricorn Coast in central Queensland, before moving to Brisbane to join the Fortitude Valley club four years later. He made an instant impact with Valleys.

His interstate debut in Sydney that year was a real eye-opener—and probably set the foundation for his reputation as a bloke who never retreated from a confrontation, no matter how big or fearsome the player who eyeballed him. Although normally a second-rower, Hall was a late inclusion in the Maroons side as a prop. As he packed down for the first scrum of the match he found himself looking straight into the eyes of Frank 'Bumper' Farrell, the fellow who three years earlier had allegedly bitten off part of the ear of an opposition front-rower (see 'What's This Ear?'). Hall would later tell friends how, while he was frightened about Bumper's reputation, he knew he could not show any hint of apprehension.

In the first two or three scrums Farrell gave the young Queenslander a thorough workout. Solid head-butts. Liberal use of what is euphemistically called 'the squirrel hold'. Knees to the groin. Boots raking down Hall's legs. Nevertheless, Hall gave plenty back to the old warhorse. As the workout continued, Farrell smiled: 'Well, son, do we understand each other?'

To which Hall replied cheekily: 'We certainly do. And you know what? I'm a lot younger than you—and I can keep doing it all afternoon.'

It seems Farrell was impressed: 'Yes, son, I'll admit we certainly *do* understand each other!'

It was an inspiring start.

When the visiting Kiwis surprised Australia by winning the First Test in the Trans-Tasman series 21–19, Hall was one of five chosen to make their international debuts for Australia in the second encounter (Bumper Farrell was one of those dropped). Hall came in at the expense of South Sydney's Jack Rayner and performed so well it was a foregone conclusion that at the end of the year he would be chosen in the squad for the first Kangaroo tour of Great Britain and France after World War II.

Once in Old Blighty, he quickly attracted the attention of the English fans, who were convinced the Australian forwards were little more than a gang of thugs. In a fiery encounter at Castleford three days before the First Test, Hall was one of two Kangaroos and two players from the home side who were sent off. Castleford had not been beaten on their home ground that season and the Australians knew before kick-off the 'Cas' players weren't going to surrender their record without a fight. The respected *Sydney Morning Herald* journalist Tom Goodman described the game as 'the most foul affair I have seen in my 30 years of reporting football'.

Hall was not alone when it came to dishing out the heavy stuff. The maestro Clive Churchill wrote in his autobiography: 'Nothing will ever efface the foulness of that Castleford match . . . it developed into an all-in brawl in which players stood toe to toe punching the daylights out of each other.'

For the record, the Kangaroos won 10–8 with winger Johnny 'Whacka' Graves defying a shower of stones thrown by angry fans to boot the winning goal as the referee was about to whistle full-time.

Hall was lucky not to have been sent off again in the Kangaroos' 10–8 loss to St Helens. One of the home side's centres was Doug Greenall, whose main weapon of defence was his well-padded right forearm (see 'Give 'Em Mammy'). Early in the match Greenall aimed a classic stiff-arm tackle at Australia's diminutive five-eighth Wally O'Connell. It missed, but that did not stop O'Connell falling like a sack of potatoes and feigning unconsciousness. Hall was fooled by the dive and took it upon himself to exact revenge. A well-timed right hook sent Greenall spinning to the turf.

It was on the French leg of the tour that Hall was switched to prop and made such a success of the role that he stayed there for the rest of his time in football.

Despite playing as captain–coach for a small country club at Home Hill in North Queensland, Hall was chosen in the Test sides to take on the touring British Lions in 1950, when the Australians won an Ashes series for the first time in three decades. They won the deciding Third Test 5–2 on a Sydney Cricket Ground quagmire and celebrated for almost a week.

Hall then moved to Toowoomba to play under the legendary coach (and former great half-back) Duncan Thompson, and from there gained selection for the 1952–53 Kangaroo tour. This time he knew what to expect. In every game the opposition forwards would niggle him. Hall explained:

> It was a waste of time—I was never a hot head. Never did I start a blue, but if someone whacked me I would certainly belt them back. I threw a few stiff-arms. Everyone did. On the other hand, I never gouged an opponent in the eyes . . . I never put my knees into another player's kidneys . . . and I never kicked a bloke who'd been tackled. That sort of rubbish could permanently maim a bloke.

In the First Test of the 1952 Ashes series he was baited continually by Warrington prop Jim Featherstone but kept his temper because the Kangaroos had been warned the Great Britain forwards saw him as a danger man and wanted him to be sent off. But eventually in the Third Test, an encounter so brutal it became known as the 'Battle of Bradford' (see the following story), his fuse finally blew. He was, indeed, sent off and had to be protected from British fans as he left the field.

Hall played a prominent role when Australia regained the Ashes in Australia in 1954 and later that year in the inaugural World Cup, staged in France, when the Australians didn't have the same success. They had been behind the eight-ball, as the tournament was played a month after the Sydney and Brisbane grand finals and several of the players whose teams didn't make the play-offs had been without a game for nine weeks.

Hall had hoped to make a third Kangaroo tour in 1956–57. Only one player had previously managed the hat-trick—Newcastle lock Wally Prigg (in 1929–30, 1933–34 and 1937–38). But Hall injured a knee in a 1955 trial game and from then on he had trouble getting onto the field on a regular basis. Eventually in 1957 he decided enough was enough and called it a day.

After hanging up his boots, Hall carved out new careers as a leading publican and bookmaker in Brisbane. And he remained involved in rugby league, serving as the Queensland team's manager in the inaugural State of Origin match in 1980. Hall's son, Duncan Junior, followed his father into the Test arena—but in rugby union.

His old mentor Duncan Thompson was in awe of Hall. Near the end of the prop's career, he wrote: 'Hall had an equal distribution of brawn and brains which put him in the near genius class. There certainly was never a better ball distributor. Whatever a champion prop needed Hall had. He was surprisingly fast and truly tough.'

The Battle of Bradford

Every generation there seems to be a rugby league Test match in which all sanity goes out the window and the players decide to resort to thuggery rather than play football. Such was the Third Test of the 1952 Ashes series at Odsal Stadium, that giant arena in Yorkshire capable of holding around 120,000 spectators. No one is quite sure who dubbed it the 'Battle of Bradford'. But the cliché perfectly summed up the encounter on that cold, misty December afternoon.

The match reports in the so-called 'Pink-Uns' (local Saturday afternoon sporting newspapers) that afternoon and in the Fleet Street papers the following morning were liberally peppered with such words as *nauseating*, *shameful*, *disgraceful*, *reprehensible*, *disgusting*, *vicious*, *sickening* and *abhorrent*. There was little description of the game itself, in which Australia beat Great Britain 27–7, but plenty about the foul play by both sets of forwards.

In typical British fashion, journalist Vincent Firth wrote in *The Rugby League Review*: 'What might and certainly ought to have been a grand game of rugby quickly degenerated into an ugly and unseemly brawl which nearly ended in a blood-bath.' The renowned league broadcaster and writer Eddie Waring noted: 'The all-in brawl will put the rugby league code back 20 years in public estimation.' And the correspondent for the *Sydney Morning Herald* explained: 'Veteran pressmen who have been reporting Test matches since the First World War said this match was the worst example of unruly and distasteful football and weak refereeing in their experience.'

Even one of those involved, Bradford Northern lock Ken Traill, who was playing on his club's home ground, was embarrassed:

No one could say our forwards or the Aussie pack were footballers today. We acted like twelve animals . . . like twelve busy bears fighting for a bun. I have never played in a rougher match and I was surprised that referee Dobson let it get that way.

Albert Dobson came in for criticism from all quarters for not stamping out the violence after an early clash involving British second-rower Charlie Pawsey and Kangaroo winger Noel Pidding. The Featherstone official was one of Britain's most experienced referees, having controlled the first of his four Championship and two Challenge Cup finals back in 1934. And he had been the man in the middle in the first post–World War II Ashes Test in Britain four years earlier. Yet when the biggest brawl broke out early in the second half, he took almost five minutes to restore order and get play underway again. The *Sydney Morning Herald* match report commented: 'Although [Australian prop] Duncan Hall was the only man sent off by referee Dobson, there is no question that at least half-a-dozen English and Australian forwards deserved to be sent to the sidelines more than did Hall.' Hall, by the way, was the first Australian ever to get his marching orders in an Ashes Test on English soil.

Such was the feeling between the two sides that British centre and vice-captain Ernest Ward, a player noted for his good sportsmanship, refused to shake hands with the Kangaroos' skipper Clive Churchill after the match. It was a sorry end to the Test career of Ward, who had appeared in 40 internationals for Great Britain and England. As rugby league historian Robert Gate poignantly noted: 'Ward could hardly have envisaged bowing out in such an unsavoury encounter.'

Give 'em mammy

DUGGIE GREENALL WAS NOT A BIG MAN—weighing just 70 kilograms, wringing wet. But the tough British centre certainly had a huge right forearm that would have done cartoon character Popeye proud. Greenall went into every game with it heavily strapped with layer upon layer of solid padding. But was it just padding? Duggie would explain how it was necessary to protect an arm that had been badly broken early in his career. Opposition players reckoned it came in handy when Greenall hit them with a stiff-arm tackle—part of the defensive talents of most players in the 'bad old days'.

The fans at Knowsley Road, home of the famous St Helens club, dubbed the forearm 'mammy'. 'Give 'em mammy, Duggie,' they would roar from the terraces. And Greenall would duly oblige! Whack . . . thud . . . wallop . . . thump . . . and his opponents would fall like ninepins.

Australians who were on the receiving end of mammy reckoned Greenall played with a plaster cast on his right forearm. Such was the destruction that he inflicted! But on the odd occasion that referees were forced to investigate, all they found was thoroughly legal padding. And Greenall would smile a knowing smile. English folklore has it that when he arrived in one town on the 1954 Lions tour of Australia, he was greeted by a headline in the local newspaper proclaiming: 'Bad Man Arrives Today.' No one has been able to verify this—but who am I to spoil a good story.

Nevertheless, Greenall looked just as you would expect a hardman to look. Sports reporter Gordon Hughes of the London *Daily Mirror* newspaper once described him thus: 'The face looks like an ordinance survey map. The limbs are bent, gnarled and twisted like an old oak.'

It was to be expected. Once, when asked which bones in his body had been broken, Greenall paused momentarily before replying: 'Every last one of them. And if I had my life to live again, I wouldn't complain if each was broken a second or third time.'

Doug Greenall was destined to be a rugby league player from the day

Duggie Greenall wasn't known just for his brutal defence, he also had plenty of attacking class. Here he scores one of his eight tries in 12 appearances for Great Britain and England.

he was born back in 1927. He lived for the first five years in the pub his father ran in St Helens before the family moved to a house near the Knowsley Road ground, where his mum used to charge fans sixpence to leave their bicycles in the backyard while they walked down the road to watch their footy heroes, such as the illustrious winger Alf Ellaby and tough second-rower Jack Arkwright (see 'Arkie Had the Last Laugh'), battle it out. Greenall went to Rivington Road School, one of England's finest nurseries for rugby league talent. In 1946, he was sent off in a trial match giving the St Helens fans a preview of things to come. The Saints officials were undaunted and signed him on the spot as a five-eighth.

When the legendary Jim Sullivan took over as coach in 1952, he switched Greenall to centre. It was at that time that he came face to face with the Aussies. When the Kangaroos played Lancashire at Warrington he so incensed them with his deft use of mammy that at full-time they chased him up the tunnel to the dressing rooms. To his horror he found the door locked and it was only the arrival of his team-mates that saved him from a towelling.

But, like so many other hardmen, Duggie Greenall had a soft side. He loved to sing. And his favourite right until the day he died in 2007 was the famous Al Jolson hit . . . yes, you guessed it . . . 'Mammy'.

I'd walk a million miles for one of your smiles my . . . um . . . Duggie!

Opposite: Duggie Greenall, wearing his Great Britain cap

Whack! And it was on!

July 10, 1954. It was a black day in the history of rugby league. That afternoon at the Sydney Cricket Ground, a rain-drenched crowd of 27,869 witnessed possibly the most disgraceful international match ever played. So vicious, so unruly, so uncontrollable was the clash between Great Britain and New South Wales that referee Aub Oxford did what no other had done before or since—he walked off the field 56 minutes after the start, abandoned the match, and left the players to continue a brawl which had raged from one end of the field to the other.

The climactic battle had its beginnings long before kick-off. Britain and Australia were level one Test all in the Ashes series and the decider was scheduled for the following Saturday. The New South Wales side contained most of those who would make up the Australian line-up. But the British management selected only three players likely to play in the deciding Test and, in an unprecedented move, included three forwards in the back line. Giant Halifax prop Jack Wilkinson was on one wing and Huddersfield toughie Brian Briggs on the other, with Hunslet stirrer Geoff Gunney at full-back. This prompted many critics to suggest the tourists planned to put the local stars—notably the match-winning full-back Clive Churchill and scheming half-back Keith Holman—out of action.

The match certainly lived up to these pessimistic predictions. Indeed, the New South Wales players later said the British had continually called to team-mates to 'kick to Churchill' and 'get Holman'. Churchill recalled: 'Beyond any doubt the Englishmen did not take the field to play football, but to injure Australian players and put them out of the Test match. The Englishmen wallowed in unrestrained vicious punching. Fists flailed and boots flew.'

'Whack! And it was on!' read the headline next day in the Sydney newspaper *Truth*.

The first half was relatively quiet. But the match exploded soon after the break when British half-back Ray Price was sent off for abusing a touch judge. The affair then degenerated quickly. Its climax came after an exchange between Churchill and British scrum-half Alf Burnell. A punch aimed at Churchill missed and hit an unsuspecting New South Wales winger, Noel Pidding. Within seconds both teams were locked in a wild melee. Churchill described it as 'a filthy brawl of back-lane thuggery'. As was his wont, Duggie Greenall raced into the fray and locked horns with New South Wales centre Harry Wells. It was a poor decision, as Wells was very capable with his fists—coming from a boxing family (his father George fought for the Australian lightweight title under the name of Dealer Wells). Churchill explained their confrontation in colourful terms: 'They were locked in a terrifying punching duel like a couple of enraged beasts of the jungle.'

Oxford, the touch judges and a couple of the calmer players tried in vain to separate the pair and the other gladiators who had joined in. When this proved fruitless, Oxford walked off, calling the match a no-contest. Disillusioned, he decided to quit refereeing for good.

The incident looked likely to wreck Anglo–Australian rugby league relations. But cooler heads prevailed. Charlie Pawsey, who captained Great Britain on that day, addressed an official New South Wales Rugby League inquiry two days later.

'My team-mates wanted me to come along and say how sorry they were. I ask you to accept the apology, with all sincerity,' Pawsey said.

The governing body did just that. Officially, nothing more was said.

Satisfaction for Dealer

Harry Wells vividly remembered his next encounter with Duggie Greenall after their punch-up in the abandoned match. Wells didn't make the 1956–57 Kangaroos side that toured Britain and France, but he was in the squad that visited Old Blighty three years later.

'Early in the tour we had a match against St Helens,' Wells recalled. 'A few days before the clash we were training and saw some familiar faces in the grandstand watching. There was the great half-back Alex Murphy and the rugged Vince Karalius. And who else but Greenall. All three were stars of the St Helens side.'

Greenall grinned at Wells: 'Are you playing against us, laaad?'

'Wouldn't miss it for quids,' Wells replied. 'I've waited five years for the moment. We have some unfinished business, don't we?'

As a satisfied smile drifted across his face, Wells remembered the moment as the two sides prepared to walk onto the field. Karalius called out to him: 'Hey, Aitch. Duggie's decided not to play today. He's dogged it!'

Referee told 'no send-offs'

Respected country referee Wal Sneddon hasn't forgotten Duggie Greenall even though almost 60 years have passed since they eyeballed each other on the football field. And Sneddon, now in his mid eighties, has always been pretty well convinced the heavy padding on Greenall's right arm was designed to hide a plaster cast. But, with Greenall no longer alive, neither Sneddon nor anyone else will ever know for certain.

Sneddon was a teacher in his twenties from Taree, on the New South Wales north coast, who had appeared in a couple of first-grade games for South Sydney four years earlier, and he controlled two of the most vicious games involving the 1954 Great Britain touring side. The matches were late in the tour during which bitterness between the Australian and British players had reached a low point, culminating in the abandoned match against New South Wales (see 'Whack! And It Was On').

On Wednesday 7 July, a record 6380 fans packed into the ground at Grafton to see the Lions take on a combined Northern Division/North Coast side. More than half the British team would be playing in the Third (and deciding) Test in ten days' time. Sneddon wondered why these players had been selected for that afternoon's match and not for the game against New South Wales three days later. He was later to realise the reason when that Sydney match achieved notoriety.

Sneddon recalled: .

As soon as the two teams came onto the field I realised it was going to be a tough afternoon. The locals had no players of international

note, although full-back Brian Graham, still at high school, was to join the great St George side the following year. The Poms had a few tough nuts, including forwards Alan Prescott, Jack Wilkinson and Nat Silcock and, of course, centre Duggie Greenall. And didn't the Poms dish it out, especially when the local forwards picked up the young superstar winger Billy Boston and threw him headfirst across the sideline. Then it was on for young and old.

Midway through the match Sneddon's patience ran out and he called out the two captains. He first spoke to the local skipper, a half-back from the Tweed named McConnell: 'You know full well I don't stand for any nonsense. Tell your fellows to stop all this rubbish or they know where they will be heading. I couldn't care less how many players have an early shower.' Sneddon then turned to the Lions captain, Ernie Ashcroft: 'If your blokes want to play in the Third Test, they had better smarten up. I'm not afraid of reputations.'

It was basically the end of the mayhem. Both sides decided to play football, with Great Britain winning easily 44–14. And, by the way, the 19-year-old Boston had the last laugh over those forwards who had manhandled him—he scored six tries that afternoon.

Sneddon's biggest test came, however, when the Lions returned from the New Zealand leg of their tour to play the Newcastle Coalfields at Maitland on 22 August. The wounds caused by the infamous abandoned match were still festering. There was also a question of pride, as Newcastle had beaten the British early in the tour.

Sneddon had torn some hip muscles while training with Taree footballers in the week leading up to the match. He kept the injury secret, for even though he knew it was going to be a tough encounter he was determined not to miss the game. The bloke who drove him to Maitland had a friend in the local hospital who gave him a painkilling injection, telling him: 'It will only last about an hour. For the final 20 minutes you will be on your own, although the adrenalin will probably keep you going.'

The Taree referee explained how a leading official in the New South

Wales Rugby League—no names, no pack drill—approached him before the kick-off with strict instructions: 'This hasn't been a real good tour, with all the fighting and mayhem. We want it to end on a high note. We don't want anyone sent off. We want to finish the game with 26 players.'

Sneddon's hands were tied and he knew it was going to be a case of anything goes:

> I was keeping an eye out for Greenall who was playing on the wing. Early in the match there was a scrum and the Newcastle five-eighth Bobby Banks darted down the blind side and gave a beautiful pass to his winger before copping a Greenall stiff-arm. It was the worst I ever saw during my career as a referee. But that was the way it was back then. Everyone threw stiff-arm tackles. Dave Parkinson, the Newcastle captain, asked me to examine the padding on Greenall's right arm. I explained to Greenall there had been an official complaint and asked him to show me the arm. He told me if I made such a demand he would walk off. When I repeated my request he did so.

As Greenall left of his own volition, Sneddon told the Lions:

> You're now playing with 12 men. Remember what you saw in the New South Wales match. I'm happy to do the same and call off the game. It won't matter to me. However, the black mark against your reputations will last forever. It could probably mean the end of all Ashes tours.

The referee's words worked. There was no more violence. Ten minutes later Greenall strode back onto the field. When Sneddon asked why he had returned, the St Helens agitator smiled. 'You want to look at my arm? Well, take a look.' And he rolled up his sleeve.

Sneddon shrugged his shoulders: 'What could I say? There was no padding at all, let alone a plaster cast.'

And a thorough search of the Lions dressing room after the game failed to find any either!

The Wild Bull of the Pampas

HOW MANY OF US AS CHILDREN were scared stiff by the bogeyman? Who was he? No one is quite sure. But we all knew he existed, if only in our minds. If we were naughty, the ethereal bogeyman would come and get us. The very thought of such a fate invoked terror in our minds.

It was a bit different in Lancashire in the late 1950s. Parents did not threaten their recalcitrant offspring with threats of the bogeyman. Around St Helens and Widnes, mischievous children were told, 'If you continue with that behaviour, Vinty Karalius will come and get you.' And such was the fear of the boilermaker turned scrap-metal merchant that the kiddies would immediately transform into little angels. They had seen the ferocious exploits of Vince Karalius on the footy fields of northern England and they didn't want to suffer the same fate as the hapless players who lined up against him every second week at St Helens' Knowsley Road ground.

'On the field he was a monster,' is the way legendary Australian lock-forward Johnny Raper described him.

'He'd rather walk on you than around you,' said Aussie Test captain Ian Walsh. 'His one thought was to hurt you.'

'Playing with him was like having one of the Kray twins as your best mate—that's how hard he was,' explained St Helens and Great Britain team-mate Alex Murphy. (The Kray twins were infamous London gangsters and murderers.)

Even Karalius himself acknowledged the ferocity of his approach to rugby league: 'I always enjoyed the game more when there was a body or two lying about. It made the job a bit more interesting.'

It was this reputation that earned Karalius the sobriquet 'The Wild Bull of the Pampas'—as he was known in Australia—but it belied his true character off-pitch. Karalius was a mild-mannered gentleman (in the true sense of the word) and a devout churchgoer, who would sing lullabies to

Opposite: Two St Helens hardmen—Vince Karalius, the Saints captain, and Alan Prescott, the club's coach—after victory in the 1961 Challenge Cup Final at Wembley

babies and was loved unconditionally by everyone who met him socially.

This approach to his fellow man cost him dearly in his first senior appearance for St Helens, in 1951, as a raw-boned 18-year-old. He explained the humiliation of that debut to English journalist Harry Edgar:

> People have asked me when I started putting myself about on the field. I think it all came down to the fact that I have never liked being second best at any time in my life. My first game was against Warrington. They had a good pack of forwards, including [former Balmain and later St George star] Harry Bath. To put it in plain words, I got a good pasting in that match and the Warrington pack knocked hell out of me.

Karalius came off the field and thought:

> It's like war. So if it's going to be like this I'd better get myself 110 per cent fit . . . if I wanted to get my own back on the fellows who had given me a good pasting, then I needed to be bigger and stronger the next time we met. From then on I nursed a grudge. I had to equal matters with the blokes who had given me 80 minutes of sheer murder in my first match. It played on my mind so much that it became an obsession. I lived practically like a hermit. I did nothing each night when I came home from work but train, train, train. I did body-building and weight-lifting exercises. Gradually I was putting on those extra pounds and hardening my muscles. I looked after myself and I had that dedication to try to be the best. I wasn't going to let anybody trample on me. Every time I played against Harry Bath after that I used to give him a bit more stick, and in his last game at St Helens I gave him a real hammering. I think I knocked him out a couple of times. It settled the old scores.

The Wild Bull made his reputation on the 1958 tour of Australia—yet his international career was almost over before it had begun. The Test selectors omitted him from the original squad of 26 and it was only at the insistence of tour manager Tom Mitchell that they changed their minds.

'I needed him to tame the Aussie hardmen,' Mitchell was to later explain. And tame them he did.

The distinguished rugby league writer for the *Sydney Morning Herald* Alan Clarkson remembered meeting Vinty on his arrival in Australia on that tour. Karalius and a couple of the other British lads were keen to get to the beach for a swim, even though it was May and most Australians reckoned the sea was far too cold. So what! For those who were familiar with the English tourist slogan 'Skegness is Bracing', Sydney beach weather in winter still felt tropical.

'The surf was pretty hairy when I took them to Maroubra Beach,' Clarkson recalled. 'When Vince was adamant he was going to have a ride on a bodyboard, I asked a lifeguard mate of mine to keep an eye on him. Anything could have happened. There had even been a few reports of sharks lurking around the Sydney beaches.'

Then a smile spread over Clarko's face: 'After Vinty's performances against us, I shook my head. If only a shark had taken him, we might have won that series.' And before British fans start baying for Clarko's blood, his postscript should be added: 'But you know what? I am glad the Noahs [sharks] didn't get him. Not only was he one of the greatest rugby league players in history—he was one of the greatest gentlemen in history. You couldn't meet a better bloke.'

Karalius quickly displayed his rampaging style, the first of four players sent off in a wild clash with New South Wales. His three-match suspension cost him a place in the First Test the following weekend, a match won easily by Australia 25–8. But he was back with a vengeance for the other two encounters.

The Second Test in Brisbane is remembered by historians as 'Prescott's Test' after British captain Alan Prescott played on with a broken forearm to help inspire the tourists to a most unlikely victory. But for Prescott's heroics it could very well have been called 'Karalius' Test'. He could not even stand up in the dressing room at half-time because of an injured back.

Tom Mitchell described the scene:

> The team went out with Karalius at the far side of the dressing room still sitting on the bench. 'Vinty, we're out—come on.' 'Sorry, Thomas, I can't—it's me back.' I got in behind him and did enough to get him standing up. Slowly across the room to the sunlit opening leading to the pitch—then a step or two and like a boxer getting up after a knockdown, he teetered with a push onto the arena, gaining movement with every stride. Without him on the field the position was the same as without the captain . . . certain defeat. How he stood up to the first ten minutes I will never know.

But stand up he did, and he worked with Murphy to score the try that set the British on the road to a 25–18 victory. And Karalius figured prominently again two weeks later when the tourists won the deciding Test in Sydney 40–17.

A month later the Lions played three more matches in Australia when they stopped off on their return journey from New Zealand to Old Blighty. One of the games was against a New South Wales Colts side that featured several future Test stars, not the least Raper and Walsh. The former was in his second season of first grade, with the Newtown Bluebags. Raper recalled:

> The first time he played the ball, I was the marker. It wasn't my go but I hit him. There was no reaction. None whatsoever! The next time I hit him again. No reaction. When I did it a third time and started to run away, he grabbed me by the jumper and said, 'Oi, there's still sixty minutes to play, lad.' From then on, when he was on the open side I made sure I was defending on the blind side. And when he was on the blind I was on the open.

Walsh agreed: 'He looked as if he was made of granite. Felt like it too!'

The Australian fans never again saw the genius of Karalius, with his frightening defence and magnificent offloads. But in England Karalius was to go on to play 384 games for St Helens and Widnes, and collect three Wembley Challenge Cup Final winner's medals (for St Helens in 1956 and 1961, and with Widnes three years later). As a coach he also steered Widnes to success in 1975.

Vinty Karalius had only one gripe about his Aussie nickname. He was not happy with the tag 'Wild Bull'. As he explained, 'I was never wild.'

Hmmm . . .

GRRRR!

Great Britain Test forward Geoff Gunney notes: 'Vince Karalius was a great player. Frightening! But I never saw him do anything dirty. But when he tackled you, he never just tackled. He grabbed you, picked you up and shook you. And he growled at you at the same time. Grrrr!'

Who gave him the name?

As a journalist you get a bit of a buzz when you give a person a nickname—and that nickname sticks. That's why I found it unusual that no one has ever admitted to being the person who first called Vince Karalius 'The Wild Bull of the Pampas'. I wish it had been me—but I was still at school when I saw arguably the toughest guy ever to play rugby league.

The moniker came from a famous Argentine boxer of the 1920s, Luis Angel Firpo—El Toro Pamporo. His great claim to fame was a fight with world heavyweight champion Jack Dempsey, regarded by many critics as the one of the greatest bouts in history, even though it lasted just two rounds. Dempsey knocked Firpo to the canvas seven times in the first round before the challenger smashed Dempsey through the ropes and into the media tables below. The champ's head smashed against the typewriter of a newspaper reporter. Dempsey staggered slowly to his feet, hardly knowing where he was, and dragged himself back into the ring. Slowly was an understatement. The referee had counted to just nine, even though flickering newsreel film showed Dempsey had been out of the ring for 17 seconds. A real reprieve! Dempsey knocked out Firpo in the next round.

So who did make the Karalius–Firpo connection?

Respected sporting journalist Alan Clarkson covered the 1958 Lions tour for the *Sydney Morning Herald.* But he admitted he had no idea. Neither did that other great league writer Ian Heads. Both thought it may have been the colourful writer from the Sunday tabloid *The Truth*, Jim Mathers. He is remembered as the ghost-writer of Clive Churchill's autobiography and a scribe noted for his colourful language and overindulgence in clichés. It has the Mathers feel about it.

But could it have been E.E. (Ernie) Christensen from Sydney's *The Sun* newspaper? He covered many a Kangaroo tour and was a regular at the Monday night fights at the Sydney Stadium. Or maybe a young Bill Mordey, from the opposition *Daily Mirror*, who later became a boxing promoter?

What about the doyen of Sydney radio broadcasters, Frank Hyde, who used to broadcast the boxing as well as the footy? Or George Lovejoy, Hyde's Queensland equivalent, who used to be marketed as 'The Greatest Name of All in the Greatest Game of All'? There was hardly a sport that Lovejoy didn't cover and he was not adverse to the use of clichés either.

More to the point—why didn't I or any other journalist ask Vinty before he died? Wouldn't that have been logical?

'I always enjoyed the game more when there was a body or two lying about. It made my job a bit more interesting.'

English forward Vince Karalius, dubbed 'The Wild Bull of the Pampas'

Prescott's naked courage

SHOULD ALAN PRESCOTT EVER HAVE BEEN ALLOWED to get away with his stoic, inspirational display against Australia at Brisbane's Exhibition Ground in 1958? It is now so much part of rugby league legend that the match that afternoon is universally described as 'Prescott's Test'. No other player from any country can boast such an accolade.

Prescott was the captain of the touring Great Britain side that had been thoroughly outplayed 25–8 in the first Ashes encounter at the Sydney Cricket Ground three weeks earlier. And it looked as if the series was going Australia's way when he broke his right forearm in the third minute of the Second Test. 'I caught it on the head of Aussie second-rower Rex Mossop,' Prescott recalled. 'It went completely numb and I knew immediately it was broken.'

But that was just the start of the British setbacks. Five-eighth Dave Bolton shattered a collarbone just 17 minutes into the action. And by half-time it was the case of the walking wounded. Full-back Eric Fraser, who in the previous two weeks had run up 81 points in three matches against country teams (31 versus Central Queensland, 20 against Wide Bay and 30 in the encounter with Far North Queensland), had burst a blood vessel in an elbow, centre Jim Challinor was nursing a badly bruised shoulder, and Vince Karalius (see 'The Wild Bull of the Pampas') was in agonising pain from a spinal injury that prevented him from standing up straight. Every one of them ended up in hospital after the game.

At the break, with Great Britain ahead 10–2, the Lions coach Jim Brough asked Prescott if wanted to head for hospital there and then, but the skipper just shook his head: 'No. I'll play on. I can be of nuisance value. The Aussies will have to run around me.' But they couldn't run around him enough to win the game. The British never looked like losing, finally triumphant 25–18. And to rub salt into the wound, Great Britain thrashed Australia 40–17 in the decider in Sydney a fortnight later to retain the Ashes.

Great Britain's team manager Tom Mitchell was in awe of Prescott's performance that afternoon:

> He gathered the ball, he ran, he dictated the pattern of play and he tackled well with his good arm. Only those present at the game had any idea of the man's naked courage. It was a selfless sacrifice for his team and country, unequalled in any sport anywhere in the world.

Be that as it may, Clive Churchill, who took over as coach of Australia the following year, was scathing of the way the home team did not force Prescott to quit. In his autobiography, Churchill noted:

> He played on as a passenger in every movement. But what a grand inspiration he was to his players. With his arm dangling at his side, Prescott kept his shattered forces together, and if ever a man earned the VC of rugby league it was England's captain in that mighty Second Test match. But the terrible joke about it all was that the Australian players told me the captain Brian Davies had requested to them to lay off Prescott's broken arm. Why, goodness me. I guarantee if an Australian had broken his arm during that or any Test match the Englishmen would have snapped off his broken arm and hurled it to the crowd . . . the Englishmen will eat you without salt to win a Test match.

According to *A Centenary of Rugby League*, the official history of the sport written by Ian Heads and David Middleton, the famous Queensland half-back of the 1920s Duncan Thompson was just as scathing in his unpublished memoirs, accusing the Australian forwards of suddenly becoming Florence Nightingales:

> Prescott had no right to be on the field. It was a most courageous con act. I know what [former Test props] Mick Madsen and Herb Steinohrt would have said—they would have taken his hand and

enquired if he wanted a compound fracture or would he like to walk quietly back to the dressing room.

But Davies rejected all the criticism, saying the Great Britain players skilfully shielded Prescott from the Aussie defenders. 'We just couldn't get to him,' the Australian skipper said.

For a man remembered as one of the most courageous prop-forwards in history, it is surprising to find Prescott started out as a winger when he signed professionally for Halifax as a 17-year-old, in 1945. But at 'Fax' he was moved into the pack as a lock. And, when Prescott was lured to St Helens in 1949, the club's coach, Jim Sullivan, decided his future was in the front row. Prescott didn't want to switch, but as history showed it was a masterful decision by the former legendary full-back Sullivan.

In an era where props were slow and lumbering, Prescott stood out because of his exceptional speed and try-scoring ability, honed in his early years as a winger. This was never more evident than in his most memorable performance in Britain. In the 1956 Challenge Cup Final at Wembley Stadium, against his old club Halifax, his deceptive running set up one try to his Welsh team-mate Steve Llewellyn and later earned one for himself as St Helens triumphed 13–2. There was an even greater reward for Prescott, the Lance Todd Trophy as Man of the Match.

In 1951 Prescott played the first of 28 Tests for Great Britain, against the touring Kiwis (he also played one international for England and another for the British Empire). Five years later he became the first forward to captain his country. His gutsy Brisbane display rang down the curtain on his Test career but he played on in St Helens colours for another two years. Sadly, all his rugby league memorabilia, including his Test caps and Lance Todd Trophy, disappeared, believed to have been stolen. A public appeal for news of their whereabouts from one of his sons failed to unearth these treasures.

Prescott tried his hand at coaching with St Helens, with success in the 1961 Challenge Cup Final at Wembley. Respected Fleet Street journalist Dave Hadfield writing his obituary in *The Independent* newspaper in

1998 noted: 'Players in his charge found that, contrary to his ferocious reputation on the field, he was perhaps a little too easygoing to make the same success of that role.'

Easygoing? Ray French, the dual international prop whose first rugby league coach was Prescott, may beg to differ. French recalled an incident in his first season with St Helens after switching codes. He had left the pitch to tell his mentor he had dislocated a shoulder in a tackle. When Prescott lifted French's jersey and shoulder pads and felt along the bone, French winced with pain. The coach nodded knowingly. 'It's not too bad, Ray. Pack on the other side of the scrum for the rest of the match.'

As French noted: 'Could anyone object to a man who had led his country to a Test triumph with a broken arm? No, he commanded everyone's respect.'

Grumpy was no grouch

AUSTRALIAN MEN HAVE THIS WICKED SENSE OF HUMOUR when giving nicknames to their mates. A red-haired bloke gets dubbed 'Blue'. A lumbering giant is known as 'Shorty'. A slowcoach becomes 'Speedy'. So it comes as little surprise that the lovable hardman Brian Hambly—popular with his team-mates and the fans barracking for the sides in which he played, if not with opposition players—was known as 'Grumpy'. If he was really a grumpy fellow he would never have made it as a successful publican later in life.

Nevertheless, early in his career he got someone offside at the South Sydney Rabbitohs. An apprentice boilermaker, Hambly had come through the Rabbitohs junior ranks, making his first-grade debut in 1956. But after three successful seasons and a game for New South Wales Colts against the touring Great Britain side (together with future Test stars Don Parish, Eddie Lumsden, Ian Walsh, Bob Bugden and Johnny Raper), he had the audacity to ask for a better financial deal and the Souths hierarchy showed him the door. These were the same legends in their own lunchtime who a few years earlier had turned their backs on Harry Wells, later to be admitted into the Australian Rugby League Hall of Fame, because one of the senior Rabbitohs had told them Wells would never make it in the sport.

But like Wells before him, Hambly let his form on the footy field do the talking. Grumpy accepted the post of captain–coach of the Wagga Magpies for 1959 and 1960. Even though he was just 21 years old, the folk in the Riverina saw something special in him. And weren't the faces of the Souths officials bright red when at the end of that first season in the country he was selected to tour Britain and France with the Kangaroos.

Hambly went away as a second-string back-rower, but his good early form saw him chosen as lock for the first two Tests against Great Britain. Then the sensational form of the rookie Raper saw him moved back into the second row for the rest of the tour. Hambly eventually bulked up and he finished his career as a prop.

The Souths hierarchy must have cringed when he returned to Australia after that first Kangaroo tour and was courted by several clubs, including the two best of the era, St George and Western Suburbs. However, Hambly surprised everyone by throwing in his lot with Parramatta. And his presence helped turn the Eels into a respectable football side after years as the easy-beats of the Premiership.

The highlight of his career was touring with the 1963–64 Kangaroos, the first all-Australian side to win an Ashes series in Britain (the only previous successful side, the 1911–12 Kangaroos, had included New Zealand prop Arthur 'Boller' Francis in two of the Tests). When the side was chosen, the *Sun-Herald* newspaper pointed out how Hambly had lost some pace but Parramatta had used him as 'a softening agent'. The newspaper added: 'His toughness will be needed in England.' That toughness was tested in the final international, at the Headingley ground in Leeds. Hambly was one of three players sent off in a fiery encounter (the others were Australian half Barry Muir and Great Britain enforcer Cliff Watson). Hambly had been involved in a punch-up with Watson and several other British forwards—although Watson did not get his marching orders until later in the game. All told, Hambly made 21 Test and World Cup appearances.

In 1967 he took over as captain–coach of the Eels but was already planning for life after football, as publican at the Albion Hotel in Parramatta. However, midway through the season, plagued by a chronic knee injury, he sacked himself as a player. He wasn't grumpy at the Eels' poor form—just pragmatic. 'I'll stick to the coaching job,' he said. 'But I'm going too bad to play anymore.'

Well, not quite. He was still good enough to run around for a couple of seasons with the Lithgow Shamrocks in the central-west of New South Wales—and invite his team-mates back to his new pub after each game.

Such is life

MEET NOEL KELLY THESE DAYS and I inevitably scratch my head. Surely this kindly gentleman is not the man who struck fear into opponents in the 1960s . . . not the fellow I watched as a teenager as he played for Australia at the Sydney Cricket Ground or for Wests Magpies at Pratten Park, Ashfield, just down the road from my home. Yes, the battered face suggests many a confrontation in years gone by. But what of the benign smile that lights up that same face?

Noel Kelly is one of the true heroes of my past. The media called him 'Ned' after the infamous bushranger. The moniker fitted the young hooker who came south from Queensland to join Western Suburbs in what was then the Sydney Premiership competition in 1961. For Kelly's credo on the field seemed to be 'take no prisoners'. His biography, published in 1996, was titled *Hard Man—A Life in Football*. Hardman? You'd better believe it.

More than four decades after he hung up his boots, Kelly's fatherly looks belie the toughness of this former hooker-cum-prop. His old mate, radio king John Laws, summed it up in the foreword to Kelly's book:

> Ned is the quintessential Aussie and if we had more like him the country would be set even more firmly on course. As a footballer during a particularly vigorous era in rugby league's evolution in Australia he was perhaps *too* direct to be seen as any sort of role model. It was a dog eat dog world and . . . he realised he was going to be swallowed up if he didn't assert himself. It was then that Noel Kelly's unspoken slogan 'Retaliate First' was born.

Kelly agreed: 'Some people condemned the tactics I used, but I wasn't going to let anyone walk over me.'

It all went back to his days growing up at Goodna, west of Brisbane. Kelly tells of how the local kids learned to swim in a creek which fed into

Opposite: *Noel 'Ned' Kelly*

NOEL 'NED' KELLY

the Brisbane River: 'A dozen willing hands would pick him up and hurl him out into the water. I reckon it's how most of the people of Goodna learned to swim. It was sink or swim . . . literally.'

And it was hardly a flash area—most families with little more than two pennies to rub together. When Kelly and his gang began playing football they had to scrounge old jumpers and get their mums to dye them black and blue, the Goodna colours.

'After two or three games the dye would have run to the extent that you wouldn't have a clue what colour the jumper might once have been,' Kelly recalled. Any frustrations were usually taken out in the boxing ring, with Kelly having 16 amateur fights and losing only three.

Years later, his team-mate Rex Mossop told Ned why football referees kept sending him off: 'The only thing you're doing wrong is you're hitting them too hard. You're knocking them out. Why don't you ease up a bit and just sit them down?'

> **'You're hitting them too hard. You're knocking them out. Why don't you ease up a bit and just sit them down?'**
> **Advice to Noel Kelly from Rex 'The Moose' Mossop**

But the real Kelly can be seen by what happened after he first played for Australia, in 1959. Most footballers covet their first green and gold jumper. Kelly was no exception. Yet he gave it away to someone else— a blind physiotherapist named Jim Bowen. Kelly had suffered some serious damage to his knee cartilage. But Bowen, who had been blinded while fighting at Tobruk during World War II, used to fix him up. He worked at a pool and sauna in the Brisbane suburb of Spring Hill.

Kelly recalled:

For a long time he propped up my football career. After I'd relaxed with a long swim, he'd put me on the table and work the bits of cartilage back into place. Fair dinkum, the bloke could see through his fingers. Match after match I'd go back to him and Jim would work his magic. When I won my first Australian Test jumper I gave it to Jim Bowen. I reckoned he'd worked just about as hard as I had to get it.

One of the most confusing rugby league contracts ever signed was that drawn up for Kelly when he decided, in 1960, a year after making that Test debut, to go to Ayr in north Queensland. He had signed to play as captain–coach. But what he didn't realise was that he was to be captain–coach of each of the five sides in the local competition. One week he would be in charge of one side, the next week another and so on. Usually his team won, but it was all very bewildering. 'An eccentric football year,' is the way he described it.

Then it was off to Sydney and a series of grand finals—all of which ended in defeat at the hands of the great St George combination, which was midway through a world record of 11 straight wins.

One defeat which has always rankled is the 1963 grand final. Kelly and all of his Wests team-mates believe they were robbed by a cheating referee, Darcy Lawler. When Lawler died a journalist rang Kelly to get a comment for his obituary. 'There is nothing good I can say about Darcy, so I'm better off saying nothing,' Kelly told the journo. But eventually Kelly spoke out:

What I know is this . . . that we got a raw deal in that grand final at the hands of Lawler—a betting man—because he had done a deal, for £600, to look after St George.

On that afternoon Jack Gibson, who was later to be named as Australia's Coach of the Century, was not only playing for Wests but also had his own SP bookmaking business. He went into the dressing room before the game and told Kelly and captain Arthur Summons: 'We can't win. Darcy has backed them. I know the bloke who put the money on for him.'

The penalties went against Wests 18–7. St George winger Johnny King scored a try after he was (as newsreel film has verified) fairly tackled, and a fair try by Wests centre Peter Dimond was disallowed. St George won the match 8–3. Kelly said:

There is a huge irony in the image by which the match is best remembered. That image is the great photo, 'The Gladiators', later to become the inspiration for the Premiership trophy, which in its moment of shared mateship after a tough game seems to capture just about everything good there is about the game of rugby league.

In fact, one of the pair in the photo (and now in bronze on the trophy), Summons, is saying to the other, St George skipper Norm Provan: 'You shouldn't have got away with that. You shouldn't have won it.'

Kelly hardly endeared himself to the fans in Britain with his brutal defence. On the Kangaroo tour that very same year, he played a part in history. There were eight Australians sent off by English and French referees, a record for any tour. Kelly was dismissed twice: in the opening match, against Warrington, for a head-high tackle, and the other time for punching, in the clash with Wigan. Kelly was also sent off a third time—in a game in which he was not even playing.

Derek Brown, the referee for the match against Wakefield Trinity, had obviously been warned about Kelly's fiery disposition. But Kelly was in the grandstand at the Belle Vue ground. The hooker that day was, in fact, the vice-captain of Australia's touring squad, Ian Walsh. Brown called Walsh out of the scrums a couple times to issue warnings to the fellow he thought was Kelly. Brown kept shouting, 'Get your feet back, Kelly,' before blowing his whistle and bellowing, 'Off, Kelly. You're off!'

Kelly was also sent off on the same tour in a game against a Provence Selection at Avignon in the south of France, but this time it was for an uncomplimentary remark about referee Robert Cassan. Kelly refused to go. Eventually, after much mutual shouting and waving of the arms, the good Monsieur Cassan just shrugged his shoulders and, with a snort, allowed him to remain on the field. Only in France!

Kelly finished his career with a year as captain–coach in the Wollongong competition and later had stints as a first-grade non-playing coach with the North Sydney Bears.

Never did he taste Premiership success. Nevertheless he was handed the ultimate accolade in 2008 when he was named as hooker in Australia's Team of the Century.

Ned explained: 'I never won a Premiership, so I'll never know how that would have felt. But, rest assured, the many, many memories still make it all worthwhile.'

Ned's new best friend

Noel Kelly has one particular story about his introduction to rugby league in England, on the 1959–60 Kangaroo tour, that he relates in most of his after-dinner speeches in Australia.

In one of the early matches on the tour, he was crunched in a tackle by two hulking forwards, who pinned him to the ground. The only part of Kelly that wasn't wrapped up tightly in the tackle was Kelly's head. He looked up to see another local player, who had a fearsome reputation for putting the slipper into opponents, beaming down at him, right foot poised.

'Hey, Kelly,' said the smiling assassin. 'I'm told you hate Pommies.'

Quick as a flash Ned replied: 'Oh, yes, I do . . . except for you. I was rather hoping we'd become good mates!'

This sporting life

ONE OF THE MOST ACCLAIMED SPORTING MOVIES ever filmed was the 1963 English production *This Sporting Life*. It was the story of a crude, violent Yorkshire coalminer who became a successful rugby league player and it won an Oscar nomination for lead actor Richard Harris.

One noted American movie guide pointed out: 'The squeamish will not like the game scenes.' And with good reason! They were filmed on Wakefield Trinity's Belle Vue ground and the 'extras' were members of the Wakefield senior team. They held nothing back as the director Lindsay Anderson strove for realism. One story tells how Anderson allegedly told Great Britain Test forward Derek 'Rocky' Turner, 'I want you to hit Richard just like you would an opposition player in a normal game.' So when Harris, in his role as a lock-forward, broke from the next scrum, Turner hit him with a screamer of a stiff-arm tackle. The actor was carried off the pitch unconscious and took longer to shake the cobwebs from his head than he took to sing his 1968 hit single 'MacArthur Park'. Filming had to be postponed for 48 hours.

The Wakefield misadventure is just one of the scores of colourful tales told about Turner, who took his nickname from the unbeaten world heavyweight champion Rocky Marciano, who knew only one way to fight: forging straight ahead absorbing every blow his opponent threw before usually knocking him out cold (winning 43 of his 49 bouts by knock-out).

The legendary St George lock-forward Johnny Raper said the only time he had seen tough team-mate Billy Wilson (see 'Bluey's Blood and Guts') wobbly on his legs was after a high shot from Turner during Great Britain's 1962 tour of Australia. 'It was a killer,' Raper recalled. 'He was gone for a while.'

And Wilson agreed: 'Rocky caught me around the throat with a stiff-arm and I thought he had taken my head off. He was the hardest player I ever faced.'

Referee George Scott, who controlled Championship matches in England during the 1960s, told members of his family that Turner was

Richard Harris in the cult movie This Sporting Life *. . . he learned the hard way how rugby league was played when smashed by Rocky Turner.*

close to being the toughest player of his time. He reckoned one time before a match he heard Rocky telling a rookie player: 'Lad, each of us gets sent off at some time in our career. But if you're going to get an early bath, make sure the other bloke gets carried off.'

Then there is the yarn about future Test star Brian Lockwood, in his younger days, playing for Castleford when Turner was the coach and ruled with an iron fist . . . literally. Lockwood had won the Man of the Match award against Bramley, but had committed the cardinal sin of not following Turner's half-time coaching instructions. After collecting his award Lockwood headed up the steps towards the dressing room. A furious Turner was waiting for him. 'I suppose you think you're good,' Turner glowered. 'Well, I've had shits that are better than you.' And before Lockwood replied, Turner is said to have hit him with a haymaker that sent him toppling back down the steps. Neither of the pair involved has confirmed the story—but, more importantly, neither has denied it.

On the other hand, while the stories abound about the might and power of Rocky Turner there was no denying his football brain. He had talent in abundance. Colin Hutton, coach of the 1962 British Lions touring side in which Rocky was a vital component, reckoned that while there was never a harder man playing rugby league than Turner, 'he was not short of skill and was as good as any loose forward [lock] who has ever played our game'. That's some praise from a man who has seen, played with and against, and coached many of the finest players in history.

The feared Englishman began his career with the Shaw Cross amateur side in Dewsbury—around the same time as his future Test team-mate, winger Mike Sullivan. Turner made his senior debut (with Hull Kingston Rovers) during the 1950–51 season, was a Yorkshire regular from 1954 and a first choice for Britain after his debut against the touring Australian Kangaroos at Bradford's Odsal Stadium in 1956. He played 24 Tests and World Cup matches (12 against France, seven versus Australia and five against New Zealand), a European Tournament match against France in 1962 and made two tours Down Under, with the 1957 World Cup side and the 1962 Lions.

Hutton vividly recalled one particular match in 1957:

I was almost at the end of my playing career with Hull FC and we took on local rivals Hull Kingston Rovers at Boothferry Park. I had played at centre or full-back for my entire career, but this day I was selected in the second row. I took on my new role with great commitment and when I saw our scrum half being manhandled in a melee by a Hull KR player I rushed in and grabbed the first player in red and white I saw. Imagine my horror when I found myself staring into the deep, dark eyes of Derek Turner. I broke out in a cold sweat and almost fainted.

But God was on Hutton's side. Turner just smiled and said, 'Don't be daft, Colin!' Hutton paused for a millisecond and made the right decision. What was it that Shakespeare's Falstaff said? 'The better part of valour is discretion; in the which better part I have saved my life.' The two were good friends from that day on, with Turner Britain's vice-captain on the 1962 tour to Australia.

In a career spanning 16 seasons in the 1950s and 60s, some 547 club matches brought Turner a host of medals—three Wembley Challenge Cup winners (he was captain each time when Wakefield Trinity triumphed in 1960, 1962 and 1963), two English Championship winners (Oldham in 1956 and Wakefield in 1962), three Lancashire Cup winners, and three Yorkshire Cup winners. Those were the days when the British understood that rugby league was the game for real men and had not been brainwashed by Fleet Street journalists into believing that the Oscar-winning performances in the penalty area by soccer celebrities were a sport. In 1960 Turner was presented with the Challenge Cup by Queen Elizabeth II and on the other two occasions by World War II heroes, the Field Marshals Viscount Montgomery of Alamein and Earl Alexander of Tunis.

After his playing days were over, Turner coached Castleford and Leeds to Championship and Challenge Cup successes.

Turner always worked as a furniture removalist for his 'day job' in an era where the football income of players was just a bonus to their weekly earnings. After lugging huge wardrobes and lounge sets all week, it was child's play for him to lift opposing forwards and sit them on their backsides on rugby league pitches. Such was his fitness throughout life that he was still moving families when he was in his mid seventies.

'I thought he had taken my head off.'
Billy Wilson on fellow enforcer Rocky Turner

Opposite: Rocky Turner, lifted high by team-mates after Wakefield Trinity won the 1962 Challenge Cup Final at London's Wembley Stadium

Bluey's blood and guts

MANY A COLOURFUL YARN WAS TOLD at the famous old Journalists Club overlooking Central Railway Station in Sydney in the years before its demise in the 1990s. Of course, you would expect that to happen as the singing syrup took its toll on the scribes who would drink there through the night before sleeping off the effects in the wonderful antique chairs in the club's Kenneth Slessor Memorial Library.

Sometimes the tall tales were recounted by celebrities—actors, politicians, PR men and sporting figures—who for some inexplicable reason seemed to enjoy drinking with journalists. One of the most intriguing was told to me by veteran rugby league front-rower Billy Wilson, one of the toughest players ever to pack into a scrum—be it with the great St George outfit that strung together a world record of 11 straight Premierships, the hapless North Sydney Bears who couldn't even win one in his era, New South Wales or Australia. I had bumped into 'Bluey' one night in the mid 1980s and inquired about his bandaged right wrist.

'What happened, mate?' I asked.

'I've had a lump on my wrist for some time and thought I'd better get my doctor to check it out,' came the reply. 'He sliced it open this morning and found part of a tooth buried half an inch under the skin. When he told me I remembered what had happened.'

Wilson was playing for New South Wales against Queensland in the late 1950s. The Maroons, he recalled, had a great front-row combination from Ipswich, props Dud Beattie and Gary Parcell and hooker Noel Kelly. 'During the match I caught one of the props, I can't remember exactly which one, with the best stiff-arm tackle I had ever made. But I thought at the time that I had come off second-best. My whole forearm was split open down to the bone.' There were no replacements in those days, so the St John's Ambulance First-Aid officer suggested Wilson go off and quickly get it stitched up. 'They swabbed it with some Dettol and sewed up the gaping wound, then I raced back on,' Wilson said. 'The

139

medico obviously missed the bit of tooth that was embedded in my wrist. And it's been there for more than twenty years.'

Bluey Wilson's career spanned 21 seasons. He began in the President's Cup for St George in 1947 and came out of retirement to help an injury-plagued Norths in 1967. And during his entire career no one messed with him . . . or his mates. He was very protective of those with whom he played.

Typical was his last game for St George, the 1962 grand final against Wests Magpies. Wests firebrand Jim Cody had flattened the Dragons captain–coach Norm Provan, who was carried off on a stretcher. The St George players were livid and planning their revenge when Wilson, who had taken over as on-field skipper, stood up at half-time with a warning: 'I don't want you going out there and trying to get square. This is a grand final and we'll win it if we keep our heads. I don't want to see any of you blokes throwing a punch. Let's play football.' And they all nodded in agreement. No one ever argued with Bluey.

Within a minute of the start of the second half, Cody was unconscious. Wilson had knocked him out cold with a perfect left hook. As he was sent for an early shower by referee Jack Bradley, he gave Johnny Raper a wink. 'I'll join you all for victory drinks after the game,' Wilson quipped. And he did, with the 12 Dragons holding on to win 9–6.

Stories about his courage abound.

Soon after half-time in the 1954 minor semifinal against North Sydney, Bluey suffered an awful gash in his right eyebrow. He rushed from the field, had four stitches to close the wound and returned to the fray to complete the match. After St George scraped in to win 15–14, the Dragons' famous secretary Frank Facer asked how the eye was feeling. Wilson grinned: 'The eye's okay. No problem there. But when I went back I broke my left forearm and that's bloody hurting like hell.' He had played with the injury for 33 minutes and no one—least of all his team-mates—knew it. Early the following season he broke the same arm again but played on for 55 minutes without whingeing. And it was the trifecta for the broken arm in 1956—this time Bluey finished on the wing and gave a one-handed pass for the winning try.

His widow, Norma Wilson, recalled another example of his heroics:

He got 17 stitches in a head wound at half-time but no one was game to tell him not to run out for the second half. He looked like a mummy. He bled easily and always had blood pouring out of him. That's why they called him Captain Blood.

Norma explained to author Larry Writer how her husband was a firm believer in the footballing adage that what happens on the field stays on the field. 'No matter what had gone on in a game he shook the hand of every opponent afterwards,' she said. 'He'd have every intention of getting square in some future game, but until then he was your mate.'

And get square he often did—never more dramatically than in a 1960 match against his future club, Norths, with which he later played his final seasons. His anger was exacerbated because of a growing injury toll in the Dragons' ranks and the fact that the North Sydney players were finding holes in the defence where normally such gaps were nonexistent. As stand-in captain he ordered full-back Brian Graham to put up a high bomb. 'Boot the bloody pill as high as you can,' were his instructions— although he used a different word from 'bloody'. As the players chased downfield, Wilson managed to iron out two of the unsuspecting Bears but when he felled a third, the referee saw what happened out of the corner of his eye. Bluey was off, and North Sydney won 17–4, one of only four defeats suffered by St George all year.

Wilson's first taste of representative football was in 1950 when he lined up for Southern Division, the only side other than Australia and Queensland to beat the touring British Lions, winning 18–11 at Wollongong. At the time he was playing a season with Picton in the New South Wales Southern Tablelands. He made his Test debut against the Kiwis in 1959 and later that year he toured Britain and France with the Kangaroos. Four years later he was Australia's captain in the first two Tests against New Zealand, but was made one of the scapegoats for the 16–13 loss at Brisbane's Lang Park in the second encounter and dropped.

He had been suffering from food poisoning and had spent most of the night before the game on the toilet. Three months later, six others who had also been sacked were chosen for the Kangaroo tour—but not Bluey. It was a disgraceful snub to the old warhorse.

Wilson died after suffering a stroke in 1993, aged 66. He had previously told Norma: 'When I go, I want no tears. And make sure everybody's got a beer.' And at his wake at the Gold Coast pub owned by that other hardman of his era, John Sattler, his wishes were fulfilled.

> **'He bled easily and always had blood pouring out of him. That's why they called him Captain Blood.'**
>
> **Billy Wilson's widow, Norma**

The big heart of Poppa Clay

IF BRIAN 'POPPA' CLAY HAD BEEN PLAYING TODAY, among the modern behemoths, he would have been regarded as something of a midget. He was just 170 centimetres tall and weighed in at 82 kilograms. But even back in the 1950s and early 1960s the rugby league scribes knew his size was misleading. The clichés flowed freely. 'Pocket dynamo' was the most popular description of the lock-forward turned five-eighth. And what about the throwaway line handed down by that great American wordsmith Mark Twain: *It's not the size of the dog in the fight but the size of the fight in the dog?* Show me a sports journalist who claims he or she has never used Twain's words and I will show you a liar!

But Clay didn't fight. He just hit opposition players with copybook tackles that left them wondering whether they had fallen in the path of an express train. Had he been alive in the 21st century, Clay would have wondered why players were taught to wrap up the ball in a tackle. He just smashed them under the ribs or around the thighs (or occasionally the ankles if they got a half-a-second start on him) and left them wondering for the rest of the match about where Clay was playing, rather than where their supports were lining up for an offload.

Clay would never compromise on the footy field. He would compete just as hard against a team of park players as he would against the might of Great Britain. This was never more evident than on the 1959–60 Kangaroo tour of Britain and Europe, when he appeared in his only five Tests. The British had been trying—all in vain as it eventually transpired—to foster the sport in Italy and asked the Kangaroos to add a couple of games against the Italians to their itinerary. They played in two cities on the outskirts of Venice, the picturesque Padua, arguably the oldest city in northern Italy, dating back to around 1200 BC, and Treviso, home of the clothing manufacturer Benetton.

The Italian Test sides were made up of enthusiastic youngsters, all amateurs who had never before come up against a well-drilled international side. Kangaroos captain–coach Keith Barnes urged his players to

go easy on the kids and hooker Ian Walsh recalled: 'In the first game we tried to encourage them by letting them score a few tries.' They managed three when going down 37–15 on a field that was little more than a quagmire caused by snow and rain the previous day.

Clay did not play that afternoon but was furious. 'We shouldn't give anything away,' he grumbled. 'We should make them earn their tries.' And the next day in Livorno he did. Playing at lock, he left the Italians bruised and battered as he smashed them with crunching tackles, sending one poor fellow into the crowd. 'Never give anyone an inch, no matter who they are,' he said. The one consolation to the hapless Italians was that some of the world's best had fared no better against the bone-crushers of Clay. Australia won the Livorno match 67–22, with the flying winger Ken Irvine scoring no fewer than six tries.

Renowned journalist, author and rugby league tragic Larry Writer summed up Clay so well in the definitive book on St George's glory years *Never Before, Never Again*: 'The tanklike, bald five-eighth's stampeding, close-to-the-ground charges battered and scattered defences. A perfect team man, Clay took it upon himself to deter with hurtful tackling any opposition dangerman.'

> ## 'Never give anyone an inch, no matter who they are.'
> ### Brian 'Poppa' Clay

Opposite: Poppa Clay ducks under a tackle from rugged Balmain forward George Piper in a 1962 club match.

Clay's widow Esme explained it even better, telling Writer:

He was a demon tackler from the word go. If they [the opposition] had a danger player he would say, 'Leave so-and-so to me.' Brian would then sweat on the poor fellow and punish him. He liked to get underneath an opponent, lift him and dump him. After the game, though, he'd be in there socialising with the opposition.

Clay's father tried to stop him playing rugby league because he thought young Brian was too small. Small maybe—but not frail! The future Test star tried his hand at other sports, and he excelled in every one of them. Tennis, golf, soccer . . . he had a cupboard full of schoolboy trophies to show how he had shone. But he was destined to play league and did so in the working-class Sydney suburb of Newtown, making his debut at Henson Park, the iconic home ground of the club known as 'The Bluebags' after the colour of their jerseys. Housewives used to put Reckitt's blue bags in with the washing to ensure that their whites came out without a trace of grey. They were also used for many years by surf lifesavers to treat victims of bluebottle stings, although modern research shows that cure was misguided. Nevertheless, the tackles by the Newtown Bluebags— Clay in particular—certainly stung.

Clay started losing his hair when he was a teenager and was often the subject of protests by opposition teams in the junior ranks who reckoned he was cheating on his age. He established himself as a first-grader in 1954. One evening that year, he fumbled a few passes at a training session and Newtown's captain–coach Col Geelan quipped: 'What's the problem, Pop? The joints are getting a bit stiff, eh, old fella!' The name stuck and everyone called him 'Poppa' until the day he died. The bald pate made him stand out on the field. Even his young children would explain how they picked out their dad: 'He's the one with the shiny head.'

Poppa was okay. It was a term almost of endearment. Baldy was not. And if an opponent dared call him Baldy he was in for a brutal bruising!

Clay had been born to succeed in rugby league. There was more than just the ferocity of his defence. He read the game like few others ever have. Esme Clay told Writer: 'Brian was a wise man. We called him *The Thinker* after the Rodin sculpture and we bought him a little one for his desk.'

After he hung up his boots (after a record ten grand finals with Newtown and the Dragons and missing out on two more for St George in 1962 and 1963 because of broken arms), he became a hard-nosed, successful businessman, never suffering fools gladly but always willing to offer guidance to friends who sought him out for advice. But he worried a lot. And the stress of that worry took its toll.

He had a massive heart attack in 1969 and a triple heart bypass five years later. For a long while, surgeons couldn't find a donor for the heart transplant that Clay desperately needed. Eventually in 1987 they did. Sadly, at the age of 52, Poppa Clay died after an operation performed by the man regarded as best in the world in his field of surgery, Dr Victor Chang. Clay had fallen victim to an associated lung problem.

But this didn't stop his old mate and captain–coach at St George, Ian Walsh, saying what everyone who knew Clay thought: 'They couldn't find a heart big enough.'

Making every tackle hurt

KANDOS IS A SMALL TOWNSHIP with a population of around 1500, located between Lithgow and Mudgee in the central-west of New South Wales. There is nothing much for the tourists. The town exists only because of a cement works set up in 1914, to take advantage of the abundance of limestone in the nearby hills. But the product was good and over the years builders associated the name Kandos with strength and daunting durability.

So you could readily imagine that a footballer dubbed 'Kandos' by his contemporaries must have been one hard, resilient fellow. That man was Kevin Ryan. There was hardly a forward who locked horns with Ryan in either rugby code in the 1950s and 1960s who hesitated to name him as the toughest, strongest and most ruthlessly inflexible opponent they had ever encountered. He wasn't dirty like some of the thugs of his era. Indeed, he claimed he threw fewer than ten punches in the ten seasons he played in the big league. Instead, he just systematically and brutally smashed opposition players one-on-one, confessing that he tried to hurt them in each and every tackle. 'Controlled aggression,' is the way he described his style.

'He took pity on no one,' said fellow prop Billy Wilson, with whom he played at St George. 'And he never expected any favours either. The only fear ever shown was on his opponents' faces. They knew he was coming for them, and they knew his tackles would hurt. Pain was inevitable.'

'He was the hardest player I ever encountered,' said John Sattler, a man so tough he played through the 1970 grand final with his jaw smashed in three places.

And a former Dragon who had helped Ryan when he first joined St George, the wily old fox Harry Bath, agreed:

They called him Kandos. But he was more like a piece of granite. And tough in his mental commitment, too! I told him to forget about the rugby union style of mauling. He had to realise it was his job—and his alone—to put the man he was tackling out of business. He could not rely on others helping him. And he put them out of business . . . did he ever!

Born near Kingaroy on Queensland's Darling Downs, Ryan's life was shaped through a no-nonsense upbringing by his dad, a tough man whose strength had been hewn in the bush. Kevin Ryan was academically successful but at an early age he told his dad that one day he would play rugby league for Australia. For a while, it looked as if his prediction had gone astray and that his international hopes would centre on the boxing ring instead. He was Queensland amateur heavyweight champion in both 1958 and 1959 and looked to have won the 1960 Australian crown, a prelude to the Rome Olympic Games, when he was caught by a lucky punch from a New South Wales fighter named Ron Taylor. As is the wont in amateur boxing, the match was immediately stopped. Taylor went on to fight at the Olympics in a team that included arguably Australia's finest amateur boxer, Tony Madigan, who lost a controversial semifinal in the light-heavyweight division to American Cassius Clay (later Muhammad Ali). Ryan had lacked the killer instinct in the fight against Taylor. He was determined it wouldn't happen again as he pursued a rugby union career.

Ryan's credo was to always win. He was determined never to give a sucker an even break. And he succeeded. He played seven seasons for Brothers in the Brisbane Rugby Union competition, toured Britain with the Wallabies in 1957–58 (with a Test against England), played three Tests against the New Zealand All Blacks in 1958 and another against the Maoris, before accepting an offer to switch codes and join St George from 1960.

He was to play an important role for the Dragons in their Premiership-winning sides for seven straight seasons. In 1962 Ryan made the Sydney side that played the touring British Lions and the New South Wales line-up that turned out against the Queenslanders later that year. He was in the Sydney side again the following season (against Country and

South Africa) before being chosen for the tour of Britain and France with the Kangaroos.

It was a miserable tour. Ryan turned out in three of the first four games—against Warrington, Huddersfield and Leeds—with performances which he admitted weren't up to his usual high standard. Before his fourth appearance, against a side chosen from the two Humberside rivals, Hull FC and Hull Kingston Rovers, four days before the First Test, he confided to room-mate and fellow Dragon Ian Walsh: 'You know, Abdul [Walsh's nickname], I think I've been treating the Poms too gently. From now on, if any one of them dares to lay a hand on me, he's gone. I'll cream him.'

Walsh always reckoned it wouldn't have been a pretty sight. However, Ryan never got the chance to carry out his threat. He tore ligaments in his right knee when fellow prop Noel Kelly fell awkwardly on him as the pair were making a tackle. The injury brought a premature end to Ryan's on-field hopes on the tour but he stayed with the Kangaroos as a frustrated onlooker.

In 1964 Ryan made his only Test appearances in the 13-a-side code in the second and third encounters with the French tourists, an outfit so disappointing that they were forced to wander among the crowds selling autographed team photos in an effort to make financial ends meet. After a solid game for New South Wales against the 1966 British Lions he was chosen in the Australian side for the First Test, but a botched treatment of a corked knee suffered in a subsequent club game against Balmain saw him hospitalised and he missed the whole Ashes series. He never got another chance in the international arena.

The following year Ryan switched to Canterbury, even though he could have almost certainly negotiated a better financial deal with the Dragons. He wanted to coach a Premiership side. With Canterbury, he adopted many of the old St George tactics and ultimately helped bring about the demise of his old club after its record 11 straight titles, with the Berries (as they were then known) beating the Dragons 12–11 in the preliminary final to head for a grand final showdown with South Sydney. There were mixed emotions that afternoon—as Ryan had played seven grand finals with St George.

Walsh, the beaten captain–coach, claimed his old Kangaroo room-mate Ryan was the difference: 'He was their strength, especially in the scrums. And he had instilled the will to win in his team. We didn't have that same determination.'

In what spare time he had from his football duties, Ryan had been studying law. And in 1970, a year after he finally hung up his boots, he was called to the bar. Another career also presented itself. In 1973 he stood as a Labor candidate for the New South Wales seat of Hurstville but failed in an attempt to unseat the sitting Liberal member Tom Mead, a former journalist and leading light in Suburban Publications, owners of the main local newspaper, the *St George Leader*. Nevertheless, after serving as Mayor of Hurstville, Ryan tried again and this time won, albeit by just 44 votes. He was to hold the seat for eight years but then resigned from the Labor party after a bitter faction fight. Ryan almost won back the seat in 1987 as an independent candidate.

Never afraid of a fight, in 1991 he organised the Players' Association to legally take on (and subsequently beat) the New South Wales Rugby League in the Federal Court over the decision to introduce an annual 'draft'.

Ryan is fully aware today that he had the status of a hardman. Yet he swears that he was never conscious of the reputation during his playing days: 'It may sound strange, but I wasn't aware I intimidated opposition players. I just saw it as making every tackle hurt.'

A hard act to follow

Kevin Ryan has always loved to tell the story about one of his parliamentary predecessors as Member for Hurstville, a colourful identity the newspapers dubbed 'The Minister for Murder'. His name was Thomas John Ley and he was the only serial killer elected to parliament in Australia.

The conservative Ley did actually hold a cabinet post—ironically, as Minister for Justice—before switching to the Federal Parliament in 1925 as Member for Barton. Once elected to serve federally he was accused of offering the defeated Labor party incumbent and close friend, Fred McDonald, £2000 worth of shares to throw the contest. To avoid conviction Ley murdered McDonald (his body was never found) and forged a suicide note to deflect any suspicion.

Next to go was MP for Coogee, Hyman Goldstein. Ley fleeced him out of thousands of pounds invested in a company that produced a bogus poison that was supposed to kill off the agricultural pest prickly pear. When Goldstein started asking questions in parliament his fate was sealed. This time the body *was* found, by fishermen off the cliffs at Coogee. It was tied up and Goldstein's face battered.

Ley then headed for Britain with his mistress. His wife followed and they lived together in a bizarre ménage à trois as Ley began ripping off UK investors. But Ley was paranoid. He thought his mistress was having an affair with a London barman, John Mudie. In 1946, Ley had Mudie kidnapped and strangled, and his corpse dumped in a disused Surrey chalkpit. This time he was apprehended by the police and quickly dubbed 'The Chalkpit Murderer' by the Fleet Street press. He was sentenced to hang but escaped the noose when declared criminally insane. Before the year was out he had died from a stroke suffered in the infamous Broadmoor asylum.

As Kevin Ryan would say, 'He was a hard act for me to follow!'

Nothing could match the savagery

HOW OFTEN DOES A SPECTATOR GET TO WHACK A TEST PLAYER on the field of play? Only once, if historians are to be believed! The player in question was Great Britain's full-back Arthur Keegan. The match was the Second Test of the 1966 Ashes series, at Lang Park—a match so violent that many critics have labelled it the 'Battle of Brisbane Mark II'.

This was an era when the authorities kept selling tickets until they had squeezed every possible fan into the ground. So many turned up that afternoon that there was an overflow, and many spectators were allowed to sit inside the boundary fence along the two sidelines. When Keegan tackled an Australian player, a middle-aged gentleman ran onto the pitch and thumped him. Needless to say the spectator spent the night as a guest of the local police and fans were never again allowed to sit inside the fence.

The Lions had won the First Test at the Sydney Cricket Ground thanks to a solid display by their forwards against an Australian pack which included two shock selections in the second row: the light-weights Angelo Crema from Tully in North Queensland and Bill Bradstreet from Manly. Neither wore the green and gold again. Newcastle five-eighth Gary Banks also joined the ranks of the 'one-test wonders' that day.

There was widespread criticism in the press about the Australians' lack of fire. The great former half-back Keith Holman, commenting in the *Sun-Herald* newspaper, called the Test a 'terribly mild affair':

In a Test match you go out there to give everything you possibly can for 80 minutes, taking and giving knocks with no beg-pardons. But the Australian team, and here I must single out the forwards, did not show any drive or determination. Most of the Australian forwards fell down in their job by their meekness in the rucks and individual efforts in attack. We needed a [Kevin] Ryan, a [Noel] Kelly and a [Arthur] Beetson out there to put some life into the forward play.

Ryan missed the whole series with injury problems, Kelly returned for the Brisbane Test and Beetson would make his international debut in the Third Test of the series. But the figurative blood-letting had its effect and the blood literally flowed freely in the next encounter at Lang Park.

Bill Ramsey, a firebrand from the Hunslet club in Yorkshire, had already attracted the attention of the referees on tour. Against Newcastle he had been cautioned twice by Goulburn-based referee Keith Lyons before the Englishman tried his luck a third time and was dismissed for a stiff-arm tackle. Ramsey was to be a target in the Second Test.

English sporting historian Robert Gate summed up the match with a minimum of words: 'The first half was bereft of spectacle as the two teams played on top of each other preferring to engage in pugilism rather than football.' After just eight minutes, debutant John Wittenberg got a dramatic welcome into the international arena. Great Britain captain Brian Edgar collared him with a heavy tackle around the neck and swung him solidly into the turf. For a while Wittenberg didn't know where he was. However, Australia's full-back Keith Barnes booted a penalty goal for the only points in the first half. Late in the first spell Ramsey gave Wittenberg a second helping of 'how's your mother'. Fellow prop Kelly went to his aid and flattened Ramsey with a crisp right hook. When Ramsey eventually cleared his head and got to his feet, both he and Kelly were cautioned.

As that true gentleman of the fourth estate, Tom Goodman, never one to reach for the journalists' cliché book, noted: 'Some tough things were done. Men were punched and thrown to the ground—sometimes when they did not have the ball. The tackling of both teams, especially in the forwards, was thorough. Sometimes it went beyond that limit.'

Five minutes into the second half, the game blew up. Ramsey was pulled up by referee Col Pearce for kicking Mick Veivers. The Australian second-rower had no idea who was responsible and staggered to his feet and lashed out at Lions prop Cliff Watson. It didn't save Ramsey, who was given his marching orders.

There were to be no tries that afternoon, with Australia managing to post victory 6–4. For the 36 minutes after Ramsey departed, the visitors held the Australians out—but there was little, if any, classic football. The great Clive Churchill stated the obvious:

> All Test matches are hard, no-quarters affairs, but today's surpassed anything I have seen. Nothing could match the ferocity, and at times the savagery, of today's clash between these two great rivals. Some of the bone-jarring tackles made me shudder. The forwards seemed intent on knocking each other out of the game and it was a tribute to their heart that they could still stand up at the finish.

Back to Robert Gate: 'All in all, the match was a most unsatisfactory affair with even the victors emerging with little honour.'

For the record, Australia won the decider in Sydney a week later to retain the Ashes.

> **'Two teams ... preferring to engage in pugilism rather than football.'**
> **English sports historian Robert Gate**

Rough Dimond

IT'S NOT A GOOD CAREER MOVE when you poleaxe a priest on a football field. In the case of Peter Dimond it was a career-ending decision when, in 1967, he hit Father John Cootes—a professional rugby league player and an ordained Catholic priest—with a high tackle that knocked him senseless.

It was in an end-of-season City–Country match that was doubling as a selection trial for the upcoming Kangaroo tour of Britain and France. Dimond had been one of the stars of the previous tour, four years earlier. Cootes, a Newcastle Catholic cleric so highly regarded in the church that he had been ordained in the Vatican by no less a figure than Pope Paul VI, had yet to make his mark internationally but would do so less than two years later.

There was a collective gasp from the crowd at the Sydney Sports Ground (the site of the current Sydney Football Stadium) when Father Cootes slumped to the ground. Referee Les Samuelson had no hesitation in immediately sending off Dimond. Cootes shook the cobwebs from his head, but the damage had been done. The chances for either of them to tour had gone out the window. After the game, Dimond was unrepentant:

He works on Sunday. We play footy on Saturday. We lined up against each other and it was my job to stop him. When we play footy it's the survival of the fittest. That's the way it has always been.

Dimond was of the old school: never give anyone a favour on the field, but be their mate once the full-time whistle blows. He was given a severe caution by the judiciary.

But the real punishment was the unwritten and unspoken orders to representative selectors for Dimond 'never to be chosen again'. It was a real blow, as rumours had suggested he was about to make another Kangaroo tour. The powers-that-be reckoned he was the type of fellow needed to 'tame the Poms'—just as he had the previous year. Dimond had been brought back into the fray after a two-year absence and played a

significant role in Australia's victory in the Ashes decider, staying on the field to cause mayhem despite three cautions.

Peter Dimond was just nine when he watched his 19-year-old brother, Bobby, leave for England as the youngest member of the 1948–49 Kangaroos. Ten years later, Peter took up the mantle Bobby had cast aside and pulled on his own green and gold Australian jersey. The Dimonds remain the only brothers to have represented Australia as teenagers. Once in the limelight, the big, tough winger-cum-centre Peter Dimond was to continually wreak havoc on opposition defences on both sides of the world.

In 1958, he graduated from Dapto on the New South Wales south coast to join Western Suburbs in the Sydney Premiership competition. After only a handful of matches, Dimond found himself in the New South Wales state side. He scored a hat-trick of tries against Queensland, but his second match, against the touring British Lions, was not so rewarding.

It was a barbaric afternoon at the Sydney Cricket Ground, especially in the second half. In an unprecedented reaction to the foul play by both sides, referee Col Pearce sent off four players. Never before or after have so many players been given their marching orders in an international game in Australia. Three of them were from the New South Wales side— five-eighth Greg Hawick, second-rower Rex Mossop and Dimond. The lone tourist was Vince Karalius, whose performance that day is believed to have been responsible for his subsequent nickname 'The Wild Bull of the Pampas'.

The judiciary gave the thumbs-up to Pearce for the send-offs. Karalius was suspended for four matches, Hawick and Dimond for ten days each, and Mossop for one match. Mossop's ban was served when his club Manly played the next afternoon, but the other three were ruled out of the First Test scheduled for the following Saturday. Dimond was devastated. Nevertheless, he bounced back to make the Australian side for the other two matches in the series.

The high point in Dimond's career came in 1963, when he was one of the stars of the highly successful Kangaroos side which wrested the Ashes from Britain. He played in all six Tests against Britain and France and, in 24 tour matches, went over for 16 tries.

It didn't take him long to impose his presence. In his fourth outing, against St Helens, he started an 80-metre movement that should have resulted in a try to team-mate Graeme Langlands. However, the big winger had bounced the referee George Philpott out of the way while storming down the sideline. And, under the rules of the game, once a player touches the referee the ball becomes dead. Philpott wasn't the only one knocked about by Dimond that afternoon. He crash-tackled Cumbrian prop John Temby, earning himself a caution, described by Australian journalists as unwarranted. 'But it probably bounced Temby right out of the Wembley Test,' said the Australian Associated Press correspondent. 'In England, a front-rower knocked unconscious by a winger is regarded as too soft for Test football.' Actually, the British selectors turned a blind eye. But after the Great Britain side was beaten in the famous London arena, Temby's Test career was as good as over, with just one more appearance, against the lowly Frenchmen the following year.

Dimond made only one other Test appearance after returning from the Kangaroos tour, the decider in the 1966 Ashes series. On the club scene, Dimond's play earned him more than his share of conflict with referees. Yet it also earned plenty of accolades before he finished his career playing in the local Premiership in Newcastle.

Western Suburbs team-mates swear he was twice robbed of tries in Sydney grand finals. Had they been awarded, each would have changed the result and meant that St George never would have posted their record 11 Premierships. In 1962 he was racing to a loose ball, but the Dragons winger Johnny King got there first. The Magpies players called on referee Jack Bradley to award a penalty try because Dimond had been tackled from behind without the ball. But their pleas fell on deaf ears. The following year, in the grand final plagued by controversial allegations that referee Darcy Lawler had placed a substantial bet on St George, Dimond reached a rolling ball kicked by captain Arthur Summons and swore he had touched down to score. But Lawler ruled the ball had slid from his grasp in the Sydney Cricket Ground mud. Newsreel film of the play seemed to suggest Dimond did score. Whenever I questioned Lawler in subsequent years, he would just grin and reply: 'Really. Would I have cheated, Malcolm?'

Whither Father John

Father John Cootes made an incredible impact on fans when he went to Britain for the 1970 World Cup. The Fleet Street press salivated at the idea that a Catholic priest should be playing the roughest, toughest sport imaginable. And this was before the days when the paparazzi followed celebrities not only from dawn to dusk, but more often in the intervening hours.

In recent years, as a weekly columnist in *League Express*, Britain's major rugby league publication, I have regularly received emails from fans in the Old Dart wondering whatever happened to Father John. And I have explained how he eventually left the priesthood to start the first of a chain of furniture stores, in western Sydney. He also was for several years a television personality on the Ten Network.

Letting the cattle dog loose

TOMMY RAUDONIKIS was a graduate of the 'old school' of rugby league . . . when Professors Pandemonium, Turmoil and Bedlam handed out the diplomas . . . and when a blue wasn't an award for sporting excellence but a full-blooded punch-up on the footy field. Tommy graduated with honours.

One of the facets of the old school of rugby league that Tommy embraced enthusiastically both as one of Australia's greatest players and later as a State of Origin coach were the get-togethers at a local pub, euphemistically called bonding sessions. It was at one of these bonding sessions that he earned a place in sporting folklore.

It was in 1997, the year of the great Super League split, in which there were two competitions in Australia. Most of the best Queenslanders were in the Super League ranks, but there were still a host of good players who hadn't defected. They may have lacked big-match experience, but more than made up for that with a spirit that would ensure it would be no walkover for the New South Wales side, which contained such names as Andrew Johns, later to be honoured as Australia's Half-back of the Century, back-rower Steve Menzies, who in 2008 would equal the then record for the greatest number of Premiership appearances, and a couple of the toughest props ever to pack down in an Origin match, Paul 'The Chief' Harragon and Mark 'Spud' Carroll.

To send these players onto the field in a 'fighting' mood, the hierarchy of the New South Wales Rugby League handed the coaching reins to Raudonikis, the man who had captained the Blues in the very first Origin encounter back in 1980. The man they dubbed 'Tom Terrific' explained why they chose him:

> People need to remember the big Super League split. They needed a coach like Tom Raudonikis. They couldn't have a coach that went to university or anything like that. They needed a real knockabout bloke . . . a coach the public could relate to . . . and that's the main reason I was given the job.

Once in camp, Raudonikis took the lads to a bonding session at the Coogee Bay Hotel in Sydney's eastern suburbs. There he fell into conversation with Australia's 1995 World Cup five-eighth Jim Dymock.

Dymock explained how he started questioning the coach about some of the infamous scraps in which he had been involved before asking him whether or not the renowned half-back had been a good fighter in his playing days. 'I was a good fighter, Jimmy,' Raudonikis grinned. Memories flooded back: clashes against the hated Manly Sea Eagles during his time with Wests and Newtown, as well as fights with the Maroons of Queensland and the traditional foe, Great Britain. 'And once I latched onto one of their legs, I was like a cattle dog. I wouldn't let go.'

Raudonikis had been looking for a rallying cry for the New South Welshman to match the simple 'Queenslander' that the Maroons would shout as they went into battle, and his eyes suddenly lit up: 'That's it. Yeah, cattle dog. That's what we'll use.' It was more than just a rallying cry. It was an exhortation to precipitate an all-in brawl in an endeavour to put the Queenslanders off their game.

Dymock recalled how most of the team easily accepted the cry:

Origin has always been about passion and pride in your jumper and Tommy certainly had plenty of that. He had always been a real knockabout bloke and the majority of our blokes were, too. We wanted to win each Origin game for Tommy.

That year they won the first two encounters to ensure a series win, although it was close call: 8–6 in the first and 15–14 in the second. In the third clash at the Sydney Football Stadium things weren't going too well. So Raudonikis sent a trainer out with a simple message: 'Cattle dog!'

'The reaction was sensational,' Raudonikis explained.

Opposite: *Tom Raudonikis slips a pass away in a 1977 Magpies clash with Eastern Suburbs.*

Spud Carroll went absolutely berserk and started jobbing blokes left, right and centre. Beaver Menzies, who didn't have a bad bone in his body, shook his head in dismay: 'Oh, no, not the dreaded cattle dog.' But he was too late. Spud and the other boys were already unloading on the cane toads [Queenslanders]. It was wonderful to watch.

Johns was forced off the field coughing up blood after Queensland hooker Jamie Goddard caught him with a perfect right cross.

Over to Johns:

The doctor put 24 stitches in my mouth and I thought my match was over. But Tommy growled and asked me if I wanted to be remembered as a wuss. So I went back out.

The words 'cattle dog' are now part of the Raudonikis legend. More than a decade later he was driving past the Gabba (Brisbane Cricket Ground) when he heard someone shouting 'cattle dog'. He turned around and there was Johns hanging out the window of a passing car with a wide grin on his face. Tommy was no fool either. He trademarked the words and sold a range of cattle dog souvenirs, including T-shirts, beer mats and stubby holders. One marketing man noted: 'He proved that you can't keep an old dog down and you can teach an old dog new tricks!'

It was a long way from Tommy's formative days. He was born in a migrant camp in the New South Wales central-west town of Bathurst. His father had been a top Lithuanian soccer player who had escaped from a German prisoner-of-war camp in the early 1940s. His mother had worked as a cook at a factory canteen in Switzerland. And the couple were among the hundreds of thousands of Europeans who looked for a new and better life postwar on the opposite side of the world.

Tommy joined the RAAF as a 16-year-old and it was while stationed at a base in Wagga Wagga that he first showed the ability that would take him to iconic status in rugby league. The boss of the local leagues club was Arthur Summons, the Western Suburbs half-back who was

Tom Raudonikis tries to rally his Wests Magpies team-mates.

captain–coach of the great 1963 Kangaroos, and he recommended the youngster to his old club.

A story is told that before Raudonikis' first-grade debut in 1969, veteran Magpies hardman Noel Kelly suggested he get one of the news photographers covering the game to take a photo of him. Raudonikis was flattered, thinking that Kelly was suggesting he would one day make a name for himself. 'No, son,' came the reply. 'You'll want the photo because you ain't ever going to be as good-looking as you are today.' Apocryphal? Maybe! But Tommy's face has certainly taken a battering over the years.

Wests struggled for much of the time that Raudonikis was with the Magpies. But from his Test debut against the Kiwis in 1972 until the last of his 29 Test appearances eight years later, he was unchallenged for the No 7 green and gold jumper.

His last three seasons (1980–82) were spent in Newtown colours after millionaire advertising guru John Singleton offered him a truckload of cash to switch. It was with the Jets that Raudonikis played in his one and only grand final, against Parramatta. The Jets looked like they could cause an upset when Raudonikis scored a try just after half-time to put Newtown ahead 11–7. That's the way it stayed until the 66th minute when the Eels took the lead. And two more Parramatta tries late in the game gave them their first Premiership since joining the big league in 1947.

Tommy admitted:

> It was very disappointing not to win a Premiership. But if that's the worst thing that happens to Tom Raudonikis I can live with that . . . I have no problems with that. It would've been nice to win one and run around the Sydney Cricket Ground with the trophy. It would've been terrific—but history shows it wasn't to be.

His Sydney career ended the following year. It was one of the lowest points of his professional life. His form had slipped and, as he pointed out, he wasn't getting any younger: 'It's hard when you're on the slippery side of thirty.' In a reserve-grade clash at the start of the season, he flattened Parramatta hooker Ernie Garland with a high tackle and was suspended for 12 matches. When he returned he found himself relegated to third grade. However his fighting heart prevailed and when the season drew to a close he was back in the top side again.

Ironically, he was to finish his playing days in the Land of the Cane Toads, as captain–coach of Brisbane Brothers in 1983. He stayed on as coach of the club before moving to Ipswich, where he mentored a young Allan Langer, then Brisbane Norths, before returning to his beloved Wests Magpies.

It was with the Ipswich Jets that Raudonikis introduced a piece of theatrics that he exploited several times in the future. Just before kick-off in one encounter he was busy with his last-minute instructions when suddenly he stopped. He reached into a battered bag, like one a passenger would carry onto an aircraft, and produced a giant ox heart dripping with blood.

'You blokes haven't got any ticker,' he screamed at the Ipswich players. 'Well, this is what a real ticker looks like. I want each of you to take a bite out of it. At least that way you might have a bit of ticker before you run onto the field.'

Alfie Langer gulped and mumbled, 'Tommy, what say we just pass it around and feel just how big it is instead?'

Tommy glared at Langer. 'Okay. But don't you dare wipe the blood off your hands.'

Although there was no doubting Tom Terrific's ticker when he played, a lifetime of smoking wrought havoc on the health of his heart and in 2006 he had to undergo heart bypass surgery. And did he get some stick from his old Magpie team-mates! News of the operation broke on the weekend of the annual Wests Magpies reunion—and the giant card sent to him in hospital had several wicked jibes: 'What f***ing heart?'

These days, it is politically incorrect to suggest players should take a leaf out of the old school of rugby league textbook, but that didn't stop

Overleaf: The Daily Telegraph's 2011 call to readers to join the NSW Origin Army of 'Major' Tom Raudonikis and cheer on the Blues against Queensland.

YOUR STATE NEEDS YOU

TODAY, THE DAILY TELEGRAPH AND "MAJOR" TOM RAUDONIKIS ISSUE A CALL TO ARMS TO ALL BLUES SUPPORTERS.

AFTER FIVE YEARS OF CANE TOAD DOMINANCE, THE TIME HAS COME FOR THE GREAT STATE OF NSW TO STAND UP AND BE COUNTED. ENOUGH IS ENOUGH.

RAUDONIKIS, ONE OF THE GREAT WARRIORS OF NSW RUGBY LEAGUE, NEEDS YOU.

BY ENLISTING IN THE TOMMY ARMY, BLUES FANS CAN SHOW THEIR SUPPORT BY WRITING A TRIBUTE MESSAGE FOR PAUL GALLEN'S BOYS AHEAD OF ORIGIN I.

IN THE WORDS OF MAJOR TOM, "IT'S TIME TO TURN THE TABLES."

- HOW TO ENLIST - PAGE 68

the *Daily Telegraph* from recruiting Tommy as the symbol of a hoped-for New South Wales revival in the 2011 State of Origin series. Using 'Major' Tom dressed in battle gear in a mock-up of the famous Boer War poster that featured Lord Kitchener, the *Telegraph* called for its readers to enlist in the Tommy Army: 'After five years of Cane Toad dominance, the time has come for the great state of NSW to stand up and be counted. Enough is Enough.' And Raudonikis told a Blues bonding session—yes, they still do have them, but well before each encounter—to head back to the future: 'Don't be afraid of them,' said Raudonikis. 'We used to bash them on their turf. That's how you win . . . you intimidate them. You scare the shit out of them.' As it turned out, they didn't. But it was well worth a try by Tommy.

Raudonikis summed up his career succinctly: 'I was never ever the greatest player in the world but I was arguably the toughest and hardest half-back that ever played. And I hated losing.'

As for any regrets—well, Frank Sinatra may have had a few, but Tommy Raudonikis, who also did it his way, had none:

Nah, no regrets whatsoever . . . whether on or off the football field. Maybe, when I look back on my life, I could have done things a bit better, but there's not much I can do about it now. Everything in life is a learning experience—there are no regrets. I still get out and about. I like a drink or two. And I love to go fishing. After all, life's too short not to have fun.

The phantom biter

IN 1976, rugby league was rocked by the accusations that Wests Magpies had a biter in their ranks. After a spiteful match against Manly, the Sea Eagles' half-back Johnny Gibbs was left with teeth marks on his nose. *Rugby League Week* magazine tracked down the phantom biter. In a front-page exposé, Tommy Raudonikis, decked out in a black mask, admitted he was the culprit. He was to explain: 'I nearly bit his nose off, poor bastard.'

The day Big Artie broke a leg

JIM HALL HAS FACED UP TO A LOT OF TOUGH FOOTBALLERS both as a first-grade player for six major clubs on each side of the world—four in Sydney and two in Yorkshire—and later as chairman of the judiciary which dealt with those who took physical confrontation too far.

He has no doubt as to which player was the most daunting. 'No one will convince me there could have been a harder man than Arthur Beetson,' he explains when fans seek out his opinion.

And to prove his point Hall relates the story of a match on Christmas Day in 1968 when he and Big Artie were playing in England during the off-season, with Hull Kingston Rovers. It wouldn't happen today—but back then some of the biggest games of the year were played on 25 December. In this case it was the traditional local derby between Hull KR and Hull FC. Despite having British Test players such as Roger Millward, Bill Holliday, Peter 'Flash' Flanagan and Frank Foster, as well as the Aussies in the squad, Hull KR had not enjoyed the best of seasons. It was a vital match to win.

Beetson had been dubbed 'Half-a-Game Artie' in the Australian media because of his 1966 Test debut, in which he played like a demon for the first 40 minutes but was then replaced by Dick Thornett. The Humberside match kicked off at 11 am to enable fans and players alike to get home for a late Christmas dinner. The Rovers' physiotherapist wasn't available, so coach Colin Hutton was running the magic sponge. Five minutes into the game Beetson went down. When Hutton arrived he was shouting expletives. According to Hall, Hutton spluttered: 'Bloody hell, Arthur, we haven't been playing five minutes . . . get up, you lazy, fat bastard. It's not going to be Half-a-Game Artie today!'

'I'll be okay with a rub,' Artie countered.

This happened about three or four times, with Hutton almost becoming demented. But the coach recalled how when he was on his feet Beetson was the best player on the field and slipped a miraculous pass to set up a try that eventually proved to be the turning point in the game and send

KR on their way to victory. Then came what proved to be the finish of Beetson's English season. He went down yet again. Hutton roared at him to get up and play the ball. Somehow Beetson managed to do so before collapsing again: 'I can't continue, boss. I've broken me leg.' And he had!

As Hull KR held on to win 11–nil, Beetson was shipped off to hospital, where the leg was encased in a plaster cast. He and Hall and a few of the single players went back to the Zetland Arms, a pub that Hutton owned and where his wife had been preparing Christmas dinner.

Hall recounted:

Arthur just picked at his meal. That's when I knew something serious had happened. Artie never said no to a feed, even when he was injured. Of course the stories about his consumption of meat pies were legendary. So when he wasn't interested in a plate full of turkey and roast potatoes I knew something was seriously wrong.

So it was back to the hospital again, where further tests showed Beetson had not only broken a leg but had also torn knee ligaments and dislocated the ankle in the same leg. This time he went under the surgeon's knife.

'Arthur played only twelve games for Rovers, but to this day he is revered by the older fans, who remember his courage on Christmas Day in 1968,' said Hutton.

Before Beetson went to England, his Sydney club, Balmain, had insisted that Hull KR insure him for $25,000 against permanent injury. Despite the horrific Christmas Day injuries suffered by Beetson, Balmain did not collect from the insurance company because his career wasn't ended.

Beetson started as a centre in the Queensland country town of Roma but switched to the forwards as a raw 21-year-old with the Redcliffe side in Brisbane. In 1966, he was lured to Sydney and made his mark so

Opposite: Arthur Beetson had the uncanny knack of slipping the ball away to supports despite being collared by defenders. Here he looks for Eastern Suburbs team-mates in a 1977 match against Canterbury–Bankstown.

quickly that his Test debut was the same year, against the touring British Lions at the Sydney Cricket Ground. He may have earned the 'Half-a-Game Artie' tag in that encounter, but it was actually one of his finest performances. He smashed his way through the Great Britain pack time and time again. He set up the first of a hat-trick of tries for the flying winger Ken Irvine, and later made a long break before kicking ahead for the other winger, Johnny King, to regather the ball and score too. The great half-back Keith Holman commenting in the *Sun-Herald* newspaper was in awe of the display: 'Beetson is here to stay. He showed how well he can mix both brains and brawn.'

He failed to make the Test sides the following season but was recalled to Australia's squad which won the 1968 World Cup.

Beetson's career got a real boost when he joined Eastern Suburbs in 1971. He thrived under the coaching of Don Furner and Jack Gibson. Shedding a vast amount of weight and reaching a peak of fitness he'd never before achieved, he became a Test regular. Later, in the early 1990s, Furner described him as the complete footballer. 'Over thirty years I have never seen a more constructive or destructive player,' Furner said. 'He was so mobile for such a big bloke. He had great hands and he could read a game like few others.'

Beetson capped it all in 1975 by leading the victorious Australian World Championship side to Britain and France for the second half of the international contest.

And he led from the front—especially when it came to taming the rough, tough Welshmen in their clash at Swansea. The Welsh side included a terrifying front row of well-known enforcers: Jim Mills, Tony Fisher and John Mantle. But in the inevitable brawl that spilled over the sideline and into the crowd, Beetson never took a backward step.

That he would ever achieve the captaincy of his country—the first Indigenous Australian to do so in any major sport—would have been unthinkable early in his career. It all started when Jack Gibson, later named Coach of the Century, began his second stint at Easts in 1974. Every player sat for a psychological test devised by National Football

League medicos in the United States. The written answers were analysed by the Americans, who told the Roosters that Beetson was a natural leader of men. Gibson took their advice, made him first-grade captain and, in the words of the cliché, the rest is history.

However, there was more to Beetson's make-up than just being a born leader. He also had strong ethics. And this caused headlines at the start of the 1977 World Championship. In some disgraceful wheeling and dealing, the selectors originally omitted him from the national squad to go to New Zealand for the first game, on a vote of three to one. The Australian Rugby League chief Kevin Humphreys was outraged and refused to accept any team without Beetson, so the selectors reluctantly included him. Beetson was understandably upset when he heard what had happened and withdrew.

'I feel I have kept someone else out,' he said at the time. 'I wouldn't feel right going to New Zealand under these circumstances. The person originally chosen should go.'

In later years he was to explain how hurt he was at being made a pawn in deals arranged between some of the selectors. He admitted his pride was hurt. He was, however, chosen as his country's captain for the remaining Championship matches, from which Australia emerged unbeaten, with Beetson thumbing his nose at the selectors with inspirational displays.

When Jack Gibson left Easts before the start of the 1977 season, Beetson became captain–coach of the Roosters, with mixed success, before he also switched to Parramatta for the 1979 and 1980 seasons.

In the latter year he achieved cult status by leading Queensland to a 20–10 victory in the first State of Origin game. Big Artie had never worn the maroon jersey for his state. He had moved to Sydney before the Origin concept was devised and in those days you turned out for the state in which you played your club football. So Beetson wore the sky blue for New South Wales 18 times. For a proud Queenslander like Artie, that truly hurt, especially as the Blues regularly creamed the Maroons.

There were a lot of critics of the Origin idea. They claimed club team-mates would never give their all when facing each other. Winning a

Premiership would take precedence over what the detractors claimed was a 'meaningless' interstate encounter.

'State against state, mate against mate' was the marketing logo. The critics were quickly silenced when Beetson, stirred by a rush of adrenalin, delivered a right hook to the jaw of Parramatta team-mate Mick Cronin, one of nature's gentlemen. Suddenly everyone realised the Queenslanders were fair dinkum. Beetson explained: 'There were a lot of cynics. Of course, they were all New South Welshmen. It was always going to be a tough game. My Parramatta team-mates were the opposition. It was just business as usual.'

Many stories now claim Artie had been plucked from Parramatta's reserve-grade side to lead Queensland in that iconic game. That was not true! On the other hand, he *was* dropped the following week. This had nothing to do with him decking Mick Cronin. Coach John Peard and the Parramatta selectors had already made their decision before Artie's historic Origin appearance.

The inaugural Origin match provided Beetson with his final appearance centre-stage as a player. But what an appearance it proved to be! By the end of the game most of the crowd was shouting, 'Artie, Artie, Artie!' The headline in Brisbane's morning newspaper the *Courier-Mail* said it all: 'Thanks a Million Artie'.

However, there was to be no fairytale finish to Beetson's career as a player. His last match in Sydney was in the Eels reserve-grade side beaten in the grand final. He then had one final year (1981) with his old Brisbane club, Redcliffe, beaten in the grand final by Souths with victory slipping from Beetson's grasp with just 40 seconds left on the clock.

But the warhorse still had plenty to give—as a coach. Under his tutelage the Queenslanders won the only Origin game in 1981 and the series in 1982, 1983 and 1984.

Unfortunately, his one chance at coaching Australia (in 1983) was soured when New Zealand scored an upset 19–12 victory in the second encounter at Brisbane's Lang Park. After a few years out of the limelight

Opposite: Big Artie Beetson

he was all smiles on his return to big-time coaching, when his beloved Queenslanders thrashed New South Wales in a 1989 whitewash of the Blues, ironically coached by Beetson's old mentor and mate Jack Gibson. But Gibbo had his revenge when New South Wales won a year later.

Beetson spent several years coaching in Sydney—with his old club, the Eastern Suburbs Roosters (1985–88 and 1994), and the Cronulla Sharks (1992–93). And he was a long-serving Australian Test selector.

In 2008 he was named in Australia's Team of the Century but refused to attend the glittering awards ball with the other living members of the hypothetical line-up. He said the boycott was his way of protesting the way rugby league was heading, with authorities not doing enough to nurture the game at the grassroots level. But a year later he relented and was presented with his Team of the Century blazer during half-time at a club game at his old home ground Leichhardt Oval.

RUGBY LEAGUE IN AUSTRALIA has never known an outpouring of grief to match that which followed the sudden death of Arthur Beetson after he suffered a heart attack while riding a bicycle on the Gold Coast on a December morning in 2011.

His rival captain in the inaugural Origin encounter in 1980 and lifelong mate, Tommy Raudonikis, best summed him up: 'Too many people in rugby league only care about themselves. But Arthur only cared about the good of the game.'

> **'Too many people in rugby league only care about themselves. But Arthur only cared about the good of the game.'**
>
> **Tommy Raudonikis, on his old mate and adversary Artie Beetson**

> **'Over thirty years I have never seen a more constructive or destructive player. He was so mobile for such a big bloke. He had great hands and he could read a game like few others.'**
> **Don Furner describes Artie Beetson**

Ian Heads, the doyen of Australia's rugby league press corps, described his on-field efforts: 'He was the maker of tries and always both the rapier and the broadsword in the way he played—tremendously physical, but with the subtle touches and skills of a concert pianist.'

Beetson will never be forgotten. The Queensland Government immediately announced it would erect a bronze statue of him to stand at Suncorp Stadium (the former Lang Park) next to the one of Wally Lewis, and the proposed statue of another inspirational player, Darren Lockyer.

A week after Beetson's death there was a funeral attended by family and friends at his old home ground, Dolphin Oval in Redcliffe. Former Australian captain Ron Coote, who played under Beetson when the Roosters were successful, told the mourners:

He was proud to be Indigenous, proud to be a Queenslander and proud to be Australian. He brought honour to all three. He leaves a mighty footprint on rugby league that will guarantee he is remembered not just now, but forever.

But the last word should stay with the great man himself. Never one to take himself seriously, he had as the voicemail message on his phone: 'Hi, this is Beets, Half-a-Game Artie, Meat Pie Artie, whatever you like to call me. Don't call me late to breakfast, lunch or dinner.'

Foster's brutal clout

EVERY ENGLISH RUGBY LEAGUE PLAYER who came into contact with Frank Foster—either as an opponent or as a team-mate—seems to have his own favourite yarn about the international lock-forward of the 1960s.

Some are quite far-fetched, like the one about when he visited a farm in eastern Yorkshire and knocked out a prize bull with a single blow. But mates who used to work with him on the Hull Fish Docks, where most employees were engaged in the back-breaking work of unloading tonnes of North Atlantic fish harvested by Britain's largest fleet of trawlers, swear to the story of Foster's favourite 'party trick'. Just before clocking off for the day, he would challenge all his co-workers to try to knock him down. They would pounce as a pack—sometimes up to 20 of them at a time. But never once did they succeed.

'Foster was renowned for standing no nonsense,' said Peter Harvey, a St Helens forward in the 1960s, on the *Era of the Biff* website. 'He didn't wait for the trouble to start . . . but set about starting it. Everyone knew that there was only one way for Frank . . . straight at you.'

Mike Stephenson, the former Great Britain Test hooker who also made a name for himself in Australia with the Penrith Panthers and has since become a respected television commentator, had no doubt that Foster was the most uncompromising opponent he ever played against, as he explained in a 2004 interview with *The Guardian* newspaper:

> He was absolutely solid. Tough as teak! I don't think I've ever met anybody as tough as Frank. As much as you tried to hurt him, you knew it was just a waste of time. He just absorbed punishment like water into a sponge. And he never complained. You've got to respect a guy like that.

The *Guardian* reporter asked Stevo, tongue-in-cheek, whether Foster was 'one of those hard but fair psychopaths'. Stephenson replied: 'Umm . . . let's just say he was . . . he was on the fringe of being penalised. But that's how it was in our day, and that's how we all were.'

The Cumbrian enforcer began his senior career with Workington Town in 1962 but was best remembered for his eight seasons with Hull Kingston Rovers, during which he helped inspire them to a 27–15 success over the 1967 Kangaroos. That year he also played against the tourists in his lone Test appearance, with Great Britain going down narrowly 17–11 at White City in London. Foster later had stints with Bradford Northern, Barrow and Oldham. At Barrow he also became the longest-serving coach in the game.

Colin Hutton, his coach at Hull KR (and later coach of the 1962 British Lions touring side), told how Foster's hard nature carried over into 'touch football' games at the club's training sessions. Foster was never afraid to give his team-mates more than a touch-up. Players would wait to see which colour jersey he would chose before making a mad rush for the same colour to ensure they were on his side.

Hutton recalled returning from France after a Test match:

It was a cold, miserable winter's night and a long coach journey from London's Heathrow Airport to Leeds lay ahead. Sitting with me in the front seats were Harry Womersley, chairman of Bradford Northern, and Bill Oxley, chairman of Barrow, and it was not long before our discussions turned to Foster. I expressed the opinion that Barrow had shown great belief in Frank's ability as a coach by keeping him on for so long despite little success. Oxley shook his head and explained that the board had sacked him three times but no one was game to tell him. Eventually the then-chairman posted him a letter and immediately went on holidays before the mail could be delivered.

When Australian legend Arthur Beetson and fellow Sydney forward Jim Hall played for Hull KR in 1968, Foster warmly greeted them at their first training session and explained, in no uncertain terms, he had no intention of stepping aside so they could get his spot in the pack. Forewarned about Foster they wisely accepted his advice without comment.

As it turned out all three were in the side when the two Aussies made their English debut in a match against Stephenson's club Dewsbury at Craven Park in Hull.

Hall learned a few things that day:

Foster had this style of play where he would take the ball forward and when he reached the opposition defenders, he would turn his back and wait for his team-mates to run off his clever passes. But, far too often, they left him on his own and he was smashed by the defenders with no bonus of a break in the defensive line. Artie and I quickly decided to go up and give him some help. As a result, there were more than a few stinks that day. From that game on, he accepted us as dinki-di mates. Frank was a master of using his elbows when he was carrying the ball. Quick, sharp blows to the side of the head left many a defender lying prone on the turf. Nothing obvious, mind you. The referees rarely saw it, but the tacklers certainly felt it. He was one tough Englishman in an era that had the likes of those two tough nuts Cliff Watson and Mal Reilly.

And Jim Hall knew some tough nuts—especially later when he was chairman of the judiciary back in Sydney. To this day, he's not too sure how he would have dealt with his former Hull KR team-mate if Foster had ever appeared before him.

Like so many of the hardmen of rugby league, there was another side to Frank Foster. One Hull KR fan told *Era of the Biff* website a story about the final of the Yorkshire Cup against Humberside rivals Hull FC in 1967. Until that game Foster had spent most of the time on the sideline recovering from a broken thumb. While he was out, John Hickson took over his role in the second row. In the final Hull FC were ahead at half-time, but Foster came off the bench to replace Hickson in the second spell and helped steer Hull KR to victory. In those days, only 13 medals were awarded to players in the winning team so John Hickson missed out. Next morning Hickson was in bed when his mother rushed in: 'John, a man called Frank Foster is downstairs to see you.' Hickson began to worry, as Foster was known to have given team-mates a working over in the past for perceived indiscretions. In trepidation he fronted Foster at the front door but was immediately disarmed. Foster smiled: 'Marra [a northern England expression for mate], you played in all the rounds leading up to the final. This medal rightly belongs to you.'

Jim Hall would not have been surprised: 'Frank Foster was a champion bloke. What more can I say?'

Planting a Liverpool Kiss

EXPERIENCE AND RAT-CUNNING, for want of a better word, will always overcome youthful enthusiasm. Or so the adage tells us. It's happened many times in rugby league. Just ask Jim Morgan!

The prop from the Eastern Suburbs club came off second-best in his Test debut in 1970. It was in the First Test of the Ashes series against Great Britain, at Brisbane's Lang Park. Morgan was 26 years old, back then a relatively young age for a Test front-rower. And until that year he had been in and out of first grade with his previous club, South Sydney.

Lined up against him was the granite-tough Cockney Cliff Watson, a veteran of 26 Test matches since he had first made Britain's international side in 1963. But there were also plenty of young players in the Great Britain line-up, including winger John Atkinson and forwards Malcolm Reilly and Dave Chisnall, all 22 or younger. Reilly, Chisnall, full-back Terry Price and second-rower Doug Laughton were all making their Test debuts.

The likes of Watson would have to guide these youngsters through their baptism of fire after a succession of one-sided victories against weak opposition in the early tour matches. Coach Johnny Whiteley told the newcomers: 'It's like you're going into a bullfight and you're a bull with no horns. Waiting for you is the bull with the horns.' Whiteley obviously had never been to a bullfight, but the young Lions got the message.

As with so many Ashes encounters it was a spiteful match with a surfeit of head-high tackles and niggling fouls by both sides. Some 25 minutes into the action, Australian second-rower Ron Lynch was forced off the field with a broken jaw. Then eight minutes before the break, all hell broke loose. One of the tourists landed a kick on Morgan. He erroneously believed Watson was the culprit and tried to head-butt the big Englishman, who decided to show the true nature of a 'Liverpool Kiss'. Watson later explained: 'Jimmy tried to put the head on me. So I thought I'd turn around and show him the correct way to plant a Liverpool Kiss. Which I did! Consequently he had a funny nose.'

Well, funny nose is one way to describe it. Morgan's snout was spread across his face with blood spurting from the gaping wound. Morgan recalled: 'Never in my career was I so badly injured. Several bones in my nose were shattered. One of my cheeks was split open. And I lost heaps of blood.'

Nevertheless, Morgan stayed on the field. His reward was two tries, as the Australians emerged easy winners by 35–15. 'They can break my nose in every Test provided I can score two tries,' Morgan quipped after the game as the Australian team doctor tried to push the broken proboscis back into some semblance of a normal shape.

The tourists squared the series at the Sydney Cricket Ground with a 28–7 victory, playing one man short after centre Syd Hynes was ordered off 16 minutes into the second half. They then took out the Ashes with a 21–17 win at the same ground, after Australian Arthur Beetson received his marching orders in the 61st minute for attacking Watson. By 2012, the British have never again won an Ashes series.

Cliff Watson's rugby league career is unique. It only began as the result of a newspaper advertisement. He had played some rugby union in the English Midlands, but had never even seen a game of league until he answered the call for 'big, fast, men to consider playing rugby league'. Watson was an instant success and became the backbone of the St Helens club pack and the British international six.

His first Test was against Australia, in 1963. And he went on to play 30 internationals (14 against Australia, nine against France and seven versus New Zealand). He captained Britain several times. In 11 years with St Helens, Watson figured in the sides which won two Challenge Cups (1966 and 1970) and two English Championships (1965 and 1967).

St Helens and Great Britain Test team-mate Ray French was to later ponder the way Watson would terrorise opponents with his lung-bursting tackles:

He would take up a defensive position on one side of the play-the-ball and I would be on the other side. I had to do so much tackling as few opposition players seemed to relish the thought of running in the direction of Cliff's all-consuming bear hugs.

Watson's performances in the 1970 Ashes series and in the World Championship in Australasia two years earlier encouraged the Aussie clubs in a bidding war to secure his services. But one club was able to deal a trump card. In 1971, Watson headed south to join former St Helens clubmate Tommy Bishop, who was captain–coach of the Cronulla Sharks. The pair were instrumental in lifting the side from near the bottom of the Premiership table to the 1973 grand final, one of the most brutal in history, where the Sharks took on the Manly Sea Eagles. And Watson led by example. Such was the violence that referee Keith Page twice issued a mass caution to all 26 players. Watson's old 1970 Ashes team-mate Mal Reilly, playing for Manly, sustained a painful rib injury after an incident in back play and ultimately had to retire from the fray. Eventually the Sharks were beaten 10–7.

The following season Watson could not broker a new deal with Cronulla and left, finishing his career as a player–coach of Wollongong Souths in the Illawarra competition.

Journalist Neil Cadigan told a wonderful story about Watson in the book *Rugby League Yarns*. It concerns a 1972 match against Penrith at Endeavour Field (now, in its fifth metamorphosis, Toyota Stadium). Early in the action Watson had his jaw broken in two places but continued playing until half-time. 'A Penrith player cracked me with his elbow, and as I had broken my jaw two years earlier I knew that it was gone,' Watson explained. 'But it was okay to play on for a while until it cooled down.'

At the interval he broke the news to the team medico, Dr Peter Malouf, who decided to personally drive him to hospital where he would get it wired. However, before leaving, Watson ran upstairs into the grandstand to explain to his wife what was happening. 'I just thought I had better tell Barbara I wouldn't be home for tea,' Watson said. 'In fact, tea wasn't quite what it used to be for the next couple of months.'

That probably hurt as much as the broken jaw. Ray French recalled

Opposite: Frenchman Marcel Bescos was the toughest opponent Watson ever encountered.

Watson's gargantuan appetite, especially before a game: 'Not for Cliff the lightly boiled egg or the medium-rare steak. No, he preferred a full four-course lunch, often less than an hour before kick-off. And extra portions of chips were always welcome.'

Watson confronted many of the game's toughest forwards during his career and has gone public to air his respect for the likes of Aussies John Sattler, John 'Lurch' O'Neill, Kevin Ryan, Brian Hambly and Bob O'Reilly. But when it comes to hardmen against whom he had squared off, he admitted none could compare with a Frenchman from the RC Albi club, Marcel Bescos.

He told Cadigan that he discovered Bescos' looks were very deceiving when the pair first locked horns in a 1966 Test match:

He was a short, stocky prop with thinning hair. And I was young and cocky so I thought to myself, 'I'll rip into this lad and make his life a misery.' So in the scrums I head-butted him, wrenched his arms, squeezed the muscles under his ribs . . . all I could do to unsettle him.

Eventually, after one scrum broke up, Bescos looked Watson in the eye and suggested: 'No more, monsieur. No more!' But Watson was a slow learner. He had no intention of being swayed by the Frenchman's entreaty. He laid about Bescos with even more vigour in the next scrum. It was a big mistake.

'From that moment on, he punched me, strangled me and threw my body around like a rag doll,' Watson explained. 'He was the strongest player I ever faced. He absolutely exhausted me. I couldn't control him at all.'

At full-time Bescos approached Watson, nodded politely, shook the young English prop's hand and smiled while uttering the simple words: 'Thank you for the game, monsieur.'

Watson was to later find out that this short prop with the deceiving looks was something of a Jekyll-and-Hyde. Off the field Bescos was a mild-mannered antique dealer whose hobby was the study of French history.

Sattler's broken jaw

THE ICONIC IMAGE OF COURAGE on the rugby league field in Australia is that of South Sydney captain John Sattler embracing coach Clive Churchill after the Rabbitohs had won the 1970 grand final. Sattler is obviously happy despite the blood oozing from his mouth and a jaw that doesn't sit straight. His forced smile disguises the intense pain of an injury that would have had a lesser man rushed to the nearest hospital at least an hour earlier for immediate surgery. For Sattler had been the victim of a vicious late tackle in the fifth minute of the game—a tackle that had shattered his jaw in three places—but he refused to quit, staying on to inspire his team-mates to a famous grand final victory over Manly.

When the injury occurred it was touch and go whether Sattler would be able to stay on his feet, let alone see out the 80 minutes of the grand final action. He had pleaded with team-mate and fellow Test star Mike Cleary: 'Mate, I'm dizzy. Hold me up, hold on to me, don't let me fall. I don't want those bastards to know I'm crook.' Cleary obliged, Sattler shook the cobwebs out of his head and the rest is now a rugby league legend.

Sattler is the only one who has ever told the full story. The man responsible, regular Manly lower-grade player, John Bucknall, is the only other person who knew everything that happened—and, predictably, he's never wanted to elaborate. Others saw part of what happened, but Sattler saw it and felt it:

> Bucknall only got into their team because a couple of other blokes were missing, injured. I think he went onto the field looking for easy pickings. Maybe make a name for himself on the biggest day of the year. Their prop Bill Hamilton made a burst and Bucknall loomed up inside him, screaming for the ball. But Hamilton didn't pass it. Then as Bucknall ran back for the play-the-ball he hit me with the best forearm jolt imaginable. It knocked me off my feet. Then, as I was on one knee trying to get up, Bucknall belted me again. He finished up breaking my jaw in three places. There was one break on either side and the third was in the middle. And six of my teeth were smashed.

But Sattler has always downplayed the courage he showed by staying on the field:

> I wasn't getting any mad pain. Of course, it was very uncomfortable, but I knew I could put up with that. Most of my team-mates were unaware of how serious it was. Clive [Churchill] did and at half-time asked if I wanted to call it a day. But I knew I could get through the match and went back on for the second half. It was only at full-time when I started to cool down and the adrenalin rush was over that the pain really set in. I was taken to hospital and stayed there for two weeks. And my jaw was wired up for another 14 weeks. It should have healed quicker, but I'd often wake up at night with a jolt and break the wiring.
>
> It wasn't about trying to be a hero that afternoon. In fact I don't really know what it was. I just battled on. It was a grand final and nothing was going to stop me. Some blokes can play through the pain barrier and others can't. But league is a hard game and I think your mind and your body just get used to it. You get used to the toughness, the big knocks, and you learn how to take it.

Another famous South Sydney forward, Bob McCarthy, was well aware what had happened in those opening minutes of the 1970 grand final. He was determined to wreak revenge and waited for the chance. Five minutes before half-time he got that opportunity and creamed the Manly forward. Bucknall staggered off the pitch and never returned. In league-speak it's called 'Looking after your mates.'

The injury cost Sattler the captaincy of Australia's side which won the World Cup in Britain six weeks later. But he did get to hold up the JJ Giltinan Shield, the symbol of Premiership superiority—and was back again 12 months later to lead the Rabbitohs to another success.

Opposite: A bruised, battered and bloodied John Sattler is chaired from the field by team-mates after Souths won the 1970 grand final.

'It wasn't about trying to be a hero that afternoon ... It was a grand final and nothing was going to stop me.

John Sattler, explaining why he continued playing with the broken jaw

Ironically, for a player with such a fearsome reputation, Sattler originally detested rugby league because it was too rough. He lost count of the number of times he was punished for skipping winter sports afternoons at school because he didn't want to play footy. But a neighbour in Kurri Kurri, the coalfields town west of Newcastle, helped change his attitude by asking him to play a game of touch football with some other local youngsters. Sattler accepted and found he actually enjoyed the sport. And he soon made his mark, never taking a backward step no matter who was the opponent.

As a lock-forward, he was one of the stars in the Newcastle representative side which beat the touring 1962 Great Britain side 23–18 in a vicious match. It wasn't the Lions Test line-up, but it was captained by Derek Turner, who didn't get his nickname 'Rocky' for nothing, and it boasted a rough, tough front-row combination of Jack Wilkinson, John Shaw and Ken Noble, keen to show raw 19-year-olds like Sattler who was boss.

St George and Canterbury both tried to woo the young Novocastrian, but it was South Sydney that eventually got his signature on a contract. He started at Redfern the following season and was soon beating a regular path to the judiciary hearings at the New South Wales Rugby League headquarters in Phillip Street. As Sattler later explained: 'I had a bit of a reputation. I had the habit of exploding every time something went wrong. And, as a result, I was given a few holidays.'

It all changed when he was handed the Souths captaincy in 1967. He was still not averse to dealing out a bit of 'Larry Dooley' but it was no longer random mayhem: 'Instead of acting on impulse I'd stop for a moment and think it over before taking a calmer approach. It was a new-found responsibility and something that I found I enjoyed.' Sattler was to lead Souths to four Premierships, in 1967, 1968, 1970 and 1971.

Sattler toured Great Britain and France with the 1967–68 Kangaroos, even though he had not yet played for New South Wales. He was captain of the Australian side which toured New Zealand in 1969, and he also skippered Australia in a Test against the touring 1970 Englishmen before his horrific injury. His career spanned 14 seasons, two in the Newcastle competition, nine with Souths and the final three in Brisbane. In that period, he achieved a record of being sent off 15 times. Suspensions cost him 30 weeks of play, a huge period in his era. Yet his wife once described him as being 'as gentle as a lamb'.

Noel Kelly, another old hardman who roomed with him on the Kangaroo tour, agreed. He once told Sattler: 'For such a fiery bloke on the field, you're awfully quiet off it. I think it's your mouthguard. When you put it in, it's like flicking a switch and you go off your head.'

Sattler could never believe Kelly's summation: 'Can you imagine that coming from Ned Kelly? He was a fine one to talk!'

Sattler recounted a time when the pair were chatting about the modern game and all the video coverage. 'It's just as well we're not playing these days, Satts,' Kelly said. 'We'd only get a game every leap year!'

> **'For such a fiery bloke on the field, you're awfully quiet off it. I think it's your mouthguard. When you put it in, it's like flicking a switch and you go off your head.'**
> **Noel Kelly's unusual take on Sattler**

Dog eats dog

THERE ARE SO MANY OF LIFE'S LITTLE MYSTERIES that confront us as we go about our day-to-day existence. Like, why do you only lose one sock from each pair in the laundry? Why do cars move at their slowest during 'rush hour'? Why do you park in a driveway? And before they invented drawing boards, what did they go back to?

So it is with rugby league. Why did Canterbury's record-breaking five-eighth Terry Lamb snap a field goal in the closing minutes of a match against Newcastle when the Bulldogs trailed by two points in 1992? Why was Len Smith good enough to be captain–coach in the Third Test against New Zealand in 1948, but when the Kangaroo touring side was selected a few hours later he wasn't regarded as being among the best 26 players in the country, missing the squad completely?

Then there is the case of a British journalist with an unfathomable analysis of a game that unfolded before his very eyes. On Challenge Cup Final Day every May, in the press box that used to hang from the grandstand roof at Wembley (accessible only by a scary shuffle along a narrow catwalk some 30-odd metres above the crowd below), the scribes would be asked to cast their votes for winner of the Lance Todd Trophy awarded to the Man of the Match. In 1969, when Castleford took on Salford, this fellow kept telling everyone in a loud voice that the Lance Todd Trophy winner was a foregone conclusion. 'There can be only one winner,' he roared over and over again. 'Colin Dixon!' Admittedly, Dixon, the Salford back-rower, played very well in a beaten side. But then, with the clock ticking down, a Cup official collected the votes and counted them before announcing to the journalists: 'Lance Todd Trophy winner . . . Colin Dixon of Salford, one vote . . . Malcolm Reilly of Castleford, 27 votes.' The expression on the face of Dixon's admirer had to be seen to be believed.

Opposite: Mal Reilly in his 1969 Challenge Cup Final jumper . . . the year he won the Lance Todd Trophy as Man of the Match.

That afternoon, the 21-year-old lock Mal Reilly truly came of age. His pen-portrait in the match program said:

Is regarded as the most promising young loose forward in the game. Was selected for the England v France Under–24s international recently and has played for Yorkshire. Castleford people confidently expect him to represent Great Britain in the World Cup later this year.

He didn't. The World Cup was postponed for 12 months. But he did make the British side to tour Down Under the following year.

It was on that tour that the Australian fans were introduced to the headstrong Reilly via some newspaper headlines he would have rather not appeared. They related to off-field scuffles—one with a Brisbane businessmen and another with South Sydney full-back Kevin 'Lummy' Longbottom.

But all this paled when stacked up against his uncompromising play on the field. To this day many keen judges reckon it was young Reilly's no-nonsense approach that provided the foundations for the Lions' success in that Ashes series, winning the final two Tests in Sydney, after losing the opener at Brisbane's Lang Park. At the World Cup in Britain later in 1970, Manly secretary Ken Arthurson, who was manager of the Australian team, talked Reilly into joining the Sea Eagles (St George had also been trying to woo him).

It took Reilly just two games in Sydney to set the scene for the rest of his career in Australia. It was against a tough Wests Magpies side. In his autobiography *Reilly: A Life in Rugby League*, he explained:

I had arrived [in Sydney] with something of a reputation and everyone was hell-bent on fixing me up. The game was survival, a matter of looking after yourself. I have always found the best avenue of defence was attack—getting the ground rules square to start off with. Looking back now, some of the things that went on in those seasons make me shudder. No way it could happen in the modern game . . . I don't condone many of the things that happened then. Really, it was dog eat dog . . . It wasn't as if I had a quiet way with some of the things I did—it was blatant.

His Manly team-mates dubbed Reilly 'Kiss', as in 'Liverpool Kiss'. Enough said!

In that game against Wests Reilly admitted he fell for the 'thimble and pea' trick. The Magpie forwards baited him, he retaliated, and the referee gave him his marching orders. A few weeks later he was sent off again, this time against Canterbury. But to give him his due, he adapted his aggressive game . . . although not enough to prevent being sent off seven or eight times in club matches.

In that first year in Australia, Reilly suffered an injury to his right knee which was to plague him for the rest of his career—and beyond. The knee became the most famous in Australian sport—so well-known that *Daily Telegraph* columnist Mike Gibson even conducted a spoof interview with it, the knee replying to Gibbo's questions in what could be construed in print as a Yorkshire accent. Reilly admitted that he was in severe pain every time he played—but pain never stopped a genuine hardman.

Reilly was involved in one of the most vicious of all grand finals in the history of the game in Australia—the 1973 encounter between Manly and Cronulla. During one flare-up, Reilly walked away from a fight for the only time in his football career. It involved his former Great Britain team-mate Cliff Watson, who was one of the Sharks props. Reilly explained in his autobiography:

Cliffy Watson and I suddenly found ourselves face to face. In the same instant we turned away and found someone else to sort out. Being tour friends [on the 1970 Ashes tour] creates a powerful bond—and that camaraderie doesn't snap easily, especially when you're both far away in another country. I think had we been in England then we would have probably tested the water with each other but when you're playing the game away from home, well, it's all Pommies together.

The Manly enforcer didn't last long. In the 25th minute, he had chip-kicked over the defensive line and intended to follow through. Instead he was flattened by Cronulla (and Australia's Test) hooker Ron Turner, who planted his knees into Reilly's pelvis. It was a payback for a stiff-arm Reilly had planted on Turner in a previous match—causing a wound that required 27 stitches. 'To put it simply, I got my comeuppance. What goes around . . . comes around,' said Reilly. Manly won the grand final 10–7.

But to paint Reilly as just a backyard brawler would be a terrible injustice to one of the classiest players ever to grace a rugby league arena. He possessed some amazing footballing skills. No one could better offload the ball to team-mates running in support. His kicking game would do justice to the finest halves of the modern game and the supreme full-backs of yesteryear, when they were expected to use the air to relieve pressure in defence. None could produce a better chip-kick. Reilly was master of the up-and-under before the media renamed it the 'bomb'. And when he successfully turned his talents to coaching, notably with the Great Britain Test side and the Newcastle Knights in Australia, he proved to have a tactical brain second to none.

Renowned sporting journalist Ian Heads, who ghosted *Reilly: A Life in Rugby League*, reckoned he was the greatest English player of his time and arguably the most outstanding Great Britain player in three decades.

Heads retold a story about a game at Brookvale Oval that remained etched in the mind of Arthurson, the man who snared Reilly's signature for Manly and was later the game's supremo:

> Arthurson can still conjure up with ease an image of Reilly beseiged by a swarm of angry Western Suburbs forwards intent on destroying him. Suddenly from the melee an arm pops out, football in hand. In the twinkling of an eye the ball is on its way and a Manly team-mate is over between the posts for a try.

Ken Arthurson has always been an unabashed fan of the Yorkshireman, rating him one of the toughest players he had ever seen—and Arko saw some tough men in his long career as a player, coach and administrator.

'He never asked for any quarter, never got any,' Arthurson explained. 'His attitude was that if he was going to hand it out, then he was going to cop it back. And that's the way he lived.'

But Arthurson also saw another side to Reilly:

A bloke for whom such things as family, love of home, loyalty to friends always meant the world. In every possible respect he was an ideal citizen—a considerate, modest and responsible bloke. A gentle man and a gentleman.

'It wasn't as if I had a quiet way with some of the things I did—it was blatant.'

Mal Reilly

A boot full of blood

JOHN O'NEILL'S TEAM-MATES DUBBED HIM 'LURCH'—and that says it all! Lurch, of course, was the tall, shambling butler with the Frankenstein monster's looks in the macabre 1960s television comedy series adaptation of the long-running cartoon strip *The Addams Family*.

On the box, Lurch was regarded as a bit of a joke, treated in a patronising manner by his employers Gomez and Morticia Addams. Not so the big prop-forward with a record of six Premiership victories from eight grand final appearances. It is doubtful whether there has been a more feared forward in the history of the game, even though he played in an era where brutality was the norm.

His success can probably be attributed to the fact that O'Neill was never afraid of hard yakka. When he was in his prime, players couldn't pick up the riches available to today's pampered stars. You had to have a day job to make ends meet. And O'Neill was a builder's labourer—long hours of swinging a pick and digging out tonnes of soil with a shovel. It was an appropriate lifestyle for a hardman of rugby league, honing his muscles so he could be the last man standing in each and every match.

'You had to outlast the opposition,' O'Neill explained. 'You had to be standing over them after eighty minutes. These were the days when there were no replacements. It was no use being on top after ten minutes if you couldn't go on with the job.'

Lurch was going on with the job when just a raw-boned 16-year-old playing for Gunnedah in the New England area of northern New South Wales, mixing it with old hands twice his age who had a wealth of experience in the rough and tumble of country football.

In 1964, St George scouts recognised his potential. But the Dragons' famous secretary Frank Facer realised that if O'Neill moved to Kogarah the best he could hope for was a spot in the reserve-grade side—and that would snuff out his enthusiasm for the game. After all, the St George pack included internationals Norm Provan, Johnny Raper, Elton Rasmussen, Kevin Ryan, Dick Huddart (Great Britain) and Ian Walsh as well as

New South Wales representative Monty Porter. So O'Neill stayed in Gunnedah, where he played Country Seconds for the Northern Division side that beat France 17–13 and for New South Wales Colts, who beat the tourists 39–15.

Eventually O'Neill ended up a Rabbitoh. At Redfern, he joined three of his team-mates from the Colts pack—Ron Coote, Bob McCarthy and Jim Morgan—in what was to be the start of a vintage era for South Sydney.

In O'Neill's first season with Souths, the Rabbitohs reached the grand final against St George, at which a new attendance record of 78,056 was set before the police ordered the gates of the Sydney Cricket Ground closed for safety reasons. But many thousands more scaled the fences to get a glimpse of the contest. The young Rabbitohs were beaten 12–8.

In 1967, the legendary Clive Churchill took over the reins as coach and the side won grand finals that year and the next, as well as in 1970 and 1971. They were beaten in 1969, when Balmain stretched the offside rules and held down the Rabbitohs in tackles to slow the pace of the game. O'Neill was one of seven South Sydney players in the Australian squad that won the 1970 World Cup in England two months later. There would have been an eighth but captain John Sattler had his jaw smashed in the grand final.

Australia sneaked into the World Cup final against Great Britain on points-difference and triumphed 12–7 in a brutal encounter that became known as 'The Battle of Headingley' (see 'Pure Bloody Mayhem', following). O'Neill showed his courage in that match. At one stage a scrum erupted and O'Neill emerged with a gaping wound in one leg. The shin had been split open, exposing the bone, and the blood pumped out and filled the boot below.

O'Neill refused to quit:

When I ran onto the field, I was running out for the full 80 minutes. They [the Australian trainers] wanted me to quit—but I told them where to get off. It wasn't the first time that year. Earlier in one of the Ashes Test, in Australia, I played with a bung shoulder for half the game. One hand was useless, so I just tucked it into my shorts and tackled with the other arm to help out my mates.

O'Neill wasn't content just to take on opposition players. He had an aversion to many officials, too. After the Rabbitohs' victory over St George in the 1971 grand final, they returned to the leagues club in Redfern to celebrate. However, the players were segregated from the officials. The latter had a sumptuous repast washed down with fine wines. The players basically had to make do with sandwiches and beer. O'Neill takes up the story: 'I had copped it sweet the previous year. But when it happened again I blew my top and belted a couple of officials in the club. Needless to say, they didn't want me there the following year.'

That was a big mistake. That shrewd old fox Ken Arthurson was on the prowl. As Manly supremo he was plotting the Sea Eagles' first Premiership. It was perceived that Manly had a soft underbelly. Life was too good on the northern beaches. Arko wanted some players who had not been seduced by the beachside lifestyle to put some starch into the Manly pack. His first significant signing had been young firebrand Mal Reilly from the grim north of England at the start of 1971. But the Sea Eagles were still found lacking when, after being clear winners of the minor premiership, they bowed out of the play-offs with successive losses to Souths and the Dragons.

So Arko moved on cash-strapped South Sydney, whose players were not used to the good life. He had already lured Bob Moses across from Redfern and now pounced on O'Neill and fellow World Cup representative, the goalkicking utility back Ray Branighan. They were the final pieces in the puzzle and Manly won the Premiership that year. But two straight losses to Western Suburbs in the 1972 finals series saw the Sea Eagles eliminated before they were back in the grand final mix in 1973 in what was another brutal clash (see 'Men Turned into Animals). O'Neill put it succinctly: 'It was boots and all. Fans all remember it, not because it was a great game, because it was anything but great. They remember it because it was so rugged. Yet no one got badly hurt.' A magical display by Manly's captain Bob Fulton, who scored two tries, proved the difference between the two sides.

By now Old Father Time was catching up with Lurch. He played three more seasons in the big league, but slowly lost the edge he had over other forwards. 'I knew when it was time to go,' he said. 'But I had enjoyed a good innings.'

That good innings had already provided him with the cash to set up as a successful builder—an unusual builder, too, as he was never afraid to work alongside the labourers he employed. That was the measure of Lurch O'Neill.

An incident in 1971 sums up his philosophy on his beloved rugby league. He had laid out Parramatta's Bob O'Reilly, a regular team-mate in New South Wales and Australian sides. O'Reilly was lying on his back, semiconscious, when the referee, former international half-back Keith Holman, gave Lurch his marching orders.

'You must be kidding,' O'Neill said, shaking his head.

'Hey, take a look at what you've done to O'Reilly,' Holman replied.

Lurch frowned and headed for the dressing room. But as he departed he turned around and shouted back at Holman: 'What's the bloody game coming to?'

What indeed!

Pure bloody mayhem

Test matches between Australia and the traditional foe Great Britain have always been torrid affairs. Sometimes they have been downright vicious. But usually when the referee blows his whistle for full-time the antagonism dissipates and the combatants seemingly become best of friends.

This wasn't the case as English referee Fred Lindop called a halt to proceedings in the final of the 1970 World Cup at Headingley, Leeds. The shrill pierce of the whistle was the signal for another bout of hostilities to begin and within seconds almost all the 26 players, who had been at each other's throats for much of the encounter, were trading blows—and not too gentle blows at that! The mayhem was to prompt a very public post-mortem in the pages of the Fleet Street press that left rugby league in a none-too-favourable light.

The British were hot favourites for the hastily arranged tournament after they had returned from Australia a few months earlier having regained the Ashes. South Sydney prop John Sattler, who would have been Australia's captain, was missing after having had his jaw smashed in the grand final. And the next choice, Graeme Langlands, was also ruled out with a broken scathoid bone in his left hand. The new skipper would be Rabbitoh Ron Coote.

Sponsorship reared its all-embracing head for the first time in the World Cup. The magnificent trophy that had been awarded at each of the previous four tournaments was cast aside and replaced by an ugly, puny cup with the name of the sponsors, V&G, inscribed on it. That stood for Vehicle & General Insurance. And to prove that what goes around comes around, the company eventually went belly up.

In his regular column in the Sydney *Daily Mirror*, former Kangaroo Bernie Purcell summed up the arrogance of England's Rugby Football League and its secretary Bill Fallowfield:

Bill Fallowfield and Co have again treated us like lap dogs. Without even giving us the courtesy of telling us what they were up to, the English Lords of rugby league decided to wipe the World Cup. They have found a new name, new cup and a new sponsor for this world championship. It is now called the World Series, at least until Bill Fallowfield thinks up something else. From reports, the 3ft [1 metre] high cup which has been the trophy for the series since its inception in 1954 dwarfs the insignificant egg cup that has been forced on us by Fallowfield.

The prize piece of luggage with the touring party was the [World] Cup and managers Ken Arthurson and Bert Quinn were amazed by the edict that was handed to them when they arrived in Yorkshire. If I were in the managers' boots I would pack the Cup we won in 1968 and fly it straight back to Australia. Otherwise you can guarantee that Mr Fallowfield would finish up with the coveted trophy in pride of place on his mantelpiece.

The Aussie powers-that-be should have heeded Purcell's advice. No sooner had the column been published than the original World Cup was stolen from the Australians' hotel and was not retrieved until a quarter of a century later when a fossicker found it on a Bradford rubbish tip. It assumed its rightful place for the 2000 World Cup.

Australia began the tournament in fine style, thrashing New Zealand 47–11 at Wigan's Central Park, with South Sydney full-back Eric Simms snaring a record 23 points from a try (then worth three points), nine goals and a field goal (at the time worth two points). Ironically Simms only made the team when Langlands pulled out.

Great Britain then gave a warning of things to come when they beat Australia 11–4 at Headingley, Leeds, in a brutal clash better suited to a back alley on a dark night. Sadly for the Australians,

Simms had an off-day with the boot with four attempts at penalty goal and four out of five shots at field goal all going astray.

The players from both sides engaged in every conceivable act of foul play. Eye gouging, forearm jolts, stiff-arm tackles, kicking tackled players lying prone on the turf, knees in the groin and just plain full-blooded punches to the head. The first half was cold-blooded mayhem. English referee Fred Lindop issued 12 cautions, including four to Manly iron man John 'Lurch' O'Neill. Respected Sydney *Daily Telegraph* writer Ian Heads described it as the roughest session of football he had ever witnessed. And one of those involved, rugged Castleford prop Dennis Hartley, agreed: 'It was unbelievable. It was the toughest I have ever played and ever expect to play.' At half-time coach Harry Bath urged the Australians to calm down and, if necessary, turn the other cheek. They didn't go that far, but they did play with more discretion after the break.

O'Neill admitted he was disappointed when told he had to tone it down. 'After all, this was Test football and, in my opinion, you have to get stuck into it,' he said. 'There is nothing given and nothing asked. It's not playing for your club. The Chooms [British] were handing out plenty of stick themselves and I felt I was entitled to give a bit back.'

New Zealand scraped home 16–15 against France at The Boulevard, Hull. Britain confirmed a place in the final with a try-less 6–nil victory over France at Castleford's Wheldon Road and a 27–17 success over the Kiwis at Station Road, Swinton, before France provided the upset of the tournament with a 17–15 victory over a below-par Australian outfit at Odsal Stadium in Bradford. This meant that New Zealand, France and Australia all finished the preliminary games on two points with the Aussies scraping into the decider thanks to their big win against the Kiwis.

The violence in the final at Headingley had to be seen to be believed. And neither side was blameless even though Alan Clarkson, writing in the *Sydney Morning Herald*, held the British responsible:

> With the game slipping away from them in the second half, England's [sic] players turned the game into a bloodbath. In some of the most dreadful incidents I have seen on a football field, Australian players were kicked, punched, butted, kneed and jumped on by the Englishmen. The English team's play deteriorated into nothing less than back-lane thuggery.

It is true that O'Neill was singled out for special treatment—but he expected that every time he ran onto a football field, no matter where in the world it was. In one series of rapid-fire encounters, Dennis Hartley punched and head-butted him, Featherstone Rovers back-rower Jim Thompson and Bradford Northern hooker Tony Fisher followed up with solid uppercuts, Hartley returned to put in the slipper and finally Mal Reilly walked over him. All that was achieved was a desire of O'Neill to return the 'favour' . . . with interest. And he did—in no uncertain terms.

Finally Lindop decided he'd had enough and sent Australia's scrum-half Billy Smith and British centre Syd Hynes from the field. In a bizarre sight, Smith and Hynes gently patted each other on the back, as if to say 'Well done, lad,' only seconds after standing toe-to-toe trading punches.

When Lindop blew full-time, Simms offered his right hand to Leeds winger John Atkinson. But the handshake was rejected. Instead Atkinson whacked him with a solid right hook. Suddenly players from both sides raced in to join the melee. Scenes of the fighting were shown over and over again on television news broadcasts over the next couple of days, with critics appalled at the violence. And Fleet Street had a field day.

'Get these savages off our TV screens,' roared the *Daily Mail*.

The *Mail* story declared:

> Had it taken place in the street the parties would have been jailed. What the televiewers saw was not amusing, not entertaining, not edifying and certainly not sport. These were cruel assaults by Australian and British thugs dressed as rugby players, buttings, kickings, punchings, stampings. The importance of the occasion became an excuse for them to kick lumps out of each other, to commit every type of foul. This was pure, bloody mayhem paraded as sport.

Then the *Mail* showed Fleet Street's pro–rugby union bias and its constant efforts to (pardon the expression) put the boot into league: 'Rugby league is an anachronism, an excuse for viciousness and violence that debases the people who promote and organise it as much as the people who "play" it.'

The *Daily Express* was equally as scathing, with its story headlined 'The day British Rugby League winced with shame':

> [Rugby league] lost its reputation. A reputation for playing a rough, tough game without aiming for revenge, where the game, however tough, is the thing. Instead there was blatant punching, kicking and butting. It was not pleasant. The punches instead of handshakes at the end was the final shame.

It was left to Alf Drewry, the insightful *Yorkshire Post* sports writer, to put the whole affair into perspective:

> Rugby league matches between Great Britain and Australia have so often degenerated into brawls that to assume a posture of righteous indignation over the squalid goings-on that disfigured Saturday's World Cup final at Headingley is little more than an academic exercise.

Drewry went on to report a scene after full-time. 'Another soothing note' is the way he described it:

While a doctor was stitching away at deep cuts as busily as a cobbler on piece work, players with swollen faces and black eyes were exchanging quips and bottles of beer as readily as they had been trading punches only a few minutes earlier— yes, even into overtime at the final whistle. It's a baffling world.

After Dennis Hartley had thrown everything at John O'Neill bar the kitchen sink, late in the game there was a conversation that would have had psychologists scratching their heads. Hartley made a legitimate tackle on the Australian prop and, as they got to their feet, the Englishman mumbled: 'Hey, John, do you want to swap jumpers at the end of the game?'

Manly's monster

RUGBY LEAGUE PLAYERS often get a bit confused when handing out nicknames, especially to the hardmen of the sport.

Sometimes they get it right. The granite-hard Englishman Derek Turner was dubbed 'Rocky' after the world heavyweight champion Rocky Marciano. The moniker 'Lurch' was a perfect fit for Souths prop John O'Neill. He was a giant who on the pitch looked every bit as frightening as the character in *The Addams Family* television series, the family butler whose great size and strength caused plenty of trouble. Bill Hamilton, a team-mate of O'Neill on the 1973 Kangaroo tour, was dubbed 'Herman' after a similar character in *The Munsters*.

But one of the backs (who are supposed to be smarter than forwards) got his wires crossed on that very same tour when he turned to Manly Man Mountain Terry Randall and noted: 'You look like an Igor.' And the name stuck.

Igor was the definitive character in most of the Frankenstein movies. The fellow who came up with Randall's nickname thought Igor was the name of the monster created by the evil scientist Dr Frankenstein, made famous by several Hollywood stars such as Bela Lugosi and Boris Karloff.

In fact, Igor was the scientist's ugly hunchback assistant who would shuffle around the laboratory dragging chains tied to his legs while doing Dr Frankenstein's every bidding with a subservient, cringing bow and the words 'Yes, Master!'

He was nothing like Terry Randall. Randall had a face that set female hearts aflutter . . . a physique the envy of most men . . . and a raw, even brutal, presence on the field that intimidated opposition players. Many critics believe he was the toughest tackler of his era.

Randall certainly stretched the rules when it came to some of his on-field actions, typified by two long suspensions handed out in 1981 and 1982, his final two seasons in the big league. In a spiteful semifinal

Opposite: No one wanted to tackle Terry Randall.

between Manly and Newtown there was an infamous punch-up between Mark Broadhurst (Sea Eagles) and Steve Bowden (Jets). Bowden made a real mess of Broadhurst's face and Randall saw red. When Bowden went down in a melee, Igor rushed in and kicked him—getting a six-match ban for his brain explosion.

On his return from the suspension the following season Randall came out of the dressing room hating the world and went onto the field ready to cause trouble. It didn't take long. He later explained what happened:

A young Cronulla kid came down the blind side. I saw him coming and decided to get him. I almost took this kid's head off. He never saw it coming. About twenty-four stitches were needed to stitch up the wound. I knew it was the wrong thing to do, but at the time I just snapped. He was carried off on a stretcher. I was handed a ten-match suspension.

FOR THE LOVE, OF GOD! ...DON'T PASS IT TO ME!

It was then that Randall decided it was time to call it quits after 12 seasons in Manly's first-grade squad. He knew his time had come!

But despite all this, the most lasting memories of Igor are his copybook—and quite legal—tackles. It was a case of up under the opposing players' ribcages, often breaking more than a few ribs in the process.

A few are etched in the memories of his contemporaries.

Ken Arthurson, Manly's 'Godfather', has often talked in awe about one tackle in a wild match in the Welsh city of Swansea during the 1975 World Championships. Wales had a pack that would have frightened even the Mafia, with one of the toughest front-row combinations in the history of the game—Jim Mills, Tony Fisher and John Mantle. Mills was one of the old school of front-row forwards whose motto was to retaliate first.

Arthurson explained:

Terry hit Mills so hard I thought he would break him in two. Mills was a giant of a man . . . so big and so tough. But Terry hammered him, leaving him gasping for breath. The timing of that tackle was perfect.

Randall remembers the match clearly: 'I'd played against Mills when he was at North Sydney, so I knew what to expect . . . a powerhouse. But I got on top of him.' It is one of the greatest understatements of the past half-century.

Randall's former Manly team-mate and later a respected radio commentator, John Gibbs, arguably best sums up Randall's effect on his chosen sport:

He gave us an incredible psychological advantage over our opponents. You have never seen players pass the ball as quickly as they did when they saw Igor heading in their direction. You could see them trembling. He most certainly put the fear of God into them.

Mills a boon for Wales

THAT DOOR-STOPPER OF A BOOK that lists every man who has ever played first grade in the 100-plus years of what is now the National Rugby League (NRL) Premiership, the *Encyclopedia of Rugby League Players*, can't always tell the full story. There simply isn't enough room.

So, sadly, a few of the great characters of the game don't achieve the real recognition their lives on the football field deserved. Like Welsh international Jim Mills. Two lines across half a page explain how he played 37 games for North Sydney from 1970 to 1972 and scored eight tries. Actually, it was an unremarkable period very early in the fiery prop's colourful career—a career that was later laced with rugged encounters in which more than a few buckets of blood were shed, teeth were dislodged, eyes closed and cheeks and jaws broken. And that was only the players with whom Mills came into contact.

As Mills explained several years later in a television interview:

> I'm certainly a big lad . . . 17 stone [108 kilograms]. If I don't take a few lads out of the game, there's something wrong. If they are having a go at me, I just do my best and count to three. Sometimes I only get to two.

Big Jim was a former rugby union forward with Cardiff with a reputation of having a short fuse. He had stints with Halifax, Salford and Bradford Northern after switching codes in 1963 and had played four games for Wales during 1969 and 1970. At the end of that northern hemisphere season, former Leeds coach Roy Francis persuaded him to knock back a chance to tour Australasia with the 1970 British Lions (the most recent Great Britain side to win the Ashes) and join him at the North Sydney Bears on a three-year contract. Money was important in luring him to

Opposite: *Jim Mills*

Sydney because the tourists received only nine dollars a week spending money and North Sydney had plenty of cash to throw around to bolster their player ranks. Norths did attract a few good players—but the recruits were unable to win any silverware for the trophy cabinet.

No sooner had Mills arrived to start his Aussie career than he was in trouble with the judiciary. Turning up for the first time at the New South Wales Rugby League headquarters in Phillip Street he was confronted by his none-too-impressive English disciplinary record. He apologised profusely for his action on the field, blaming jetlag and the oppressive heat of Sydney compared with the wintry weather he had left back home. He was given the benefit of the doubt and his sending-off was deemed to be sufficient penalty. Mills was promptly sent off again and once more pleaded that he was having trouble coping with the heat. But he knew the excuse was never going to work a second time.

It was a wretched stay Down Under. As well as his constant brushes with referees and the judiciary, Mills spent most of his final season in reserve grade (under the tutelage of another British prop, Merv 'The Pale Whale' Hicks, who had replaced Francis). He managed only seven first-grade appearances.

That year another of Britain's legendary enforcers, Vince Karalius, took over as coach of Widnes, a tough city located on the banks of the River Mersey in the midst of scores of chemical factories. And he demanded that the Lancashire club sign the returning Mills. Karalius wanted Mills to put some mongrel into the Widnes forward pack. And he certainly did, with 'The Chemics' reaching the final of the Challenge Cup at Wembley three times in five years between 1975 and 1979. Mills was on the winning side on the first and last of those occasions.

He also made it back into the international arena, touring Australia with the 1974 Great Britain side and then turning out for Wales in the 1975 World Championships, played on a home-and-away basis. This was arguably the most violent of all the international tournaments in rugby league history—with Wales involved in a succession of vicious confrontations.

The first came when the Welshmen took on England at Brisbane's famous Lang Park, an arena noted for a couple of violent Anglo–Australian Test encounters in the past. The line-up in the Welsh pack was as tough as ever played for the principality. As well as Mills there were rugged hooker Tony Fisher (Leeds), dual-international prop Bobby Wanbon (Warrington), second-rower Colin Dixon (Salford) and substitute John Mantle (St Helens), all of whom had reputations for their respective clubs as enforcers. They ripped into the English from the kick-off and on a rain-drenched field there was no way the Welsh could lose.

Australian referee Don Lancashire said after the match he would have been justified in sending off every player in what he described as a 'shambles' of a game. England coach Alex Murphy was livid, saying the Welshmen didn't want to play football. 'They only wanted to maim my lads,' Murphy said.

The other two violent run-ins came when the tournament moved to Britain and France for the return games. And Mills was always in the thick of the action. England gained revenge for the Brisbane loss with a 22–16 victory over Wales at Wilderspool, but Warrington five-eighth Ken Gill didn't know it after being laid out by a Welsh late tackle. 'They tell me we won and that I played a major role in the victory,' he said. 'But I can't even remember running onto the pitch. I've had some bad cracks in the past, but that was one of the worst.'

International rugby league returned to Wales in 1975, after a break of almost a quarter of a century. And the locals soon saw how tough the professional game could be, with a brawling match between Australia and Wales. The venue for this glorified punch-up was Vetch Field at Swansea. Three major brawls erupted during the match, involving more than half the players. One spread over the touchline and into the grandstand, with several officials, including Australia's coach Graeme Langlands, joining in.

That the match was so violent came as no great surprise. The Australians had a tough pack of forwards that could match the Welsh in any melee, led by probably the greatest of his era, Arthur Beetson. Rugged second-rower Terry Randall and hooker George Piggins could also handle themselves when the chips were down. And the locals lacked nothing when it came to brute strength, especially in the front row, with Mills, Fisher and Mantle. New Zealand referee Jack Percival was found lacking, unable to prevent the skirmishes. Several players were lucky not to get early baths.

The match, nevertheless, had moments in which both sides showed they could play top-class football. Its star was the 19-year-old blond Australian winger Ian Schubert, playing in only his second international. Amid all the tumult he helped himself to three tries, half of Australia's 18–6 winning score.

Wales bowed out of the World Championships in a match against New Zealand that had no bearing on which side would win the tournament. It was also played at Vetch Field. In the final minute of the match, Mills stood on the face of prop John Greengrass as he dived across the tryline to score. The Kiwi needed 15 stitches to sew up the gaping wound. Mills was sent off by French referee Georges Jameau and suspended for six months by the England's Rugby Football League (RFL). Greengrass never played Tests again.

'I only saw film of the incident once and I cringed,' said Mills. 'I can't explain it. Brainstorm? Stupidity? Moment of madness? The only thing I can think of is I blamed myself for him scoring.'

The New Zealanders vowed they would never play against Mills again, and this came to a head two years later when he was chosen for the Great Britain side to play in the next World Championships, staged in Australasia. Defiantly the RFL pointed out the Kiwis had no authority to ban Mills. However, the Australian Rugby League threatened to give Aussie clubs the right to sign British players without paying massive transfer fees to their English counterparts if Mills toured. Suddenly Mills withdrew from the team 'for personal reasons', but admitted the possibility of the New Zealand ban was the real cause.

Some 33 years after the incident at Swansea, Mills and Greengrass met up again when the latter was on his first visit back to Britain. In the meantime,

Mills had established himself as a successful nightclub owner and chairman of Widnes before retiring with homes in both England and Spain.

Mills said:

I really appreciated John making contact because that incident niggled me all my rugby career and in the years since I hung up my boots. I didn't just upset John and New Zealand, I upset a lot of people. You couldn't get a worse incident. And to have him come over here and offer the hand of friendship meant a lot. It made me feel a lot better.

Over to Greengrass:

Back home it was brought up all the time. They'd talk about the worst incidents in football and that was always shown on television. I was bitter for a couple of years, but it is all water under the bridge. Life is too short to hold grudges.

Men turned into animals

WHEN MIDDLE-AGED FANS DISCUSS VIOLENT MATCHES over a few glasses of the singing syrup at their local drinking hole, there is universal agreement as to the most frightening of all grand finals. None can compare for ferocity and wilful aggression to the 1973 encounter between Manly and Cronulla. *The Sun* newspaper headlined one story on that afternoon's clash 'The Game That Turns Men Into Animals'.

And when you look at the two line-ups there is little wonder that there should have been such violent behaviour. Some of the roughest and most uncompromising hardmen in the history of the game were on show at the Sydney Cricket Ground that September afternoon. Five of the six Manly forwards had Test experience—including three of the hardest enforcers around, Mal Reilly, Terry Randall and John O'Neill. Reilly and O'Neill had played in the infamous 1970 World Cup final—the so-called Battle of Headingley (see 'Pure Bloody Mayhem')—as had the Sea Eagles centre and five-eighth Bob Fulton. So they were well-versed in what could happen when tempers got out of control on the football field. Cronulla had two veterans of that black day at Headingley, too—hooker Ron Turner and English prop Cliff Watson (see 'Planting a Liverpool Kiss').

It was inevitable that the Sea Eagles and Sharks would face off in the season finale. Manly had just pipped Cronulla to take out the minor premiership by one competition point. They met in the major semifinal and the Sea Eagles were first into the grand final with a 14–4 victory, with Fulton in magical form scoring a wonderful try and snapping two field goals. The Sharks beat Newtown 20–11 in the preliminary final and it was on again.

But no one really expected the anarchy of the decider. It was a case of anything goes as the players resorted to every conceivable foul as they tried to soften each other up. *Sun-Herald* journalist Alan Clarkson described the game as 'the most vicious grand final in years'. Had he replaced the words 'in years' with 'in the history of the game' no one would have quibbled. 'Punching, kicking and kneeing were evident as the teams ripped into each other in unrestrained fury,' Clarkson added.

And an appalled Eddie Burns, the tough Canterbury front-rower of the 1940s, an era when no quarter was expected nor given, weighed in: 'Punch-ups are expected in grand finals and the public love it, but there is no place for knees and kicking in rugby league.'

Had it not been a grand final, referee Keith Page would undoubtedly have sent two or three players for an early shower. About ten minutes before half-time even his patience ran out and he called all 26 players over to issue a general warning. But his counselling fell on deaf ears as the players continued to rip and tear at each other.

Once again, amid all the bedlam, it was the sheer brilliance of Fulton that proved to be the difference. He scored late in the first half, off a crisp pass from Manly hooker and captain Fred Jones. And Fulton was in again midway through the second spell. A try to replacement Rick Bourke, who came on for the second half and scored two minutes later, got the Sharks back to 8–7. But the Sea Eagles held it all together and a late penalty goal by full-back Graham Eadie ensured a Manly victory.

Yet, despite the memories of the Fulton genius, most of the 52,044 fans at the SCG that day were left with a bitter taste in their mouths. Rugby league legend Johnny Raper, who had always ignored the bruises and pain of football conflict at the highest level, spoke for all of them: 'It was the most disgusting game I have seen.'

> **'It was the most disgusting game I have seen.'**
> **Rugby league legend Johnny Raper,**
> **describing the 1973 grand final**

The lovable larrikin

SO MANY STORIES ARE TOLD ABOUT JOHN 'DALLAS' DONNELLY that it is almost impossible to separate the fact from the fiction. And with the big fellow gone, there is no way for historians to work out which incidents involving this larger-than-life character actually happened. Even those that can be confirmed still sound like tales written by Damon Runyon, the American newspaperman and short-story writer who was world-famous for creating characters such as 'Harry the Horse', 'Tobias the Terrible' and 'The Lemon Drop Kid'.

The huge Wests Magpies forward Donnelly fitted the Runyon mould. To this day, a quarter of a century after his untimely death, no true-blue rugby league fan would ever think of calling him John. He was—and always will be—Dallas, a moniker allegedly bestowed on him because that was the name of the biggest television series being shown at the time Donnelly was playing. When young Canterbury prop Peter Kelly first came to Sydney, one journalist called him 'Texas'. The logic was that, while the city of Dallas was big, the state of Texas was bigger. Donnelly sorted out the newcomer in their first confrontation and no one described Kelly as 'Texas' after that!

Injuries never seemed to bother Dallas too much. A favourite story told by his Western Suburbs team-mates concerns a fractured cheekbone he suffered in a match at Wests' home ground, Lidcombe Oval. But he played on. At the end of the game, the club doctor ordered him off to hospital . . . no one is sure which one. But an hour or so later when coach Roy Masters arrived at the Wests Leagues Club in suburban Ashfield, he found Dallas quaffing schooners of beer. This time Masters left nothing to chance. He ordered a cab, escorting Dallas out of the club, and stressed to the driver he should take him to St Vincent's Hospital in the inner city. This was the best establishment to deal with smashed faces—because of the number of walking wounded who would arrive every night from nearby Kings Cross, victims of either drunks in the street or overzealous nightclub bouncers.

There was no stopping Dallas Donnelly once he got up a head of steam.

Hospital X-rays showed just how serious was the injury. 'You'll be with us for at least four or five days,' the doctor in the emergency ward told Donnelly.

The big prop gave a knowing nod of the head: 'Well, if that's the case, could you have a look at my ribs? I'm pretty sure I broke a couple of them last weekend.' Then he added: 'And while you're at it, can you check out my right knee? For the past month, it's kept locking up during matches.' Donnelly's stay at St Vincent's was a bit longer than he (or the doctor) originally expected.

Donnelly began his football career in the New England town of Gunnedah. In 1973, while still a teenager, he represented New South Wales Country in the annual clash with Sydney, made his interstate debut in Brisbane (during which match he broke an arm) and was named Country Player of the Year. Gunnedah also won the Clayton Cup as the best club side in New South Wales that year. In 1975 Donnelly joined Wests and stayed with the Magpies until the end of his Australian career a decade later.

Throughout his life Donnelly was plagued by epilepsy but kept this a secret from the fans until late in his football career when he made his illness public in an effort to inspire fellow epileptics. But his team-mates all knew about the problem, although at first they weren't too sure about how bad it was. On one occasion, just before a pre-season cross-country run, they thought he had faked a seizure to escape the torture. But he went out the very next day and made the agonising run on his own. Many of the scars that 'adorned' Donnelly's face weren't from clashes on the football field but from his wild epileptic fits.

Donnelly played in Australia's winning 1975 World Championship side in home matches against France, Wales and England. Twelve months later he toured New Zealand as a member of a Sydney representative side chosen from teams that failed to make the Premiership play-offs. There are conflicting stories about one particular incident on the tour. Some suggest it was at an official New Zealand Rugby League reception, others describe it as happening when the players arrived back at the foyer of the hotel at which they were staying. Where all stories agree—Dallas happened to see a giant fish tank, reached into the water and grabbed several goldfish, which he then swallowed in one gulp. All versions also end with the postscript that Donnelly's rugby league passport was stamped 'Never to tour overseas again'. But he did manage one further Test, against New Zealand in Brisbane in 1978.

Donnelly's career started in the era when referees and the judiciary virtually turned a blind eye to brutality, although he did manage to incur a lengthy suspension in 1978 for kneeing an opponent. Then, in 1980, the New South Wales Rugby League hierarchy decided the game's tarnished image needed to be cleaned up. The NSWRL bosses turned to a leading solicitor and 1930s first-grade centre turned prop, Jim Comans, to bring about the change. He was installed as head of the judiciary and immediately started handing out draconian sentences. One of the first targeted by Comans was Donnelly, who received a 14-week suspension in 1981. Others followed, including two of his Wests team-mates, Les Boyd and Bob Cooper. The former was eventually forced to head for England when it became clear that his career in Australia was as good as over under the Comans regime.

Donnelly soldiered on, but with his style of play no longer tolerated, opposition players weren't intimidated like they were in the past. Even though Wests won only one first-grade match in 1984, Donnelly's last year in Sydney, he was permanently in the reserve-grade side. After his last match at the Magpies' home ground, Lidcombe Oval, he was driven on a lap of honour and presented with a painting of himself on the rampage during his prime. The following week, he was elevated to the firsts for the one and only time that season to play his final match for his beloved Magpies, against Cronulla at Endeavour Field.

Donnelly was awarded life membership of Western Suburbs. But there was a major problem. It was a tradition that life members—be they players or officials—were always honoured at a dinner at the Western Suburbs Leagues Club. And Donnelly had been banned for life from the leagues club. It took some hard talking from the football club hierarchy to persuade the directors of the leagues club to grant a special dispensation for Dallas and lift the ban for one night.

Many of the stories about Donnelly were repeated that night.

Like the time coach Roy Masters was fronting each player in the dressing room before a vital match and getting them to tell their team-mates what they intended to do with the blokes who were about to mark them on the footy field. Masters turned to Donnelly and asked, 'Dallas, what are you going to do?'

Dallas didn't hesitate: 'I'm going to rip his head off and poke him in the eyes. I'll bite him and kick him and smash him across the face. Then I'll really get serious.'

Masters gave a knowing nod and then turned to a pint-sized Terry Lamb, who was sitting next to Donnelly: 'Baa Baa, what are you going to do to your bloke?'

Quick as a flash Lamb replied, 'I'm going to give him to Dallas!'

Then there was the one about Masters, who was leaving the leagues club after celebrating a Wests home win when he saw a young hotdog seller standing forlornly outside waiting for customers. It was a cold and wet winter's night and Masters took pity on him, bought a hotdog and said: 'You might as well go home, son. There's virtually no one left inside.'

'I know that,' said the kid. 'But Dallas Donnelly is still there . . . and when he leaves he'll buy seven or eight.'

And the pizza shop owner in the suburb of Burwood who had to call police to remove Donnelly after he had uprooted a table that was bolted to the floor. The officers persuaded Dallas to leave and asked the pizza man if he wanted to press charges. 'Shit, no,' came the reply. 'He's my biggest customer. I make a small fortune out of him.'

After Donnelly left Wests he had a season playing for English Second Division side Southend Invicta and was a real hit with the fans in the resort town east of London. One of them, Sara Threadgold, wrote to the *Era of the Biff* website about him. She was only eight years old when she met Donnelly for the first time. 'I remember this huge guy in a flowery shirt, tall as a house with the biggest head I had ever seen. From the moment I saw him I loved him,' she recalled. 'I also remember on our local field, him playing rugby with the kids. They all loved him. Dallas, without a doubt, will stay in our hearts forever.'

Donnelly returned home after one season in the Old Dart to accept the job as captain–coach of Byron Bay for the club's 1986 campaign in the Northern Rivers competition. A month before the season's kick-off the big fellow went surfing alone on one of the town's beaches. He suffered an epileptic fit and drowned in just a few centimetres of water. He was only 31 years old.

Wests chartered an aircraft to carry players, officials and the media to his funeral in Gunnedah and a fleet of buses took fans from Lidcombe to his home town. As a mark of respect in their opening match of the 1986 Premiership, the Magpies did not have anyone wearing Donnelly's traditional number 11 jumper. Instead it was draped over a chair near the halfway line as a tribute to the lovable larrikin who had lived life to the full.

With a touch of journalistic licence when it came to Dallas' age, Roy Masters had the last word on him: 'He put sixty years of living into his thirty.'

Overleaf: 'It wasn't me, sir!' Wests Magpies prop Dallas Donnelly appeals to the referee, denying any knowledge of what happened to the prone South Sydney player in this 1977 encounter.

PLAY BY THE RULES, SON

The sporting career of my second son Murray Andrews started when he was only five years old, playing Under–7s rugby league for Burwood United Tigers in the Western Suburbs junior competition in Sydney.

About every second or third week, one of the Under–7s matches was played at half-time in the reserve grade and half-time in the first grade at Lidcombe Oval, at the time the home ground for the Western Suburbs Magpies.

The Under–7s players were allowed to sit in the dressing room with their Wests heroes as they prepared for the first-grade game. Murray particularly liked Dallas Donnelly. The big fella would ruffle his hair and tell him: 'You must not copy me, Muzz. I do rough things I shouldn't do. As a result I get sent off a lot, and that sometimes costs Wests a win. Play by the rules, son, and you can't go wrong.' No wonder the kids loved Dallas.

Too long on the sidelines

LES BOYD KNOWS ONLY TOO WELL about the fickle finger of fate. For fate regularly played a capricious role in his rugby league career . . . with others deciding his destiny.

People such as judiciary boss Jim Comans, who handed him two of the longest suspensions in the history of the Australian game. And others like Roy Masters, Boyd's mentor during his teens and later a leading Premiership coach.

When the paths of Masters and Boyd first crossed, the former was just an unknown schoolteacher in Tamworth in the New England area of northern New South Wales. Masters had inherited a talented footballing side that had been nurtured through high school by another teacher, who reluctantly handed over the reins to the future coach of the Wests Magpies and the St George Dragons. And after Masters took the kids to the pinnacle of schoolboy success, he was appointed coach of the first Australian schoolboys side to tour Great Britain, in 1972.

In one of the selection trials Boyd, a kid from Nyngan in the north-west of the state, had been sent off for punching an opponent. And the selection rules for the Australian squad demanded that anyone given an early shower was ineligible. Masters, who realised just how good Boyd was, argued that the youngster had only retaliated after an opponent had punched him. Boyd was given a dispensation and toured. While on tour Masters and Boyd formed a proxy father–son relationship that was to see the kid join Masters at the Magpies four years later. Boyd made the move to Sydney even though he was a country boy at heart and would have been happy to stay in his new home town of Cootamundra where his family had relocated.

The 19-year-old Boyd won himself a contract after an impressive display in a trial match against South Sydney, matching it in a series of

Opposite: Les Boyd's baby-faced looks belied his no-nonsense approach to rugby league.

fiery encounters with international utility player Paul Sait, a veteran of 16 Test and World Cup appearances for Australia. The following season he began to regularly attract the attention of the referees and was marched three times for fighting. The opposition realised that the youngster had a short fuse.

In 1978 the Magpies took out the minor premiership, but lost their way in the play-offs. Their feud with controversial referee Greg Hartley had a lot to do with it. Hartley had been controlling reserve-grade games when suddenly he was recalled to the elite ranks to referee a mid-season Match of the Round between Wests and Manly. The Sea Eagles won and the Wests players were furious. In the finals both Wests and Parramatta seethed about Hartley's appointment to their games against Manly. There was even talk of the Magpies forfeiting the preliminary final. The Sea Eagles went on to take out the Premiership.

It was a mixed season for Boyd. Early in the year he took the New South Wales Rugby League to court to protest a four-week ban for gouging and stomping on a Manly player. The Equity Court ruled Boyd had been denied natural justice and overturned the suspension—but the NSWRL retried him under terms acceptable to the court and found him guilty a second time. 'It left a bitter taste in my mouth,' said Boyd. 'I realised then that, in the long run, you couldn't beat them.'

Nevertheless the year finished on a high when he was chosen in the Kangaroos squad for the 1978 tour of Britain and France. He made his Test debut in the Second Ashes Test, at Odsal Stadium in Bradford, and played two other Tests, against Britain at Leeds and France at Carcassonne. The finger of fate pointed once again. There were seven Manly players in the Kangaroo squad and Boyd became firm friends with several of them. He saw another side to the traditional enemy in what had become an ongoing battle between the down-trodden 'fibros' of Wests and the high-flying 'silvertails' of Manly. ('Fibros' because of the fibro houses in which so many of the Magpies supporters lived; and 'silvertails' because of the rich lifestyle of residents living in Sydney's north.)

Boyd was one of the best of the Australian Test side which thrashed the touring British Lions the following year. At the end of that season, Manly offered him a king's ransom to leave Wests. He wanted to stay at Lidcombe but the cash-strapped Magpies did not have enough money to get anywhere near the Sea Eagles' offer. So Boyd moved to Brookvale and joined his mates from the Kangaroo tour. So, too, did his Wests team-mates, full-back John Dorahy and hooker Ray Brown.

The move across Sydney coincided with the start of a campaign by the NSWRL to stamp out foul play, which it believed was causing many parents to direct their children into other sports.

And, like his erstwhile Wests team-mate John Donnelly, Boyd was to feel the wrath of judiciary boss Jim Comans.

On the field Manly missed the semifinals in 1980, was knocked out in the first week the following year and then beaten by Parramatta in the 1982 grand final. However, Boyd went from strength to strength in the representative arena. He played in the series against New Zealand (1980 and 1982) and France (1981) before making a second Kangaroo tour in 1982. His five Tests on that tour were the last of 17 international appearances.

The players in that touring squad earned themselves the nickname 'The Invincibles' because they were the first to complete a tour undefeated, winning all 23 matches. Respected British player-turned-commentator Ray French noted:

He [Boyd] proved a fearsome competitor and helped the Kangaroos establish a dominance up front through their fitness and technique that was never questioned by any club or national side. Few players, either, questioned Les Boyd's dominance over them on that tour as he scattered numerous defences with his 30-metre bursts or his crunching tackles. Mostly within the laws, I would add!

Then came the defining moments in Boyd's career. On 7 June 1983, in the State of Origin match against Queensland at Brisbane's Lang Park, Boyd hit opposition forward Darryl Brohman with an elbow, badly smashing the Queenslander's jaw. Boyd was cited after the match and suspended for 12 months. Then, after only his fourth match following the ban, he was again cited—for gouging one of Canterbury hooker Billy Johnston's eyes. This time he was suspended for 15 months.

Although Boyd admitted he was stupid on occasions, he believed some of the sentences handed down by Comans were over the top. 'The NSWRL let things get out of hand,' he claimed. 'I reckon even some members of the League hierarchy were shocked by the size of some of the suspensions.'

Boyd knew his days playing in the Premiership were as good as over. The NSWRL wanted to ensure the game was squeaky clean—at least on the field—and Boyd was the whipping boy. Another indiscretion would have the same dire consequences.

Boyd later said:

I never believed I was as bad as some people made out. I wasn't the baby-faced assassin as some journalists like to portray me in their newspaper headlines. I probably deserved to be suspended a couple of times—but not to have been hit with those incredibly harsh sentences. And that's what people have always remembered about me.

After his 15-month suspension ended, Boyd quit Australian football to play in England with Warrington, where he proved to be a great inspiration to the club's younger players. In his first season he was sent off just once—and was exonerated by the judiciary. That same season he captained Warrington to a 38–10 success over Halifax (captained by fellow Australian Chris Anderson) in the Premiership final. In the process, Boyd won the Harry Sunderland Medal as Man of the Match. The respected English sporting journalist Harry Edgar wrote in *Open Rugby* magazine:

There was only going to be one winner, and for Boyd it was a remarkable turnabout. Banned out of Sydney League, his behaviour was impeccable, his inspiration total, and his own performance outstanding, resulting in the very first winners' medal of his long eventful career.

In 1991 Boyd was offered the job as coach of Warrington but he had already bought into a business back in Cootamundra and returned to play out his career in the Riverina. It was a hard decision. 'I enjoyed the lifestyle over there, the people and the football,' he told Aussie writer Tony Adams. 'The game suited me more over there.'

What does the 19th century proverb say? Every cloud has a silver lining. Boyd always knew that to be true:

If I hadn't copped those two long suspensions I would never have gone to England. And had I not done so I would have missed out on the best five years of my life. Yeah, I lost a lot of money sitting on the sidelines serving out those bans, but I've never been bitter.

There is that other adage—life goes on!

Facing up to a hammering

IT'S BEEN SAID MANY A TIME that Mark Broadhurst had—and still has, for that matter—a face that only a mother could love. Or to put it another way, he's no oil painting. And Broadhurst is unlikely to disagree with either cliché.

We're not quite sure what he looked like when he was born . . . whether or not he was a bonny baby. But years as a boxer and rugby league player certainly took their toll on Broadhurst's looks. A butcher by trade, he enjoyed slugging it out in the ring and was, for a time, the amateur light-heavyweight champion of New Zealand's South Island. He also seemed to enjoy slugging it out on the footy field, even on the occasion in 1981 when he was on the receiving end of one of the most notorious hammerings in the history of rugby league.

Three decades later fans still gather in pubs and over a beer or six to share their memories of that September afternoon at the Sydney Cricket Ground. Broadhurst, at the time a veteran of 12 Tests for the Kiwis, was in his first season with the Manly Sea Eagles. They had reached the play-offs, where they came up against the Newtown Jets in the minor semifinal.

In the week leading up to the encounter there was a lot of 'trash talking' in the pages of the Sydney tabloids. According to the newspapers, Broadhurst had promised to sort out Steve Bowden, a renowned hardman, in the first scrum. Broadhurst has always claimed he was misquoted. It mattered not—the damage had been done. The headlines only served to get Bowden fired up.

The first scrum was packed less than a minute after the kick-off and Bowden decided to get in first and head-butted Broadhurst. It was a perfectly executed Liverpool Kiss. For an added 'bonus' Bowden connected with a crisp right hook. And, once the big Kiwi went down, Bowden

Opposite: Mark Broadhurst ready to hand out a 'don't argue' to a would-be Cronulla defender

jumped on top of him and rained several more blows on his victim. In the meantime all 26 players were at each other—arms flailing, knees raised and heads smashing into the cheekbones of opposition players. Referee John Gocher took more than two minutes to bring an end to the mayhem.

A former Manly hero, Rex 'The Moose' Mossop, who was providing the television commentary, noted: 'That's the most frantic opening to a rugby league game that I've seen in thirty-five years.' And, believe you me, The Moose had seen some violent openings in both Britain and Australia. Bowden received his marching orders, as did tough Manly second-rower Terry Randall. The former was to receive a seven-match suspension for his efforts and missed Newtown's victory over Eastern Suburbs in the preliminary final and loss to Parramatta in the grand final.

After the match Broadhurst's face looked like a fellow butcher had used it to procure the meat for a weekend barbecue. His left cheekbone was badly fractured and he couldn't see out of the corresponding eye, which had blown up like a black balloon. But the Manly doctor had earlier managed to drain enough of the blood to restore a blurred sight and enable the big fellow to eventually see out the game.

Broadhurst had a second season with the Sea Eagles and one with the Illawarra Steelers before heading to Britain to join a star-studded Hull Kingston Rovers side. And in only his second appearance in Old Blighty he was at it again. This time his sparring partner was hooker Shane Bernadin from the Redcliffe club in Brisbane. The Queensland representative side, under coach Arthur Beetson and captain Wally Lewis, was making a short swing through England at the end of the 1983 Australian season. And their first match was against the Humberside club. The Hull KR team was a beauty—with the entire starting line-up either past or future Test players for Great Britain, Australia or New Zealand.

Queensland led 6–4 just before the break, with Steve Hartley, David Watkinson and Roy Holdstock from the home side all having been replaced injured. But there had been a lot of niggling in the scrums and rucks. Eventually Broadhurst decided he'd had enough. After being tackled by Bernadin, he got to his feet, calmly played the ball and then hammered the unsuspecting Queenslander with a perfectly placed hook to the jaw. Bernadin was out like a light. Incredibly, Broadhurst was allowed to stay on the field—with just a penalty being awarded. The referee had seen the blow as a 'get-square'. The incident rattled the visitors and Hull KR went on to win 8–6.

A very early shower

AN INCIDENT LESS THAN TEN SECONDS INTO A PREMIERSHIP GAME earned Peter Kelly, the tough prop of the 1980s, a place in sporting folklore. That's the time he took to lay out an opponent and receive his marching orders—the quickest send-off in any senior game played in Australia, if not the world.

Details are sketchy about what happened on Anzac Day 1986. And because there is no television footage of the incident—and most of the officials and journalists were still settling into their seats—only the basic facts can be verified.

Kelly was playing for the Canterbury Bulldogs, the club with which he won two Premierships (in 1984 and 1985). The Bulldogs were playing South Sydney at the Sydney Cricket Ground and, after both teams stood for a minute's silence to remember Australia's war dead and listen to the 'Last Post' played by an army bugler, Canterbury kicked off. Straight away, Kelly charged into the fray and hammered Souths winger Ross Harrington with a high tackle. Harrington was out cold and eventually carried off on a stretcher. But, by that time, Kelly had already been sent off. He reached the entrance to the Members Stand at the same time as the bugler, who opened the gate to let him through. According to Kelly, Canterbury's president, Barry 'Punchy' Nelson, who had been on the field for the Anzac ceremony, turned to the soldier and commented: 'Oh, Kel must have forgotten his mouthguard.'

The quickest ever dismissal? Well, there were no electronic ground clocks in those days. And no one had a stopwatch to time the action. But to this day it is regarded as a record.

But Kelly, while accepting his place in the history books, has always pleaded his innocence. He told journalist Tony Adams: 'Harrington brought the ball up, and I launched myself and hit him at what I thought was shoulder height. I absolutely creamed him. I still regard it as the best tackle I made in my career.'

It's just one of a multitude of stories told about Kelly and his hard-hitting image. Like the one which concerns an appearance at the judiciary after he had been sent off on another occasion. He was charged with making a late tackle and is said to have pleaded, 'But I got there as fast as I could.'

Another, almost certainly apocryphal, was about his first game in Sydney after several years learning his trade on the New South Wales south coast and in Newcastle. He was playing for the Newtown Jets against Wests Magpies, who boasted one of the biggest, toughest packs of forwards in the competition. The first time Kelly had the ball in his hands he charged up-field, only to see several of the Magpies forwards coming at him, hell bent on roughing up the young newcomer. Uncharacteristically, Kelly dropped the ball. Wests hardman John Donnelly looked at him straight in the eye and laughed: 'What happened? Shit yourself, did ya?'

Black and gold will never fold

AUSTRALIAN SPORT HAS KNOWN MANY CHAMPIONS: Don Bradman, Roy Cazaly, Betty Cuthbert, Walter Lindrum and countless more. Scores of names known to even those with little interest in sport.

But only occasionally has a person who followed a sport become as famous as those he or she watched. Stephen Harold Gascoigne was one. This rabbitoh from the Sydney suburb of Balmain, better known as 'Yabba', became a legend in cricket through his theatrical performances on the Sydney Cricket Ground Hill. Laurie Nichols achieved a similar status in rugby league. And it was perhaps befitting that Balmain was involved, too. In Nichols' case, it was his beloved Balmain Tigers. His performances in the grandstands of the Tigers' home ground, Leichhardt Oval, and at other rugby league arenas both in Australia and overseas, were every bit as theatrical as those of Yabba.

Nichols was instantly recognisable—dressed in a singlet even when the temperatures dropped well below zero. Talk about a hardman. Laurie felt no cold. It was a throwback to his early days as a shearer on the Monaro. Shearers have always worn singlets: Jacky Howe singlets, named after the gun shearer of the 1890s, who set records never to be matched until electric shears and wide combs made the backbreaking work just a little bit less taxing.

On freezing cold winter nights, Nichols would shadow-box in his singlet at the front of the grandstands and shout rhymes about the Balmain club and the stars that helped make it famous:

'Black and gold will never fold.'

'Artie Beetson, Artie Beetson. First he beats them, then he eats them.'

'Garry Jack, the world's greatest back.'

'Peter Jones crushes bones.'

Of Paul Sironen, who played more first-grade games for Balmain than any other Tiger in history: 'Sirro, he's a hero.'

And when Nichols was in Britain with the Australian touring side: 'Kangaroos give Poms the blues.'

Corny? Maybe. But they came straight from the heart.

Nichols' sideline performances and his simple rhymes belied the fact that he was a very intelligent and caring man. And he was fond of a joke. There is the story of the time he was in the United States, barracking for world boxing champion Kostya Tszyu, whom he supported with the same fervour he showed for the Tigers. A bystander at the gym where Tszyu was training was intrigued by Nichols and asked if he had appeared in the movie *Crocodile Dundee*. 'No, but I train kangaroos to work as couriers—they can get to places cars can't,' Nichols replied.

'Goddam! Do you mean you ride 'em?' the incredulous American asked.

'Ride them? How do you think we get around during petrol strikes?'

Nichols, one of 13 children, began his working life as a sheep shearer around his home town of Cooma (he later moved to Springwood in the Blue Mountains and then to The Entrance on the New South Wales Central Coast). His roots as a shearer led to a career as a well-respected wool-classer.

The involvement with Balmain began in the early 1960s when he went to Sydney looking for a club for Sid Williams, the brother of his best mate, who was playing junior football in Springwood. Williams joined Balmain on the field—and so, too, did Nichols off it. The young Williams was to become part of Tigers folklore by scoring the only try of the 1969 grand final, when Balmain caused an upset by beating the fine South Sydney combination that had won the Premiership the previous two seasons.

A little-known side of Nichols was his tireless work for charity. Radio broadcaster and former Balmain coach Alan Jones once told him, 'Laurie, you can't save the world.'

The ultimate Tigers fan replied, 'Maybe, but I can always do something.'

That something was the Laurie Nichols Trust Fund for the disabled and disadvantaged. Nichols was at a charity dinner at a Sydney restaurant in 2000, helping raise money for a young disabled girl, when he had a coughing fit. An ambulance rushed him unconscious to hospital where he died.

Nichols had given an emotional speech at Balmain's extraordinary general meeting the previous year, arguing against the proposed merger with Western Suburbs Magpies. His pleas fell on deaf ears and he swore he would never watch another game of rugby league. 'This merger will deadset kill me,' he told friends. But only a day before his death, Nichols was at a training session of the merged Wests Tigers, explaining, 'I couldn't desert my boys.' He promised the players he would be on the sideline for their debut match against the Brisbane Broncos, telling them: 'Balmain are no more. Wests are no more. It's now Wests Tigers.'

He never made it to see the new entity. Laurie Nichols was also no more. But as Jones said at his funeral at The Entrance—a funeral attended by more than a thousand, including half-a-dozen players who had captained Australia—'No one ever dies until the memories fade away.' And the memories of Laurie Nichols won't be fading for a long time yet!

Wanna-be hardmen foiled

Every weekend in country towns around New South Wales and Queensland there are players eager to emulate the hard nuts of the big league. Each and every team has its 'enforcer'. But somehow most never learn how to manage their role, as a Queensland country referee, Kevin Hauff, found out in 1990.

Hauff created rugby league history in a match that year when he sent all 26 players to the sin-bin for ten minutes. Hauff was in charge of a game between Barcaldine and Blackall in the central-west of the state. He had just sin-binned two players when their team-mates started an all-in brawl. So Hauff ordered each side to go behind their own tryline and think about whether they wanted to play football or fight. And the cooling-off period worked—except in the case of one Barcaldine player, who was sent off later in the match for throwing a punch.

Blocker's brawls, battles and bacon

FOR A BLOKE who was one of the roughest, toughest props in the history of the game it is ironic that Steve 'Blocker' Roach is arguably best remembered for a lighthearted moment when he patted a referee on the top of his head, while sporting a smile as wide as the Sydney Heads.

It was at Brookvale Oval in July 1990. For much of the match the Balmain star had been involved in a series of one-on-one battles with Manly's Kiwi prop Adrian Shelford. Then, five minutes before the final siren, Roach laid out his opponent in an off-the-ball incident. Touch judge Lance Harrigan raced in to report the incident and referee Eddie Ward had no hesitation in dispatching Roach to the sin-bin. As he left, Roach grinned and patted Ward, who was many centimetres shorter, on the top of the head. Roach also told the touch judge in no uncertain terms what he thought about his intervention.

After the match all hell broke loose. After all, every rugby league player knows that, unlike in soccer, you must never, ever touch a referee. The media went into a frenzy, baying for Roach's blood. He was probably lucky to escape with a $5000 fine and a four-match suspension, even though it was obvious that there was no malevolence intended.

'It was stupid thing to do,' Roach later admitted. 'It was a spur-of-the-moment gesture. There was no malice in it. I just wanted Eddie to know I wasn't dirty with him, only the touchie. But everyone gave it to me . . . and how!'

But the career of Roach, the happy-go-lucky, larger-than-life character off the field who seemed to turn into an ogre once he ran onto the pitch, was plagued by controversies. On one occasion he head-butted a newspaper photographer who had snapped a shot of him arguing with a Balmain doorman. Roach admitted that was a stupid thing to do, too, and in typical Blocker style donated $1000 to the charity of the photographer's choice to make amends.

Then there was the sneaky attempt to cut the length of a suspension to enable him to play in the 1988 grand final. In the midweek play-off with

Penrith for the fifth and final spot in the finals' series, Roach was sent off for allegedly head-butting his opposite number Matt Goodwin. Blocker was exonerated but worse was still to come. He was cited for a high tackle on centre Chris Mortimer. Roach claimed Mortimer was falling at the time and the challenge was merely a collision not a tackle. The judiciary did not agree and suspended him for four matches. That meant he would miss the grand final if Balmain managed to make it through.

An elaborate plan was then hatched by Roach and the Balmain officials. He would fly to England for a guest appearance with Warrington, sitting out one match for his new club before flying straight back to Australia, where he would serve out the other three. This would make him available for the grand final. Furious New South Wales Rugby League officials hearing of the plan set their legal eagles to work and the scheme was quickly abandoned. But the Warrington officials still wanted Roach for an off-season stint to join another controversial Australian, Les Boyd. And, for the trifecta, they added Souths enforcer Les Davidson. They tell the story around Warrington that the coach Tony Barrow had seen a video of a stoush between Roach and Davidson and noted: 'We've done well with Boyd. These two madmen are out of the same mould. We've got to have them.' Like many of the yarns about Blocker, no one is sure if it's true—but it sounds close to the mark.

One that Blocker swears is ridgy-didge occurred on the 1986 Kangaroo tour of Britain and France. After playing in Australia's 38–16 thrashing of the old enemy in the First Test at Old Trafford, Blocker suffered a dislocated elbow that kept him out of the other two internationals. But he was back in action in France, where one night he got together with his old Balmain team-mate Kerry Hemsley, who was winding down his career with several seasons in the French competition. Roach told journalist Tony Adams:

> We were having a quiet drink when in walked three or four blokes who had beaten the crap out of Buckets [Hemsley] in a club game a few weeks earlier. They had given it to him boots and all. Buckets thought this was too good an opportunity to pass up. I was glad to help him even the score.

BLOCKER KNEW THE ONLY WAY he would achieve success in life was through football. After all, he openly admitted he was no Rhodes Scholar. Hence the embarrassing gaffe on the 1989 tour of New Zealand that still comes back to haunt him today. Roach explained his red face in his autobiography, *Doing My Block*. At breakfast one morning a team-mate had remarked how in New Zealand they served bacon with almost every meal. Quick as a flash, Blocker replied: 'Why wouldn't they? They've got 40 million sheep in this country.' Roach later said: 'My only defence is that I was very hungover that morning and I may have left my wits in the bar.'

He certainly did have a successful life thanks to rugby league. He graduated from the junior ranks in Wollongong to join Balmain as a 16-year-old. He made his first-grade debut, ironically against the Illawarra Steelers, in 1982, and went on to make 185 appearances in the black and gold before calling it a day in 1992. Only six stars played more often for the Tigers. He played 17 State of Origin games for New South Wales and 20 Tests for Australia.

His one great regret was being replaced by coach Warren Ryan near the end of the 1989 grand final against Canberra. The Tigers led 14–8 at the time and Ryan decided to swap Roach and fellow international Paul Sironen with two fresh players he thought would defend the lead. Sadly, that didn't happen. Canberra winger John 'Chicka' Ferguson scored and the conversion sent the game into extra time, where the Raiders snatched victory. 'I am convinced had Sirro and I stayed on the field we would have won,' said Roach. And, to this day, Balmain fans agree.

They also agree that his original nickname was wrong, too. When he started at the Tigers he was dubbed 'Blockhead' because he had no problem taking on anyone, no matter what their reputation. Somewhere along the track he became 'Blocker'.

Roach admits: 'I'm not too sure about Blockhead. But Blocker, I can certainly live with that. Indeed, I wear it with pride!'

Tamati leaves his mark

Anyone who saw the Brisbane trans-Tasman Test of 1985 will never forget it—even though most will never remember the score. The match is remembered for one of the most ferocious exhibitions of fisticuffs between two players in the history of the game. The combatants were Australian prop Greg 'Dish-head' Dowling and Kiwi Kevin Tamati. But there was also a third player who made a cameo: 21-year-old Test debutant Steve 'Blocker' Roach.

Blocker explained what happened at Lang Park that evening in his autobiography:

Tamati was as tough a man as ever wore the black and white New Zealand jumper. A former champion boxer and a true hardman. Did he give it to me! We shaped up to sort each other out and he just belted me all over the place. He gave me the worst hiding I have ever had on a football field. By the time Tamati had finished with me I felt like one of those cartoon characters who take such a belting the lumps all pop up on their heads. To add to my embarrassment, I realised he only regarded me as a preliminary boy, someone to warm him up for his main event with Greg Dowling.

And what a stoush that turned out to be! They went hammer and tongs at each other. Eventually the referee's patience ran out and Tamati and Dowling were sent to the sin-bin. But that didn't stop the two old warhorses. As they left the field something was said and the two props got stuck into each other again, like a couple of backstreet brawlers. No one was game to intervene as the fight continued off the pitch—and along the tunnel leading to the dressing rooms.

The Brick with Eyes

NO BROADCASTERS UNDERSTOOD THE OBSESSION Australians have for sport better than H.G. Nelson and 'Rampaging' Roy Slaven. The comedy pair—real names Greig Pickhaver and John Doyle—lived by the credo 'Too much sport is never enough' and achieved cult following for their radio show *This Sporting Life*, their irreverent parodies of rugby league's State of Origin encounters and grand finals (*The Festival of the Boot*) and their Olympic television efforts (*The Dream*).

The meaning of the nicknames created by H.G. and Roy for many Origin players can never be revealed in print as they could be viewed as libellous or obscene. But the listeners understood them all too well. One which would never have been actionable was that given to tough prop Glenn Lazarus. H.G. and Roy dubbed him 'The Brick with Eyes'. It was a fitting description—and a profitable one, too, as 'The Brick' later used it in advertising campaigns for products he endorsed.

Lazarus was the vital brick in the foundations on which Premiership success at three different clubs was built. The classy backs at the Canberra Raiders, Brisbane Broncos and Melbourne Storm may have grabbed the newspaper headlines, but they wouldn't have been able to bask in the limelight if not for the hard graft of Lazarus.

The Brick was Canberra born and bred, making his first-grade debut with the Raiders in 1987 and helping the 'Green Machine' to grand final victories in 1989 and 1990.

Indeed, he was a major factor in the Raiders' successes. Under the tutelage of coach Tim Sheens he had emerged as one of the great new breed of front-rowers of the modern era. Despite being a target for opposition defences, he repeatedly made the crucial breaks to give his backs room to move. And didn't the likes of international superstars Ricky Stuart, Laurie Daley and Mal Meninga enjoy the freedom Lazarus gave them in attack. For such a big man he was deceptively quick in

Opposite: *Glenn Lazarus, 'The Brick with Eyes'*

short bursts through the rucks. And his defence was terrifyingly brutal—but legitimate.

Wayne Bennett, Canberra's co-coach before Sheens, had recognised these talents back in 1987, Lazarus' first season in first-grade. The raw youngster had eagerly embraced every piece of advice offered by the coaching staff and the experienced Test players in the ranks of the Raiders. Bennett had since moved on to Brisbane and it came as no surprise that when he was looking for a replacement for the retiring Test prop Greg Dowling for the 1992 season at the Broncos, he turned to Lazarus.

There were a lot of critics. They reckoned Lazarus wasn't tough enough. They equated toughness with the ability to smash an opponent's head off his shoulders. But Dowling wasn't one of the doomsayers: 'People knock him because he doesn't act like an animal on the field. But you don't need that type of player. Animals cost you penalties and penalties cost you matches.'

Lazarus smiled when he heard Dowling's comments:

Yeah, I'm not renowned for being a blockhead. I don't go around looking for trouble. If you're trying to knock some bloke's head off, you're not concentrating on your game. You're liable to miss a tackle and mistakes like that cost you tries. I go out and do my job.

As it turned out, the Lazarus signing proved a master-stroke. He provided the difference that made Brisbane a great side rather than just a good side. In his first year in the Queensland capital he tasted grand final success again as the Broncos thrashed St George 38–8. Lazarus was one of the stand-outs. He pointed out that the Brisbane players were more relieved than excited at full-time: 'We've been reading for a couple of months how we were home and hosed. But we weren't until the full-time whistle on grand final day. Now we've won it and can feel satisfied.'

Lazarus was to be part of the Broncos side that retained the Premiership title with another victory over St George in the grand final the following year. In the post-match celebrations team-mate Allan Langer got himself offside with the Sydney media for chanting, 'St George can't play,' from the stage of the Broncos Leagues Club in the Brisbane suburb of Red Hill. These days Langer regrets having led the chant: 'The whole thing got blown out of proportion. It was just footy . . . just one of those things. Footy was different back then. I don't need to apologise.'

But how would the Sydneysiders have reacted had the journalists realised what Lazarus was singing at the previous grand final celebrations at the club? After off-key renditions by his team-mates of 'Hey, Hey, We're the Broncos', 'You'll Never Walk Alone', 'Simply the Best' and 'Nothing's Going to Stop Us Now', The Brick grabbed the microphone and belted out a risqué version of the Southern American backwoods folksong 'Campdown Races'. The lyrics suggested Sydneysiders had a certain unfortunate sexual bent.

Sadly a broken leg forced Lazarus to miss sharing Brisbane's success in the 1997 Super League grand final, when there were two opposing competitions.

The following year he signed to captain the Melbourne Storm in their debut season. Again he was that vital brick in the club's foundations. Twelve months later, in his final match before retiring, he led the fledgling side to a surprise victory over St George Illawarra in the grand final. In doing so, Lazarus became the first (and still only) player to have won Premierships with three different clubs.

Changing face of league

THERE CAN BE NO BETTER EXAMPLE of how the size of rugby league players has changed over the years than two Australian captains of different eras three decades apart—John Sattler and Andrew Johns.

Sattler, who captained the Australians in 1970, was a prop, usually the biggest player on the field. Johns, who was skipper in 2002 and 2003, was a half-back, usually the smallest. But both were the same height (179 centimetres), weighed almost the same (89 kilograms) and were of near identical build.

They are not the only similarities. Both turned in incredibly courageous efforts to inspire their clubs to grand final victories. Sattler's 1970 effort of playing with a jaw broken in three places has become part of football folklore (see 'Sattler's Broken Jaw'). That was in an era in which blokes shrugged off horrific injuries and did not have highly paid medical teams to dissuade them from heroics.

Johns ignored the medicos' logic and signed himself out of hospital to play for the Newcastle Knights in the 1997 Australian Rugby League grand final against Manly. He had suffered rib injuries the week before, during the Knights' victory over North Sydney in the preliminary final, but when the treatment—a cortisone injection—went wrong, he had ended up in hospital recovering from a perforated lung. Respected rugby league doctor Nathan Gibbs was reported as warning Johns about the dangers of playing: 'You could die.'

But 'Joey' Johns ignored the advice. He was used to serious injury. He had already missed more than half the season after injuring an ankle in a pre-season trial match—he wasn't going to miss the most important game of the year. He turned up at the Sydney Football Stadium and not only did he inspire his team-mates, it was a piece of sheer Johns genius that won them the grand final right on full-time.

Opposite: The best in the world . . . Andrew Johns shows off one of his two Golden Boots.

With Newcastle and Manly locked at 16–all, the match seemed destined to go to extra time, when Johns suddenly darted out of dummy half. The Sea Eagles' would-be defenders charged at him, certain he would attempt a field goal to win the match. Johns had other ideas. He dummied to kick before sending a crisp pass to winger Darren Albert, who swooped on the ball and was across the tryline to score. There were just seven seconds left on the clock and the ground-record crowd of 42,482 exploded.

In a *60 Minutes* television program in 2006, reporter Tara Brown asked him about all the injuries he had suffered during his career and then listed them for viewers. 'A broken back, a broken shoulder, broken jaw, played with broken ribs and a punctured lung . . . groin operations, ankle reconstructions, a dangerous neck injury, and a knee injury so bad he had nightmares,' she said, cataloguing the setbacks. 'What were the nightmares about?'

Johns was matter-of-fact about it: 'Just the pain I went through, the snapping noise, it just . . . yeah, when I'd go to sleep it'd come back all the time. It really shook me up.'

But despite drug problems, mental anguish and later allegations of racial taunts, Johns is still regarded as one of the greatest of all those who have played the sport. He was the first player to be twice awarded the Golden Boot as the best player in the world (in 1999, and again in 2001) and was named as a member of Australia's Team of the Century. Johns also received three Dally M Medals (in 1998, 1999 and 2002) as the best in the National Rugby League Premiership—and these were just a few of the honours bestowed on the Newcastle genius before he finally accepted the experts' advice and retired in 2007 after a frightening neck injury that, if exacerbated, could have left him in a wheelchair for the rest of his life. He went out holding the record for the highest number of Premiership points (2176) scored by any player in the league.

And would he have pushed himself through that pain barrier over all the years had he known how excruciating that agony would be? Johns had no doubt. He told *60 Minutes*: 'If someone were to come to me at 18 and said, "These are the injuries you are going to have," I wouldn't have thought twice about it. I would have said, "Yeah, no problem."'

Oblivious to pain

THERE WAS NEVER ANY DOUBT that Shane Webcke would grow up to be a hardman. When he was nine years old he accidentally drove a garden fork through one of his feet while digging the vegetable patch in the backyard of his home on Queensland's Darling Downs. It took two of the neighbours to hold the foot steady while another pulled out the fork. Yet there was not a single sob from young Shane, only a detached interest in the whole proceedings. He then washed the wound and was ready to return to his digging until wiser adult heads decided otherwise. To this day Webcke has always claimed it didn't hurt. But that was the way the man who was arguably the greatest prop of his era looked at life. He would block out any thought of pain, on or off the football field.

Dr Peter Meyers, the renowned Queensland orthopaedic specialist who operated on so many of Webcke's football injuries sustained during his career with the Brisbane Broncos, claimed he had never treated a tougher man. And, rest assured, there were many, many injuries—most of which would have floored a lesser man.

There was the celebrated broken left arm in 2000. He suffered the injury during a match against St George Illawarra at Wollongong's WIN Stadium in the third last round of the season proper. Soon after half-time Webcke had tackled future international prop Luke Bailey and had caught the arm awkwardly on the Dragon's right elbow. Webcke left the field with the damaged arm flopping uselessly at his side.

X-rays revealed the worst. There was a deep crack in the forearm that would take six to eight weeks to heal. Worst of all, the grand final was only six weeks away. It would be a miracle for Webcke to be there if the Broncos made it through to the gala occasion. He was determined that miracle would happen.

Neil Smith, a boxing trainer from the Sydney suburb of Marrickville, had made special protective devices for players in the past and Webcke turned to him for a custom-fitted armguard made from plastic, resin and foam. Broncos coach Wayne Bennett told him he would have to prove himself in the preliminary final against Parramatta even though the arm had not completely healed. Webcke did so, making 24 tackles and 14 hit-ups as Brisbane accounted for Parramatta. He later revealed that he hadn't used the injured arm, tackling with the other shoulder and arm and carrying the ball only in the right arm. But no one noticed.

It was a repeat performance in the grand final against Sydney Roosters. The Roosters captain, Brad Fittler, had warned that his forwards would target Webcke and they did. But the broken arm held up as the Broncos won the grand final 14–6. Webcke said he had felt incredible relief—that Brisbane had won the Premiership, but more importantly that the risk he had taken paid off and he had not let down his team-mates.

Four years later there was another stoic effort on the part of the big fellow. In the qualifying final clash against Melbourne Storm on the first weekend of the play-offs, the Broncos were thoroughly outplayed, losing 31–14. But unbeknown to his team-mates, Webcke had gone into the game with a knee problem. He had discovered on the morning of the match that there was a piece of floating bone which caused his left knee to regularly seize up. Eventually he had to leave the pitch. Dr Meyers was contacted and Webcke went under the knife the next morning to remove the bone fragment (which he kept as a souvenir). He would have only six days to recuperate before the next match, against North Queensland. By Tuesday he was running, albeit tentatively, with the knee badly swollen. He knew that there would never be a 100 per cent recovery by Saturday night's encounter but was determined to play. A run on Saturday morning convinced him he could take to the field. It was all in vain, as the Broncos went down 10–nil.

Bennett was astounded by the recovery. He wrote in the foreword to Webcke's autobiography, *Warhorse*: 'What he did was one of the most courageous and toughest things I have ever seen in football . . . it wasn't a case of him just going through the motions, he played better than most of the guys who were fully fit.'

But more was to come at the Tri-Nations Tournament in England a couple of months later. A similar problem arose on the morning of the final against Great Britain—only this time it was a bigger piece of bone that had the knee locking up while he was walking from the breakfast table. The team physiotherapist worked on the knee all day and the pain was so intense that Webcke threw up in his hotel room. But when he went out for the warm-up at Elland Road Stadium in Leeds, he was okay. There was no hurting at all and no need for a painkilling injection. Everything went well that evening. Webcke played the entire first half as the Australians rattled up a match-winning 38–nil lead. Veteran journalists described it as the finest half of rugby league in the history of the modern game. When Webcke returned to the field for the second spell, the knee finally seized up and Bennett gave him an early mark.

What a valiant display on an almost unbelievable evening! No wonder Bennett often said, 'The bloke has true grit.'

Was it an omen that when Webcke played his first game of rugby league in the Under–9s in Queensland's Warwick competition, his club's colours were green and gold? He was to wear the 'ultimate' green and gold jumper 26 times in Tests for Australia, in both Australian Rugby League and Super League internationals.

Webcke was discovered by Bennett in the Toowoomba Under–18s grand final in 1992 when the supercoach made a special trip to watch another future Test prop, Steve Price. However, Bennett came away determined to sign Webcke. He was impressed with the way the youngster terrorised the opposition forwards, ripping into them without any fear for his own safety and lifting his team to success in the season's finale. It was to be that way from the moment Webcke signed with the Broncos—he would train and play at full throttle, pushing himself to exhaustion. As Bennett noted in *Warhorse*: 'In those early days he didn't want to just tackle, he wanted to smash whoever had the ball . . . back then he just wanted to inflict pain.'

The selective intimidation came later as the prop matured both physically and mentally. He made his first-grade debut for Brisbane in 1995 and burst onto the international scene two years later, at the height of the Super League war. He was a member of the Australian Super League Test team that played the Kiwis in the second Trans-Tasman encounter. But injury forced him out of the end-of-season trip to England for the Ashes series.

Nevertheless Webcke subsequently made three visits to Britain with the unified Test squads, appearing in all six matches (against England, Fiji, Russia, Samoa, Wales and New Zealand) in the 2000 World Cup, all three of the Ashes Tests in 2003, and each of the five games in the 2004 Tri-Nations Tournament, his last appearances for Australia. He was also chosen for the 2001 Kangaroos but decided not to tour in the aftermath of the September 11 and Afghanistan crises.

An indication of Webcke's dominant role as a front-row forward in the Test arena during the early years of the 21st century is shown by the annual world ratings in *Rugby League World* magazine (published in conjunction with the award of the Golden Boot to the world's best player). Webcke first made an impact when rated second in listings for props in the 1998 ratings. In the next six years, until his retirement from international football, he was rated Number One every single time. He never won the Golden Boot, but history shows that the toilers in the engine room rarely win top awards in rugby league—that kudos usually going to the flashier back-line stars.

Webcke continued at club level until the end of the 2006 season. He had a fairytale finish to his career, with the Broncos beating Melbourne Storm 15–8 in the grand final to give Webcke his fourth Premiership success. He was previously on the winning side in 1997 (in Super League) and 1998 as well as in that heroic 2000 performance.

Bennett was understandably delighted: 'Over the years I've said enough about him. His record is wonderful. He's a four-time Premiership player. He's got every accolade in the game and deserves every one of them.'

And Webcke was modest to the end: 'To end my career like that . . . it's a privilege. I didn't deserve it but I'm grateful for it.'

Hard man—soft heart!

'The bloke has true grit.'
Queensland Coach of the Century
Wayne Bennett describes Shane Webcke

Croker's courage

IN THE MODERN ERA there are very few stories about players staying on the pitch after suffering horrific injuries. Of course, until the mid 1960s injured players couldn't be replaced. Today, with four replacements on the bench, there is usually someone to send out to ensure no team plays a man short.

But occasionally it does happen—as the Canberra Raiders found out one Sunday afternoon in June 2001. The home side was taking on the Sydney Roosters and slowly but surely the Raiders' injury toll rose. Yet the Canberra players were able to lift and, against all odds, turn a 22–10 half-time deficit into a 32–22 victory.

More than a decade later, Raiders fans still remember that afternoon with awe and astonishment. By the interval their bench had been reduced to just one possible substitute. Five-eighth Mark McLinden was nursing what looked like a broken jaw. Centre Ken Nagas couldn't stand up. The club doctor had diagnosed a broken leg. Second-rower Ruben Wiki was suffering from concussion and a neck injury, and none of the medical staff would risk him returning in case he ended up as a quadriplegic.

Five minutes into the second spell, prop Sean Rogerson was assisted off the field with a match-ending knee injury. It was then that lock Jason Croker, already limping from a knee problem, went down in a crumpled heap. He had rolled an ankle. That would normally have meant the end of his match. However, rather than leave his team-mates a man short for the final 30 minutes, he got the trainers to strap the ankle and returned to the fray. The Raiders coach Mal Meninga explained:

> He was in trouble but just had to hang in there because we couldn't play with twelve men. And he just kept putting himself in the line of fire. In defence he was particularly impressive. The Roosters were smart enough to aim their attack at him, time and time again. But he kept coming up with the tackles. They couldn't get past him. It was an extremely brave effort.

Brave, indeed! It was only after the game that the extent of Croker's injuries became clear. There was no serious lasting damage to the ankle, but as far as the knee was concerned it was a very different matter. Scans showed that not only had he ruptured one ligament but another was badly torn. Understandably it brought about a premature end to Croker's season. He was to become the first recipient of the John Sattler Award, an honour occasionally bestowed for a player's extraordinary courage on the football field.

Pain is temporary, glory is forever

FEW FOOTBALLERS HAVE HAD A FEARSOME REPUTATION to match that of Ruben Wiki. Watch him perform the pre-Test haka with his fellow Kiwis, eyes glaring, tongue protruding and those giant hands slapping his thighs with a sound resembling a mortar explosion, and you'd hope he'd never get too close and personal with you.

Ka mate, Ka mate, Ka ora, Ka ora!
I die, I die, I live, I live!

As far as the *Ka ora* part of the war cry is concerned, Ruben Wiki reckons it all comes down to his regular enjoyment of bowls of kava—a part of his Samoan cultural heritage. The traditional beverage plays an important role in day-to-day living in Polynesian communities in the South Pacific and has a special spiritual significance for the Samoans.

The narcotic drink is also recognised for its medicinal properties, especially for the relief of stress, anxiety, depression and insomnia. It is made from the root of one of the plants in the pepper family. The root is crushed and soaked in water. The resulting liquid has an unpleasant taste and resembles muddy water. And it numbs your mouth and tongue. Does it ever!

'It's a well known fact that kava tastes pretty ordinary,' as one website devoted to kava explains. 'Really, there is no dancing around this topic, it tastes like absolute rubbish, and if it didn't deliver that sweet delicious buzz then there's no way you'd put it anywhere near your tastebuds. In fact, the more you drink, the more repugnant the taste becomes.' That is why most of the *nakamals* (or kava bars) of the Pacific sell food such as pineapple or banana cake to mask the awful aftertaste.

Indeed, a soft drink company in Vanuatu has perfected a cola that is laced with kava. The manufacturers of Lava Cola claim it produces the calming effect of kava without the muddy taste. In short it's a liquid valium.

Ruben Wiki drank kava after every game. It wasn't to calm him. It

was to mask the aches and pains of the wholehearted effort he put into his every appearance on the field. His determined displays during 15 seasons in the big league made him arguably the greatest player ever to pull on a New Zealand Test jersey. At least that's what his team-mates reckoned. So often they would quote the perennial cliché: 'He led from the front.' When the going got tough, a characteristic charge from Wiki would lift the Kiwis' spirits. Or maybe it was a bone-jarring tackle that caught an opposition star under the ribs and left him gasping for breath. And, so often, a few well-chosen, inspirational words in the dressing room at half-time.

When Wiki retired in 2008 he had played 316 first-grade games in the Australian Rugby League and National Rugby League Premierships, the most by any New Zealander, and a world record 55 Tests for the Kiwis, including 18 as captain.

In every encounter he left a lasting impression, usually on a sick-and-sorry opposition player or four. As one fan noted on a rugby league website: 'Hey, imagine bumping into him at night. Oh, my God! You'd run the other way—FAST.'

It was the astute Canberra coach Tim Sheens who first noticed the potential of Wiki as a 19-year-old Junior Kiwi when he was playing for the Aotearoa Maori in the 1992 Pacific Cup. After some legal problems were ironed out, Sheens took him across the Tasman to play for the Raiders, where he was brought along slowly, making just three first-grade appearances in his first season, including two off the bench. But then his career took off. Playing alongside his schoolboy hero Mal Meninga in the centres, Wiki was a vital cog in the Green Machine's unrelenting push to the 1994 Premiership. At the end of the season he was chosen for the Kiwis' brief tour of Papua New Guinea and was one of the stars in New Zealand's two victories over the Kumuls. From

Opposite: Ruben Wiki raises the trophy after captaining New Zealand to a shock 24–0 victory over Australia in the final of the 2005 Tri-Nations Tournament, his last Test appearance.

then on, until he bowed out of the international game in 2005, he was a Test regular.

In 2000, Kiwi coach Frank Endacott moved Wiki into lock, thus beginning his new career in the forwards. And by the time he hung up his boots he had moved into the front row. In each and every position in which he played, he excelled. After his first year in Test football he finished as third-best centre in the annual world ratings by the respected English magazine *Rugby League World* (behind Steve Renouf and Mal Meninga), and the year he bowed out of the Test arena he was rated the best prop in the world.

He remained heavily involved in the sport after finishing as a player. In 2010 he was a vital member of Stephen Kearney's coaching staff as the Kiwis pulled off an upset victory in the Four Nations Tournament. Winger Jason Nightingale claimed some inspirational words from Wiki were ringing in his ears as he raced down the sideline to set up the winning try in the final against Australia. In the first half Nightingale was in agony after he was winded by a crunching tackle by Australian half-back Cooper Cronk. 'I was hurting, my guts were killing me,' Nightingale said.

Wiki, working as the Kiwis trainer, offered some advice: 'Just remember, pain is temporary, glory is forever.'

The winger said those words were resonating in his head as he raced towards the tryline before unloading. Just seconds later, half-back Nathan Fein was across the line to score.

Wiki was no stranger to pain. And he also tasted glory. He would have survived in the bad old days when forwards ripped and tore each other with no regard for the rules. That he struck fear into opponents in an era when such barbarism was not accepted speaks volumes for Wiki's approach to the game. It was an approach that won him recognition as an Officer of the New Zealand Order of Merit in the 2007 Queen's Birthday Honours list and the kudos of becoming a New Zealand Rugby League 'Immortal'. Wiki shrugged it all off with a laugh: 'Not bad for a fellow who only wanted to play football.'

The last word on Wiki goes to his former captain at the New Zealand Warriors, Steve Price:

People had told me about him—how great he was. They weren't wrong. Ruben was a better bloke than a football player, and everyone knows how good a football player he was. You couldn't get a more gentle or more genuine bloke off the field. But on the field he was nuts . . . he was an animal. He'd do anything for you.

'You couldn't get a more gentle or genuine bloke off the field. But on the field he was nuts . . . he was an animal.'

Ruben Wiki's captain at the New Zealand Warriors, Steve Price

King of the kids

IT WAS A COLD WINTER'S EVENING IN WIGAN when Adrian Morley smashed his way into the history books. It was 8 November 2003—a date that has since remained indelibly etched in Morley's mind. The tough English forward had been playing for three seasons with Sydney Roosters in the National Rugby League but was back in familiar territory, convinced Great Britain could beat Australia to win a full Ashes series for the first time in almost a quarter of a century.

'Because I'd had a good year Down Under, I thought it was my duty to show the rest of the team that the Australians were beatable,' Morley explained. 'But, as everyone now knows, I was far too aggressive.' Well, that's one way of putting it!

Great Britain had kicked off and Melbourne Storm prop Robbie Kearns made the first hit-up of the match. Morley was determined to put him on the seat of his pants. 'I was at least six or seven metres ahead of my team-mates,' Morley explained. 'If I had hit him cleanly, he would have ended up in the stands. But he stepped me and we all know what happened then.' Morley caught Kearns flush on the chin with a blatantly reckless forearm jolt and the Aussie went down in a heap. Referee Steve Ganson quickly sought the opinions of touch judge Steve Wright and video referee David Campbell before showing Morley the red card.

It all took just 12 seconds—to this day the fastest send-off in more than a century of international rugby league. 'At the time I was bitterly disappointed, but I eventually got over it,' Morley admitted. 'We lost that Test by just four points and the other two by small margins. It was the Ashes series that got away.'

Debate still rages over the influence that send-off had on the final result of the Wigan Test and, indeed, the whole series. Would the British have won with a full complement of players? And had they won, would the success have provided the impetus for them to continue in a winning vein?

Opposite: 'Who are you looking at?' Adrian Morley stares down an opponent.

270

At the very least, the incident confirmed Morley's reputation as arguably the most feared player of his era. That status was perhaps predictable as he grew up in the tough Eccles area of Salford near Manchester, where for most kids success on the sporting field was the only escape from a life of confrontation with the police.

Morley made his first-grade debut for Leeds in 1995 before his 18th birthday. He was already a clever ball player with a tactical football brain that defied his youth. In attack his explosive power ensured opposition sides needed more than one tackler to halt his long-striding runs. However, it was always his ferocious defence that caught the eye.

Typical of this was an incident in 2004. Morley was playing for Sydney Roosters in a game against St George Illawarra. Referee Paul Simpkins placed him on report for an alleged high tackle on Dragons rookie Aaron Wheatley. The action was taken on the advice of video ref Graeme West, who had checked a replay of the incident, which seemed to show a good, hard tackle with Morley connecting around the shoulder and chest. The fans at the Sydney Football Stadium showed what they thought of West's decision by chanting, 'Morley! Morley! Morley!' Had the tackle been vicious the chant would most certainly have been, 'Off! Off! Off!'

Roosters coach Ricky Stuart was fuming, but chose his words well:

I don't go and defend him [Morley] when I see he has hit them high. But I will certainly be defending this. If the attitude is the way it is now with Adrian Morley, we're going to wipe this guy out of the game and I think it's very unfair.

His words fell on deaf ears. The judiciary suspended Morley for two matches—because of his previous record.

Luckily Morley has not been wiped out of the game and the big hits continue—on both sides of the world. Like the one on Mark Carroll in Morley's third season with Leeds, when Aussie enforcer Carroll was playing for the London Broncos. Fourteen seasons on, Leeds fans still talk in awe about the monster crash-tackle that left Carroll seeing stars.

Morley made his international debut when England thrashed France 73–6 at Gateshead in 1996, a month after his 19th birthday, and there was no looking back. By 2011 he had played in 45 Tests for Great Britain or England. He would have played many more but for a sternum problem restricting him to two appearances in the 2000 World Cup and a broken arm ruling him out of the 2001 Ashes series against Australia. He was the first Englishman to win the three major world club titles: the Challenge Cup and Super League Championship in England and the NRL Premiership in Australia. He won the Cup Final with Leeds Rhinos at Wembley in 1999, and again with Warrington Wolves in 2009 (as captain), the NRL Premiership grand final with Sydney Roosters in 2002, and the Super League grand final with the Bradford Bulls in 2005 (a success only made possible by cameo appearances for the Yorkshire club in six games after the Roosters had missed the NRL play-offs). Only Australian Harry Bath (with Warrington in England, and Balmain and St George in Australia) had previously managed the trifecta.

Morley had reversed a trend when he was lured to Australia in 2000 by his former Leeds coach Graham Murray. For the previous 15 years it was a case of a flood of Australians going to Britain because the money was so much better than under the restrictive salary cap Down Under. There were also some questionable but quite legitimate ways of avoiding full income tax, with payments into offshore superannuation funds. But Morley was happy to drop money to prove himself in the world's toughest club competition.

The rugged no-nonsense forward had a tough time with the NRL judiciary, with a dozen suspensions in his six seasons in the competition. Most were for high tackles. But Morley's successful transition to football in Australia began a trend and others, notably England internationals Gareth Ellis, Sam Burgess and James Graham, followed in his footsteps.

Even though Morley was an expatriate Brit, he was a hit with the young fans. A good example of this was his appearance at a 2004 pre-season match between Wests Tigers (NRL) and Widnes Vikings (UK) in the twin towns of Forster–Tuncurry on the New South Wales north coast. It was stinking hot and there was little shade. But there among the crowd—looking a bit out of place—was Morley, just back from a visit to England, where he had been awaiting the renewal of his Australian visa. Morley had been in Forster for a charity luncheon the previous day and, because the Roosters weren't playing a trial game that weekend, had stayed on to say hello to a few of his old mates in the Widnes side.

Throughout the match he was never alone as hundreds of kids—the vast majority of them Indigenous—lined up either to ask for an autograph or to question him about 'The Greatest Game of All'. For many of the overpaid show ponies in rugby league this would have been too much. They would have got impatient with the youngsters. Not so Morley. He answered all the questions and asked plenty of his own of the budding Preston Campbells and Arthur Beetsons of the north coast. Here was an Englishman who was not only a genuine bloke but a genuine hero in the eyes of Australian kids.

Every time Morley hits someone around the shoulders and the do-gooders bay for blood, visions of that afternoon at Forster are conjured up. A chance to meet with their hero Adrian Morley meant so much to those hundreds of north coast kids. Do you think they would have lined up for a chat with him if he were a thug?

> **'If I had hit him cleanly, he would have ended up in the stands.'**
> **Adrian Morley on the tackle that earned him the quickest send-off in Test history**

Hard man with tender heart

THERE WAS HARDLY A SEASON when tough forward Mark Geyer wasn't in the headlines. A succession of suspensions for stretching the rules that extra centimetre. Shooting off at the mouth over what he saw as injustices in rugby league. Signing with English club Sheffield Eagles during an off-season to cut the length of an Australian ban. A classic on-field confrontation with the legendary Wally Lewis during a State of Origin match. A spell on the sidelines for failing a drug test for marijuana. And a string of injuries.

But the stirrer from Penrith still managed to make a Kangaroo tour of Britain and France (1990), appear in the Test arena three times against France and New Zealand, and boast a club career of more than a decade.

It is ironic that this firebrand will probably be best remembered by historians (and not only those chronicling sport) for an incredibly unselfish effort to help thousands of people he never knew recover from a natural disaster of catastrophic proportions.

In early January 2011, three-quarters of Queensland was devastated by floods, including much of the Queensland capital, Brisbane. More than 40 people died or went missing. It was then that Geyer leaped in to help the victims of the floods. Within a week he managed to lure a who's who of State of Origin history out of retirement for one final game. And, in doing so, the greats of seasons past raised more than $455,000.

There was 'The Guru', Eric Grothe, the great former Parramatta winger. Could almost three decades have passed since he terrorised the Great Britain players in the 1982 Ashes series? Kerry Boustead pulled on the Queensland shirt again, 27 years after his last Origin appearance. Big Sam Backo, the only forward in history to score a try in each of the three Tests in an Ashes series (1988), had put on a lot of pudding since his last Origin appearance, in 1990. But there was no doubting his commitment. Former Australian Test cricketer Andrew Symonds managed to get a gig and typified the spirit of Queensland with a fiery confrontation with former Test hooker Ben Elias. 'Queenslanders never surrender,' Symonds was to later explain. Gorden Tallis showed just why he'd been dubbed Gordzilla. And Mal Meninga was the Queensland skipper.

But this galaxy of stars couldn't hold a candle to the 43-year-old owner of a small chain of fruit and vegetable shops in western Sydney who had last played a game of rugby league as young teenager at school 30 years ago—Tony Trim. Trim had 'won' a place in the New South Wales Origin Legends side by bidding $14,600 in an online auction. And his efforts on that January night made him an instant cult hero among rugby league fans.

He may have been crunched in a bone-rattling tackle by dual-international Mat Rogers—who represented Australia in both rugby league and union—but just before half-time Trim scored the Blues' first try. Former Test captain Brad Fittler put in a chip-kick towards the right wing, where an out-of-breath Trim was having a bit of a breather. Then came the adrenalin rush. He pounced on the ball and touched down. 'I called for it,' he laughed after high-fiving several of the Blues legends. 'What's more I beat [the flying ex-Test winger] Nathan Blacklock in the race for the ball.'

But Trim didn't stop there. After being hit by a hard tackle, he jumped up and eyeballed the Queensland player involved. What the hell was he thinking? There he was chesting Gordzilla Tallis himself. Trim laughed:

I had no idea it was Gordie until those eyes were glaring at me. It was too late. The other New South Wales players said I should have decked him. Sure . . . a chance would have been a fine thing! As I was walking out the door to head for Parramatta Stadium, my wife had joked about checking my life insurance. I'm not sure she realises how close she came to a payout.

His efforts had the fans shouting, 'Trimmer! Trimmer! Trimmer!' It was music to his ears: 'I felt like Wally Lewis. It was magic.'

The fans should have been chanting, 'Geyer! Geyer! Geyer!' That night the former *enfant terrible* truly became a rugby league legend.

Pint-sized men of steel

OH, TO BE ABLE TO WRITE LIKE MARK TWAIN! The 19th century 'Father of American Literature' left us with hundreds of famous one-liners. It seemed there was at least one on every page of his books and magazine articles:

Reports of my death are greatly exaggerated.

Get your facts first—then you can distort them as much as you please.

Never put off until tomorrow what you can do the day after tomorrow.

And, *It's not the size of the dog in a fight, but the size of the fight in the dog.*

Rugby league fans can certainly appreciate the last quote. How many times have we been amazed at the raw courage of the tiniest of players? Pint-sized half-backs taking on the biggest of forwards—and ending up triumphant! I remember when I was but knee-high to a grasshopper, watching my beloved Western Suburbs playing the mighty St George outfit in a Saturday Match of the Day at the Sydney Cricket Ground. At one stage the smallest man on the field, Wests half Keith Holman, went low on the tallest, St George captain Norm Provan, lifted him in a tackle that would not be allowed in the modern game and drove him headfirst into the turf. The whole arena seemed to shudder with the force of the impact. Around 7.6 on the Richter scale, perhaps. Holman just bounced up, dusted himself off and waited for the next giant forward to run at him.

If that was something of which memories were made, how incredible it must have been for fans watching around the time of World War I, when the smallest man ever to play first grade was in action. His name was George McGowan, and he played eight seasons between 1915 and 1922 for Eastern Suburbs, South Sydney and Wests. McGowan weighed just 7 stone 7 pounds in the old Imperial measure (the equivalent of 47.6 kilograms). He was lighter by about 10 kilograms than a couple of other flyweights of the time: Joey Murphy (Glebe, 1922–23) and Tiger Gillespie (Newtown, 1916–19, and South Sydney, 1920–23). But they were never overwhelmed by their bigger opponents. If only we had a time machine to go back and see how they handled themselves in the thick of the action!

To put the size of these players in perspective, check out the weight of some of the modern stars. Former Wests Tigers captain Brett Hodgson, who later moved to the Super League competition in Britain, where he played for Huddersfield Giants and Warrington Wolves, tipped the scales at 78 kilograms. So did Queensland full-back Matt Bowen. Test half-back Brett Kimmorley weighed in at 80 kilos.

Rugby league historian George Crawford reckoned that, on the international scene, the smallest player to pull on a green and gold jersey would probably have been Arthur 'Snowy' Justice, the St George hooker. He was only 63.4 kilograms when he first played for Australia, against Great Britain in 1928. Half-back Dennis Ward was 55.2 kilograms when he was called into Canterbury's grade ranks in 1962. By the time he reached first grade he weighed 61.6 kilograms and when he played for Australia in the 1972 World Cup in France he was still only 65.2 kilograms.

Gold Coast Titans folk-hero Preston Campbell tipped the scales at 76 kilograms. But there is no doubting his ticker. In August 2008, Campbell played 43 minutes of a match against the Brisbane Broncos while nursing a broken jaw. Campbell brushed aside pleas from members of the Titans' medical team who wanted him to sit out the second half, and then put on a remarkable display on the field. Neither coach John Cartwright nor any of his team-mates knew of the injury as the full-back regularly took kicks from the opposition and ran straight back into the fray. His courage was all in vain, as the Titans eventually went down 25–21. It was the end of his season.

Campbell explained:

I copped a whack on the left side of my face and all of a sudden my jaw locked up and wouldn't move. I knew there was a problem there. I couldn't align the top of my mouth with the bottom of my jaw. I think my jaw may have just popped out and popped back in. I saw the doctor at half-time and he didn't want me to go back on, but

I didn't give him a choice. I was out there before he could stop me. I was hoping I wouldn't get another knock around the head in the second half and I didn't, so I'm thankful it wasn't any worse.

Cartwright was amazed: 'I thought he was probably the best player on the field. He did an enormous amount of work. It was high energy. He was very brave.'

'If you ask guys like Preston or Alf [Allan Langer, yet another pint-sized dynamo] how they survive in our game, they wouldn't be able to tell you,' former New South Wales Origin coach Craig Bellamy said. 'They just do. They adapt. They learn little tricks. It's like being the smallest animal in the jungle.'

Before his debut in representative football, for Country Origin in 2005, Campbell told respected journalist Steve Mascord that he had never given a thought to his size—or lack of it—until he cracked it for a first-grade spot with the old Gold Coast Chargers. He just wanted to play footy:

As a kid I wasn't that much smaller . . . no, I lie. I was a fair bit smaller than those guys back then. But you don't really think about that stuff. When it gets competitive like this, though, I wondered a little bit about whether I'd be able to survive. I played at 62 kilos. It was scary but I played at full-back and on the wing so I wasn't involved too much in the defensive role. The scary part about it was running at big blokes and them getting you and swinging you around. And what about when they come at you? They don't actually say to your face they are running at you. They don't actually look at me and tell me they're coming. But you can hear them say, 'Run at Campbell.' And they do!

Brett Hodgson said he had never been scared because of his size. 'I was always quick enough as a kid that I could skirt around the bigger guys and not get hit too much,' he said. 'But there have been occasions when they grabbed hold of me.'

The most famous of these occasions was during the 2003 State of Origin series, when big Queenslander Gorden Tallis grabbed him by the jumper and threw him over the sideline like a rag doll. It is an incident that gets replayed almost every year in the Origin build-up. Not that Hodgson would forget it:

> The way I look at it is that I was fortunate enough to be there so he could do that to me. Ironically, a lot of people would want to be in that situation. Not necessarily getting dragged over the sideline—but actually being there to play Origin football. Being there in Origin is the thing that sticks out in my mind. I can forget easily being dragged. But other people don't let you forget it.

And in supreme irony, in 2009 Hodgson, the man with the stature of a jockey, was named 'Man of Steel' in the British competition. It was a deserved honour.

Back to Mark Twain: 'Courage is resistance to fear, mastery of fear— not absence of fear.'

Shouldering his way to the top

FOOTBALL COACHES ARE OFTEN VERY HARD TO PLEASE. Snare a hat-trick of tries or make 60 tackles in a match and they will most surely find a way to suggest you should have touched down four times or point to a tackle you missed at a vital stage of the game.

New Zealand Test coach Stephen Kearney was delighted when the Kiwi captain Benji Marshall engineered two late tries to snatch an unlikely victory over Australia in the final of the 2010 Four Nations Tournament, in Brisbane. There were just 93 seconds left on the clock when the New Zealanders managed to get in front for the first time all night. But until then, Kearney had not been a happy chap. The maestro Marshall revealed after the game that in the closing minutes of the encounter the normally mild-mannered coach had been sending him messages liberally laced with expletives.

'I was getting messages from the coaching box that weren't very nice,' Marshall said with a laugh—although he wasn't laughing when he received them. 'I'm not going to say what they were. It was "get your hands on the ball" or something like that, but with a few other words in there. But they got me into gear.'

Kearney made no apology for his four-letter tirade: 'Everyone is aware of what Benji can do on the footy field. That's why the messages were quite strong. I think he needs to understand the impact he can have on a game.'

The Kiwi coach had taken a leaf out of the book of Tim Sheens, the only club coach Benji had known and something of a father figure to the electrifying New Zealander. A couple of weeks after the Four Nations final, when Marshall was awarded the Golden Boot as the best player in the world and journalists were lavishing praise on the Wests Tigers five-eighth, Sheens suggested he had plenty of room to improve.

Opposite: Benji Marshall overcame a series of awful injuries that would have finished the careers of lesser mortals.

But with both Kearney and Sheens there was an unstated respect and admiration for what the young man had done to achieve Golden Boot status. He was never a big player—only 82 kilograms when he made his first-grade debut. Even after seven seasons in the big league he still only weighed in at 89 kilos, wringing wet. And, in the meantime, he had been the victim of a host of injuries that would have finished the career of anyone who did not possess Benji's incredible determination.

His medical file would have to be one of the biggest of any player in the history of the game. Some minor—but several serious—knee and ankle problems, a fractured cheekbone, a fractured shoulder and a succession of serious shoulder dislocations that required three reconstructions. Few players come back from one reconstruction, let alone two. Records suggest Marshall's effort in returning after a third and leaving the rest of the world in his wake is unprecedented.

Yet Marshall was always modest about his incredible talents. After winning the Golden Boot he noted: 'To win this award after coming back from three shoulder reconstructions, winning the Four Nations and having my best ever year since I've started in the NRL is pretty overwhelming. It's definitely something I won't take for granted.'

Every now and then fans and members of the media are privileged to witness the debut of a future superstar. There were just 9378 at Campbelltown Stadium on a Sunday in 2003 to see Wests Tigers thrash Newcastle Knights 52–12. The score means little. But that afternoon the select few were able to witness for the first time the Benji Marshall magic. David Middleton's official yearbook is to the point: 'The Tigers unleashed 18-year-old prodigy Benji Marshall for the final minutes and he showed glimpses of the potential that had him earmarked as one of the most exciting young talents of the game.'

The following week I wrote a column about Benji in the British newspaper *League Express*:

Although Tim Sheens and his Wests Tigers coaching staff are pleading with journalists not to focus too much attention on the kid—one cannot help but do so. For Marshall is a sporting freak. He hails from one of those New Zealand towns with remarkable onomatopoeic names. In his case it is Whakatane in the Bay of Plenty. Sheens has been keeping the former New Zealand Rugby Union Under–16s representative in cotton wool. But he let him out of the box last weekend and made us all sit up and take notice. He had never played league until a school trip to the Gold Coast in late 2001, when he was given a run against a classy Canberra outfit. Marshall so botched his first appearance on the pitch that the coach quickly pulled him back to the bench. But he gave him a second chance later in the game. And Marshall was so dazzling (among other great work, he scored a 60-metre solo try) that he was offered a sports scholarship to Keebra Park High School.

Many are called, few succeed. He was originally on a Tigers' scholarship but Sheens has since upgraded that to a three-year contract. In his senior debut last weekend Sheens told Marshall to play his natural game. He came on 10 minutes before half-time and promptly missed a tackle that resulted in a Newcastle try. This setback would have finished a lesser lad. But moments later Marshall made a trysaver on Mark Hughes and then proceeded to show his wares. Long passes. A side-step that reminded us all of Freddy Fittler. A wonderful kicking game. And, as the match wound down, Marshall was in at first receiver, calling the shots for the Tigers. He threw a long, cut-out pass to create a try for centre John Wilson. Then he made a side-stepping break that finished with stand-off Daniel Fitzhenry over to score. Referee Steve Clark was most impressed, noting over his two-way to Bill Harrigan up in the video referee's box in the grandstand: 'Geez, that young fellow can step, can't he!' The following day it was back to school for Marshall and final preparation for the HSC. Sheens had the last word: 'We see something special in him. But he still has a long way to go.' Maybe so! But I, for one, will cherish the memory of July 27, 2003—the day Benji Marshall was first unleashed.

Unleashed? Everyone thought that way!

Marshall came from a big family. His mother had 15 siblings, and she gave birth to Benji when she was 16. He never knew his biological father and was brought up in his formative years by an uncle and aunt, Mick and Annalie Doherty. After that dramatic first-grade debut he explained: 'I've got two families. I call them Mum and Dad. Then there's my mother and my two little brothers [Jordan and Jeremy]. I don't know my father, but all of my uncles are like fathers to me so I can't complain.'

But the uncles refused to take pity on the youngster. Psychologists would call it tough love. Uncles and cousins would regularly play what one might call backyard touch footy. Only there wasn't much touch in it . . . plenty of slamming of shoulders into the opposition. Full-blooded action.

Benji was about ten years old when one day it all became too much and he wimped off the field, crying. But ten minutes later he was back into the action. He explained to *Alpha* magazine how he went home and sat on the couch for a few minutes before he realised he was bored stiff:

So I went back and I watched the game for two minutes [from] where they couldn't see me. I was hiding behind the fence and what I saw was a game I loved playing. And I thought the best way to get them back would be to go back out there and carve them up. They pushed me over, honestly, another five or six times to try to make me cry [again]. And I just told myself don't cry, don't cry, don't cry, no, no, don't cry. And they were tough, man. They were hard on me. They just kept pushing me over. Now, of course, when I go back home, I do the pushing.

But it was good preparation for what lay ahead.

Marshall's injury worries began in his second season. After helping Wests Tigers to success in the World Sevens, he dislocated a shoulder in the fourth match of the 2004 Premiership, against North Queensland. Three matches after his return, against Melbourne, his season was over with another dislocation forcing the first reconstruction.

In 2005 Marshall was basically injury free, although hiding a shoulder problem that required off-season surgery at the end of the year. Nonetheless he etched a spot in rugby league folklore in Wests Tigers' surge to Premiership success. Benji helped them in a late-season charge that saw them reach the grand final against North Queensland. Once there he left his indelible mark, with a try in the 35th minute that will be talked about for decades to come. Marshall took a pass just two metres from his own line and his dancing feet, which would have done justice to Fred Astaire, took him to the 40-metre mark inside the Cowboys' half. There he flicked a blind pass to winger Pat Richards, who was limping after taking painkillers to mask ankle ligament damage. Richards forgot the pain and raced away before pushing off a lone would-be defender to score. 'Yeah, everyone knows about that try,' said Marshall. 'I certainly won't forget it.'

Marshall went under the surgeon's knife again during the off-season and then, in the first round match of 2006, suffered a fractured cheekbone after a head clash with a team-mate. Yet he stayed on the field and set up the winning try. Four weeks later on his return to the fray, he suffered yet another shoulder dislocation. Remarkably, he was back within a month to play for the Kiwis in the Anzac Test against Australia. But by mid-season it was deja vu—another dislocation, this time against the Penrith Panthers, and another reconstruction.

Marshall would have wondered whether there would ever be an end to this trail of chronic physical damage, especially as, in the Round 8 clash of the 2007 season, at Gosford's Bluetongue Stadium, he sustained yet another shoulder injury in a tackle when his arm was wedged between the Melbourne Storm's Israel Folau and the Tigers' Taniela Tuiaki. He managed to return later in the season but his efforts were hesitant—and with good reason.

The 2008 season started in typical fashion, with Marshall tearing knee ligaments five minutes after kick-off in the Tigers' first match, against St George Illawarra. He made it back by the seventh round and late in the season showed flashes of his exhilarating attack. The season finished on a real high, as Marshall scored a vital try as the Kiwis posted a shock 34–20 victory over Australia in the World Cup final.

The following season it all started to turn around. Even though the Tigers missed a spot in the finals series, Benji was appointed captain of the Kiwis for the Four Nations Tournament. But he lost his beloved foster dad to cancer. In his memory Marshall set up a fund during his Golden Boot year to help the victims of childhood cancer.

While dedicating his Golden Boot award to Mick Doherty, Benji also heaped praise on Sheens:

> I have plenty of respect for everything Tim has done for me. Coming from school as a touch footy player who didn't really know much about rugby league, Tim taught me everything I know. I am the player I am today because of Tim and I still have plenty more to learn. We have a great relationship on and off the field. He has definitely been like a father figure for me in Sydney.

Despite Sheens always demanding excellence from Benji Marshall, he knows only too well what a great player he has under his tutelage:

> He's mentally tougher than most people think. I saw Mal Meninga recover from four broken arms, and Ricky Stuart's groin injury was something, too. Then you've got Benji, who's come back from five shoulder operations. They all share the courage.

Marshall told *Alpha* at the start of 2010 that fans should expect something special from him. It was a forecast that was spot on:

> I've definitely got a lot more to offer. A lot of special things people won't have seen. I can feel it coming. It's coming. It's coming. I can't tell you exactly when, but I know something's coming. I just know things are going to click soon.

They certainly did—and at the start of the 2011 season, the 25-year-old said it all again: 'I've grown in maturity. I'm growing as a leader. But I think my best is still to come.'

Again, when the Tigers' hopes looked shattered midway through the season, thanks to a spate of injuries to key players and a host of rumours about alleged dissent within the club, Marshall came to the fore. He implored his team-mates to bond together to dispel the unsubstantiated media gossip. They listened and rallied, only to fall in the semifinals. But, unfazed, Benji pointed out once again—the best is still yet to come.

League's unluckiest man

BRENT TATE HAD HIS PLANS for the weeks before Christmas 2010 all carefully laid out. He was to start preparing for the return to playing football in his beloved Queensland after two seasons in the Shaky Isles playing with the New Zealand Warriors. To make sure it was all go for his new start in Townsville with the North Queensland Cowboys, he would clear up a few niggling problems.

Within days of the final of the Four Nations Tournament he would go under the surgeon's scalpel. The idea had been to clean up a troublesome ankle. But then, as had happened far too many times in his career, things took a turn for the worse. The ankle was no longer the focus of attention. Instead he underwent the third knee reconstruction of his career.

Everyone knew something was terribly wrong when the television cameras caught him at half-time in the tournament final crying on the shoulder of Australia's trainer Brian Hider. It was an intrusive piece of footage, but it served to show there is more to rugby league than players grasping for every last penny they can squeeze out of club coffers and handshake agreements conveniently ignored in the pursuit of the almighty dollar.

Tate had torn ligaments in the left knee in the opening minutes of the action against New Zealand but had soldiered on—and incredibly had been one of Australia's best players during the first 40 minutes. Indeed, he had not realised just how serious was the injury and had planned to return to the pitch for the second half. That's what so many of the great rugby league players are like. They ignore pain because they don't want to let down their mates.

However, as the team doctor did his rounds of the dressing room during the break, all that changed. 'I had felt a little pop but it wasn't like the other two [knee injuries], which dropped me,' Tate recalled. 'I wasn't even going to get the doctor to check it at half-time but he just happened to walk in front of me and because he was there I asked him to take a look.' The doctor had a good look and it was obvious the knee was gone.

And so were Tate's hopes for the next nine or ten months.

'As soon as he told me, the realisation of it sunk in pretty quickly and, to be honest, I don't even really remember what happened after that. I was just pretty well devastated,' Tate explained, fearing that his career would be over.

And everyone saw that mental devastation—including Tate's former coach at the Brisbane Broncos, Wayne Bennett. The supercoach was more than a trifle annoyed at Tate's emotions being laid bare by the television cameras:

> Players are entitled to their privacy in those situations. I was disappointed to see Brent in such a state of distress. Like everybody else, I didn't know what was going on. I remember the commentators saying he was limping a bit. If players want to shed a tear because of the sheer disappointment of what's just happened, surely they are entitled to do so in privacy. If Brent wants to show that emotion publicly, there's a place and time to do that at some other stage. For him, it's his third time. Plus he'd come back from a broken jaw this year and some years ago it was his neck. So for him, it just keeps adding up. That's some of the emotion you saw . . . the 'I'm finished here' . . . 'When is it going to stop?' . . . 'When am I going to get a good run?' That's what he was feeling. It's a raw human emotion.

Tate, a rugged three-quarter, had made it to the top wearing the maroon of Queensland and the green and gold of Australia for the first time in 2002, a season after making his first-grade debut for the Broncos. And by 2012 he had played 23 Tests and made 171 NRL appearances for the Broncos, Warriors and Cowboys.

Nevertheless there is no doubt that Tate must be arguably the most unlucky senior player as far as a succession of injuries is concerned. As well as the three knee reconstructions and the broken jaw, there was that neck injury that requires him to wear a special brace in all his matches. He has had surgery four times on his ankles and once on his nose. And he has been troubled by hernia problems caused in tackles by opposition players.

Yet the fire still burned in his belly. And after a couple of days considering where he was headed, the 28-year-old was convinced that he would not only make it back into the Premiership ranks but he would return to both the Queensland State of Origin and Australian Test sides. It was the measure of the man that he succeeded and in 2012 was one of the first players chosen to pull on the maroon and the green and gold jerseys. 'I just love playing,' is the way he describes his efforts. 'I wouldn't do it otherwise.'

He had an ally in his Queensland coach and former Australian captain Mal Meninga, himself no stranger to injury setbacks. Big Mal broke an arm no fewer than four times and fought back. Late in his career the massive padding on the arm was a visible legacy of the succession of injuries suffered by the man named as one of the centres in Australia's Team of the Century. Meninga said at the time of Tate's most recent injury:

> If I could come back from four busted arms he can beat three knee reconstructions. My last broken arm was when I was 27 or 28 years old and it wasn't the end of my career. I played for another six years after that. So anything is possible for Tatey. I can't recall anyone having as much bad luck as Brent. It's definitely a lot worse than what happened to me. His are structural injuries. Mine was just a broken bone.

Meninga did not underestimate the mental hurdles Tate would have to overcome. However, he reckoned the rewards in doing so would be immense:

> It is how you handle adversity that makes you who you are. We know he's a fighter. We know he works hard. He just needs to combine that with a determination to get back. And he's done it before. Individually, it is satisfying to overcome it all. You come back a much better player. Brent has had to endure a few hurdles. It's a bitter pill to swallow, but that's fate.

The man they loved to hate

IT'S A CLICHÉ OFTEN USED BY SPORTSWRITERS—if you were fighting in the trenches, Joe Blow would be the bloke you'd like to have next to you. For Joe Blow substitute the name of any of the hardmen in this book. In the modern era, when the game has been largely sanitised, it would most probably be Cronulla's Paul Gallen who would fit the cliché better than most.

Gal would have held his own in any of the hundred-plus seasons of the sport whose devotees like to call it 'The Greatest Game of All'. Even in the bad old days when it was a case of anything goes. Act first, worry about the consequences later.

As Gallen's State of Origin coach, Ricky Stuart, will attest:

> Paul is one of the most inspirational players I have ever coached. Gal is a player others want to play alongside. I have never met a more competitive person in my life. Gal is old-fashioned. I keep telling him he should have played twenty years ago.

Gallen wouldn't deny Stuart's reading of his psyche. As he told *Sunday Telegraph* journalist James Hooper in early 2010, before the start of what was to prove to be the best of his first ten seasons in the big league:

> I go out there every week to try to do everything I can to win . . . everything! I know I've done some silly things in the past . . . half the people hate me and half the people like me. There are times when I go out there and try to legally take out the opposition's best player. I'm not doing anything illegal, every other team does it. I've been labelled a grub, but I don't think I'm a dirty player.

But, for years, controversy plagued Gallen's life on and off the field. He seemed to be forever in conflict with referees. It was said he was overlooked for the opening State of Origin match in 2010 because of a disagreement with New South Wales coach Craig Bellamy the previous season. He

was fined $10,000 by the National Rugby League for an alleged racist comment to an opposition player—after which he resigned from the Cronulla captaincy—and was then caught in a police blitz urinating in public after a Christmas party, a misdemeanour for which the Sharks also fined him.

'To be labelled a racist was the worst thing,' Gallen told Hooper. 'Half my friends are black or Lebanese . . . from back out home in [the tough outer-western Sydney suburb of] Greystanes . . . and my brother-in-law is from Papua New Guinea. So that was pretty disgusting. I just thought it was wrong. It was something that happened, but it was something that was sorted out on the field just as quickly.' Indeed, the opposition player involved refused to make an official complaint. Instead, the NRL took action independently.

The turnaround on and off the field was dramatic. Gallen lost none of his fire. However, his performances as an 80-minute player for Cronulla were incredible, considering the fact that the Sharks were languishing near the bottom of the ladder. His 505 hit-ups and runs—he became the first Sharks player to top 500 since the recording of statistics—was over 100 more than the next best in the NRL, Brisbane's Corey Parker. Gallen made more metres than any NRL player (4060, at an average of 177 per appearance). He was among the top half-dozen tacklers, making 800, at an average of almost 40 per game. And to show there was more than just brawn involved, his 68 offloads were second only to Parramatta's Feleti Mateo (72).

On the representative scene he was also a major force. His performances in the mid-season Trans-Tasman Test and the Four Nations Tournament at the end of the year won him the Harry Sunderland Medal as Australia's International Player of the Year, and he was on the short-list of five for the Golden Boot, awarded to the best player in the world. When it came to the fans choosing the NRL All Stars side for the 2011 season-opening clash with the Indigenous All Stars, Gallen topped the poll.

Opposite: Paul Gallen was certainly hard to tackle.

And, to cap it all, he was handed back the Sharks captaincy for 2011 by coach Shane Flanagan. The Cronulla mentor dismissed suggestions he was courting danger:

> There would be some people who would be worried. But over the past twelve months he's definitely changed. He has been sensational both on and off the field. He is now one of the great, inspirational leaders and great rugby league players. He has worked very hard behind the scenes with children and for the community. And he has done so for the right reasons, not for the publicity.

Gallen proved his club coach to be right. At the end of the season he won his second straight Harry Sunderland Medal and was named as the best prop in the world by the Golden Boot judges. In 2012 it was more of the same as Gallen inspired the Sharks to become genuine Premiership contenders, making more hit-ups than any forward in the game and an average of more than 200 metres with these bullocking bursts.

'I've been labelled a grub, but I don't think I'm a dirty player.'

Paul Gallen

Thank god, it's Thaiday

SAM THAIDAY AND LUCIANO PAVAROTTI had a lot in common. Both were always big men—although Pavarotti outweighed the Brisbane Broncos captain by about 25 kilograms. The Italian was an imposing figure centre-stage at places such as the Sydney Opera House and Covent Garden in London, while Thaiday has drawn gasps of awe from the fans at Brisbane's Lang Park complex, Wembley Stadium in the British capital and other major sporting arenas around the world.

Who could forget Pavarotti's rendition of 'O Sole Mio'?

O sole
O sole mio
Sta 'nfronte a te!
Sta 'nfronte a te!

Or to give its English translation:

The sun
My own sun
It's in your face!
It's in your face!

That could well sum up the way Thaiday plays rugby league. A shining symbol on the footy field whose crunching tackles and 'take no prisoners' style of charging downfield were most definitely up in your face.

Fans marvel at the way Thaiday runs onto the pitch and immediately takes on the opposition forwards as if there were no tomorrow. Many wonder: 'Just what does he do in the dressing room to fire himself up?' Would you believe he does nothing except maybe take a nano-nap or listen to a track or six of Pavarotti? Thaiday says it is 'weird, really' and explains:

People assume I listen to some heavy metal music or bang my head against the door of a locker. But I have always been exactly the opposite. I sometimes have a sleep before a game. On other occasions I sit there listening to some opera. I just like to relax. But once I get onto the field I switch on. I know then that it is time to start working. That's when I fire up. I try to make sure that my first tackle hurts and my first hit-up is at 100 miles an hour. Then I build on that. Sometimes I need an opposition forward to put a big hit on me to get me going. If I get hit really hard the engine goes into overdrive.

When it does, it's a case of 'God help the opposition', or if you are a Broncos' fan, 'Thank God, it's Thaiday.'

THAIDAY'S SHOCK OF WILD HAIR AND WIDE GRIN make him instantly recognisable in the senior ranks. But it wasn't always the case. Even though he showed some talent at Kirwan High School in Townsville he had trouble catching the eye of the officials at the city's NRL club, the North Queensland Cowboys. In 2001, as a kid just turned 16, Thaiday attended a Cowboys' development camp. But the powers-that-be were unimpressed. The following year he returned but was again snubbed when it came to handing out scholarships. His family felt the pain of rejection, too.

His mum, Julie Thaiday, recalled the setbacks only too well:

Sam missed out the first year. Then, twelve months later, he came home with a big purple ribbon for Player of the Camp. Yet they still told him there was no money to help him continue in the game. Then we read that they'd signed someone else. Sam wanted to play for the Cowboys. He didn't want to leave home at such a young age. Unfortunately, they didn't see what was right under their nose. They were donkeys for ignoring his obvious talents.

Opposite: How about that, you cockroaches? Sam Thaiday serves it up to the New South Wales State of Origin players after a Queensland try.

Julie Thaiday refused to allow her son's dreams to be shattered and contacted the legendary Broncos talent scout Cyril Connell, pleading for the Brisbane side to give Sam a chance to prove himself. And prove himself he did! The following year Thaiday made his first-grade debut, against the Bulldogs, and there was no looking back. By 2006 he had made his debut both at Origin and Test level.

But before becoming a first-choice fixture in both the Queensland and Australian line-ups he had to overcome a personal setback. The year after his elevation to representative status he was knocked for six by the suicide of his best mate, former Broncos club-mate Joey Clarke, with whom he had shared a flat. Thaiday said he had trouble coping with the loss:

I had to step back and look at a lot of things. I turned to others for comfort. I had some counselling sessions. There were a lot of questions for which I couldn't find answers and I guess I never will. But I've come to terms with it all and I will always have good memories of Joey.

A romance with a former schoolfriend from Kirwan High, Rachel Evans, certainly helped. Thaiday said:

I was happy being single and living the single life. This involved too much partying and not enough concentration on footy. But being with Rachel I became more settled at home and it helped my football.

The couple eventually tied the knot late in 2011 after the two best years of Thaiday's career. Both seasons he was named the best second-rower in the world by the respected British magazine *Rugby League World* (chosen by the same judges who awarded the Golden Boot to the Test Player of the Year) as well as taking out the Dally M award as the National Rugby League's Second-Rower of the Year. And the Broncos announced he would be handed the first-grade captaincy for 2012, after the retirement of Darren Lockyer. Thaiday's contract would also be extended until the end of 2015.

Thaiday had been Lockyer's unofficial minder on the field, taking many of the knocks meant for his skipper before the great full-back-turned-five-eighth hung up his boots. To describe his role, Thaiday draws a parallel with the 1992 Hollywood movie *The Bodyguard*:

I'm kind of like Kevin Costner and he's my Whitney Houston. That's fine, I quite enjoy the role. We both make each other look good, I help him out in defence and he helps me out in attack.

And as to how Thaiday goes about his job? 'You want to keep your players safe. So as long as everyone's safe and no one's getting badly injured, a little bit of a face rub doesn't really hurt.'

HOW MANY FOOTBALLERS RECALL THEIR MEETINGS WITH SAM THAIDAY...

Matt finish

SUNDAY, 4 April 2004. It was the day when the life of teenager Matt King changed forever . . . the day when he played his first game of professional rugby league, for the London Broncos Academy (Under-18s) side. It was just 20 seconds into the game at Halifax that King made the first tackle of the afternoon. It was to be his last. He snapped his spinal cord and was left paralysed from the neck down. For the rest of his life he would be dependent upon a ventilator to breathe.

'I remember lying on the pitch immediately after the tackle. I knew exactly what I'd done,' he explained. Especially when the paramedics arrived and began their questions: 'Move your toes. Can you feel me touching you?'

'I couldn't feel any of it,' King recalled. 'It was terrifying. I remember thinking how I just wanted to die.' He was airlifted to a hospital in Leeds and eventually a bed was found at the internationally acclaimed spinal unit at the Stoke Mandeville Hospital in southern England.

King said that was when it really hit home what he'd done:

All my friends were planning to start university courses and there I was—stuck in hospital. My future looked really bleak. They were hard times, especially at night with your thoughts, asking myself why me, what have I done to deserve this?

But as the adage tells us . . . when the going gets tough, the tough get going. King had incredible support from his family and friends. 'These people hadn't given up on me, so it would have been wrong for me to give up,' is the way he approached it all. 'What sort of life would it be just to sit at home watching television? It would be no more than an existence.'

And, after all, while his body didn't function, he still had a very active brain. King went back to school and finished his A-levels (the equivalent of Australia's Higher School Certificate), getting straight As. He studied law at the University of Hertfordshire, and achieved a degree with

Matt King at Wembley Stadium with Sam Tompkins, full-back in the England squad for the 2011 Gillette Four Nations Tournament (Picture: SWPix.com)

first-class honours. Today he works as a solicitor with a London law firm that specialises in catastrophic personal injuries, especially those to the spine and brain. In between he has fulfilled a dream to compete in the New York Marathon.

A friend of his grandmother, a watercolour artist, taught him to paint with a mouthpiece and for the past two years he has painted Christmas cards to raise money for the Rugby League Benevolent Fund, which had given him a lot of financial support while he built a career for himself and enabled him, in his words, 'to become a taxpayer'.

In 2011, before the Four Nations Tournament match at Wembley Stadium between the home side and Australia, King was asked to present the jerseys to each member of the England side. He told them of his fight and reminded them of their responsibilities when they took the Aussies, stressing the importance of looking after your team-mates and covering for them. Coach Steve McNamara placed each jumper on King's lap and members of the team, from full-back Sam Tomkins through to the four interchange players, came forward in turn to collect their jersey.

'Matt is a truly inspirational character who has overcome adversity to become very successful,' McNamara explained. 'He has a fantastic "can do" attitude which has certainly inspired my players.'

Hooker James Roby agreed. 'This was an honour for us. This was real life and a truly humbling experience.'

In June 2012, King's charity work was rewarded with an Order of the British Empire (OBE) award in the Queen's Jubilee Honours List.

As King pointed out, 'Looking back on those early days I spent in hospital I would never have thought that I would get to where I am today. Of course, there are dark moments. But you don't have to be disabled to feel like that. It's part of human nature. Maybe my life is different now. It's certainly not the life I would have chosen. But I want to make it clear to everyone that I have a good life.'

Appendix: Career details of the hardmen

The following are the available statistics to the start of the 2012 season. Until recent years, club statistics, especially in France and for many English sides, were almost nonexistent—hence the absence of some details. Note: the Clive Churchill Medal was awarded retrospectively by a panel of experts in 2008 for grand finals held between 1954 and 1985.

Jack Arkwright (1902–1990)

Clubs:	Warrington (164 appearances, 1929–34)
	St Helens (1934–45)
Tests:	Great Britain (6 appearances, 1936–37)
Internationals:	England (5 appearances, 1933–38)
Honours:	Warrington Hall of Fame
	St Helens Hall of Fame

Arthur Beetson (1945–2011)

Clubs:	Balmain Tigers (74 appearances, 1966–70)
	Hull Kingston Rovers (12 appearances, 1968)
	Eastern Suburbs Roosters (131 appearances, 1971–78)
	Parramatta Eels (16 appearances, 1979–80)
	Also played with Roma (1962–64) and Redcliffe (1965–81)
Tests:	Australia (18 appearances, 1966–77)
Honours:	Order of Australia Medal
	Immortal
	Australian Team of the Century
	Australian Hall of Fame
	Australia's Test captain (1975–77)
	New South Wales Team of the Century

Arthur Beetson (cont.)

Honours: Queensland Team of the Century
Indigenous Team of the Century
Wests Tigers Team of the Century
Balmain Tigers Team of the Century
Sydney Roosters Team of the Century
Clive Churchill Medal (1974)

Brian Bevan (1924–1991)

Clubs: Eastern Suburbs (7 appearances, 1942–46)
Warrington (695 appearances, 1946–62)
Blackpool Borough (42 appearances, 1962–64)

Internationals: Other Nationalities (16 appearances, 1949–55)
British Empire (1 appearance, 1952)

Records: World record of 796 tries (plus 36 in 'friendly' matches)

Honours: Australian Team of the Century
Australian Hall of Fame
British Hall of Fame
Warrington Hall of Fame
One of four players depicted on British Royal Mail postage stamps for Centenary of Rugby League (1995)

Herbert Bolt (1894–1916)

Club: Newtown (52 appearances, 1912–15)

Les Boyd (1956–)

Clubs:	Western Suburbs Magpies (68 appearances, 1976–79)
	Manly Warringah Sea Eagles (75 appearances, 1980–84)
	Warrington (86 appearances, 1985–89)
	Also played for Cootamundra (1973–75 and 1991–93)
Tests:	Australia (17 appearances, 1978–82)
Honours:	Harry Sunderland Medal (UK) (1986)

Mark Broadhurst (1966–)

Clubs:	Manly Warringah Sea Eagles (44 appearances, 1981–82)
	Illawarra Steelers (24 appearances, 1983)
	Hull Kingston Rovers (97 appearances, 1983–86)
	Also played for Papanui (1975–86)
Tests:	New Zealand (17 appearances, 1979–83)

Élie Brousse (1921–)

Clubs:	RC Roanne (1939–47)
	RC Marseille (1948–49)
	Lyon (1950–54)
Tests:	France (11 appearances, 1949–53)
Internationals:	France (19 appearances, 1946–52)

Preston Campbell (1977–)

Clubs:	Gold Coast Chargers (14 appearances, 1998)
	Cronulla–Sutherland Sharks (54 appearances, 1999–2002)
	Penrith Panthers (96 appearances, 2003–06)
	Gold Coast Titans (103 appearances, 2007–2011)
Honours:	Captain Indigenous All Stars (2010 and 2011)

Clive Churchill (1927–1985)

Clubs: South Sydney Rabbitohs (157 appearances, 1947–58)
Also played for Central Newcastle (1946–47),
Brisbane Norths (1959) and Moree Boomerangs (1961)

Tests: Australia (37 appearances, 1948–56)

Honours: Member of the Order of Australia

Honours: Immortal
Australian Team of the Century
Australian Hall of Fame
Australia's Test captain (1950–55)
New South Wales Team of the Century
New South Wales Player of the Year (1949 and 1950)
South Sydney Team of the Century
Newcastle Team of the Century
Man of the Match award in Premiership grand final
named after him
Clive Churchill Medal (1954)

Douglas Clark (1891–1951)

Club: Huddersfield (485 appearances, 1909–27)

Tests: Great Britain (11 appearances, 1911–20)

Records: Most games for Huddersfield (485)

Honours: Great Britain Hall of Fame
Huddersfield Hall of Fame

Brian Clay (1934–1987)

Clubs: Newtown Bluebags (30 appearances, 1953–55)
St George Dragons (183 appearances, 1957–67)
Also played for Griffith (1956)

Tests: Australia (8 appearances, 1957–60)

Honours: Clive Churchill Medal (1961)

Arthur Clues (1924–1998)

Clubs: Western Suburbs Magpies (50 appearances, 1943–46)
Leeds (238 appearances, 1947–54)
Hunslet (83 appearances, 1954–47)

Tests: Australia (3 appearances, 1946)

Internationals: Other Nationalities (14 appearances, 1949–55)

Honours: Western Suburbs Magpies Team of the Century

Jason Croker (1973–)

Clubs: Canberra Raiders (318 appearances, 1991–2006)
Catalan Dragons (58 appearances, 2007–09)

Tests: Australia (5 appearances, 2000)

Records: Most appearances for Canberra (318)
Most tries for Canberra (120)

Peter Dimond (1938–)

Clubs: Western Suburbs Magpies (155 appearances, 1958–67)
Also played for Dapto (1957), South Newcastle (1968–71) and Maitland (1972)

Tests: Australia (10 appearances, 1958–66)

Honours: Western Suburbs Magpies Team of the Century

John Donnelly (1954–1986)

Clubs: Western Suburbs Magpies (148 appearances, 1975–84)
Also played for Gunnedah (1972–74) and Southend
Invicta (1985–86)

Tests: Australia (4 appearances, 1975–78)

Honours: New South Wales Country Player of the Year (1973)
Western Suburbs Magpies Team of the Century

Frank Farrell (1918–1985)

Club: Newtown Bluebags (204 appearances, 1938–51)

Tests: Australia (4 appearances, 1946–48)

Honours: Newtown Team of the Century

Frank Foster (1940–)

Clubs: Workington Town (1962–64)
Hull Kingston Rovers (130 appearances, 1964–69)
Bradford Northern (1969–71)
Barrow (1971)
Oldham (47 appearances, 1971–73)

Tests: Great Britain (1 appearance, 1967)

Paul Gallen (1981–)

Club: Cronulla–Sutherland Sharks (180 appearances, 2001–10)

Tests: Australia (15 appearances, 2008–10)

Internationals: Prime Minister's XIII (2 appearances, 2006–07)

Honours: Harry Sunderland Medal (Australia) (2010 and 2011)

Mark Geyer (1967–)

Clubs:	Penrith Panthers (135 appearances, 1987–2000)
	Balmain Tigers (13 appearances, 1993)
	Western Reds (32 appearances, 1995–97)
	Also played for Umina Bunnies (1994)
Tests:	Australia (3 appearances, 1990–91)

Johnny Graves (1926–1983)

Clubs:	South Sydney Rabbitohs (77 appearances, 1947–52)
	Also played for Maitland (1945–46), Charleville (1953), Cootamundra (1954), Camden Haven (1955–56) and Narrabri (1960)
Tests:	Australia (7 appearances, 1948–51)
Records:	Most tries in a Premiership grand final (4 in 1951)

Douglas Greenall (1927–2007)

Clubs:	St Helens (487 appearances, 1946–59)
	Wigan (3 appearances, 1959–60)
	Bradford Northern (4 appearances, 1960–61)
Tests:	Great Britain (6 appearances, 1951–54)
Internationals:	England (6 appearances, 1951–53)

Ben Gronow (1887–1967)

Clubs:	Huddersfield (395 appearances, 1910–28)
	Batley (16 appearances, 1928–29)
	Featherstone Rovers (23 appearances, 1929–30)
	Also played for Grenfell (1926)
Tests:	Great Britain (7 appearances, 1911–20)
Internationals:	Wales (12 appearances, 1910–23)
	Other Nationalities (2 appearances, 1924–26)

Ben Gronow (cont.)

Records:	British Championship record number of goals (147 in 1919–20)
Honours:	Huddersfield Hall of Fame

Duncan Hall (1925–2011)

Clubs:	Brothers, Rockhampton (1945–47)
	Brisbane Valleys (1948–49)
	Home Hill (1950)
	Newtown, Toowoomba (1951–52)
	Brisbane Western Suburbs (1954–57)
Tests:	Australia (21 appearances, 1948–55)
Honours:	Australian Team of the Century
	Australian Hall of Fame
	Queensland Team of the Century

Brian Hambly (1938–2008)

Clubs:	South Sydney Rabbitohs (33 appearances, 1956–58)
	Parramatta Eels (105 appearances, 1961–67)
	Also played for Wagga Magpies (1959–60)
	and Lithgow Shamrocks (1968–69)
Tests:	Australia (21 appearances, 1959–65)
Honours:	New South Wales Country Team of the Century
	Parramatta Team of the Century

Jack Harrison VC (1890–1970)

Clubs:	York (5 appearances, 1911–12)
	Hull FC (116 appearances, 1912–1916)
Honours:	Victoria Cross
	Military Cross

Brett Hodgson (1978–)

Clubs:	Western Suburbs Magpies (49 appearances, 1997–99)
	Parramatta Eels (73 appearances, 2000–03)
	Wests Tigers (102 appearances, 2004–08)
	Huddersfield Giants (45 appearances, 2009–10)
	Warrington Wolves (23 appearances, 2011)
Internationals:	Exiles (1 appearance, 2011)
Honours:	Man of Steel (2009)

Andrew Johns (1974–)

Clubs:	Newcastle Knights (249 appearances, 1993–2007)
	Warrington Wolves (3 appearances, 2005)
Tests:	Australia (24 appearances, 1995–2006)
Records:	Highest Premiership points when he retired (2176)
	Most games for Newcastle (249)
	Most goals for Newcastle (917)
Honours:	Australian Team of the Century
	Australia's Test captain (2002–03)
	New South Wales Team of Century
	Golden Boot (1999 and 2001)
	Dally M Medal (1998, 1999 and 2002)
	Clive Churchill Medal (2001)

William Johnston (1881–1951)

Clubs:	Wigan (1908–10)
	Warrington (1910)
Tests:	New Zealand (8 appearances, 1907–08)
Honours:	UK 'Cheltenham Nines' Man of the Match Award named after him

Vince Karalius (1932–2008)

Clubs:	St Helens (252 appearances, 1951–62)
	Widnes (128 appearances, 1962–66)
Tests:	Great Britain (12 appearances, 1958–63)
Honours:	Great Britain Hall of Fame
	St Helens Hall of Fame
	Widnes Hall of Fame

Noel Kelly (1936–)

Clubs:	Western Suburbs Magpies (111 appearances, 1961–69)
	Also played for Ipswich Railways (1956–57),
	Ipswich Brothers (1958–59), Ayr (1960) and
	Wollongong (1970)
Tests:	Australia (28 appearances, 1959–68)
Honours:	Australian Team of the Century
	New South Wales Team of the Century
	Wests Tigers Team of the Century
	Western Suburbs Magpies Team of the Century

Peter Kelly (1959–)

Clubs:	Newtown Jets (33 appearances, 1982–83)
	Canterbury–Bankstown Bulldogs
	(68 appearances, 1984–87)
	Penrith Panthers (40 appearances, 1988–90)
	Also played for Eden (1976–79), Lakes United (1980),
	Waratah Mayfield (1981) and Entraignes (1980–81)

Glenn Lazarus (1965–)

Clubs:	Canberra Raiders (92 appearances, 1987–91)
	Brisbane Broncos (108 appearances, 1992–97)
	Melbourne Storm (44 appearances, 1998–99)
Tests:	Australia, Australian Rugby League
	(20 appearances, 1990–99)
	Australia, Super League (1 appearance, 1997)
Honours:	New South Wales Country Team of the Century

Peter Madsen (1901–1979)

Club:	Toowoomba Brothers (1921–37)
Tests:	Australia (9 appearances, 1929–36)
Honours:	Queensland Team of the Century
	Australia's Test captain (1933)

Benji Marshall (1985–)

Club:	Wests Tigers (155 appearances, 2003–11)
Tests:	New Zealand (25 appearance, 2005–11)
Honours:	New Zealand's captain (2009–11)
	Golden Boot (2010)

Louis Mazon (1921–1969)

Club:	AS Carcassonne
Tests:	France (8 appearances, 1949–53)
Internationals:	France (1948–54)

Jim Mills (1944–)

Clubs:	Halifax (38 appearances, 1965–68)
	North Sydney Bears (37 appearances, 1970–72)
	Widnes (190 appearances, 1972–81)
	Also played for Bradford Northern, Salford and Workington Town
Tests:	Great Britain (6 appearances, 1974–79)
Internationals:	Wales (13 appearances, 1975–79)
Honours:	Widnes Hall of Fame

Adrian Morley (1977–)

Clubs:	Leeds Rhinos (149 appearances, 1995–2000)
	Sydney Roosters (113 appearances, 2001–06)
	Bradford Bulls (6 appearances, 2005)
	Warrington Wolves (104 appearances, 2007–11)
Tests:	Great Britain (30 appearances, 1996–2007)
	England (20 appearances, 1996–2011)
Honours:	Great Britain's captain (2010)
	Leeds Greats of the Millennium (2009)

Herb Narvo (Herman Nawo) (1912–1958)

Clubs:	Newtown Bluebags (48 appearances, 1937–49)
	St George Dragons (13 appearances, 1946)
	Also played for Newcastle Norths (1933–50), Cootamundra (1947) and Camden (1948)
Tests:	Australia (4 appearances, 1937–38)
Honours:	New South Wales Country Team of the Century
	Newtown Team of the Century
	Newcastle Team of the Century

John O'Neill (1943–1999)

Clubs:	South Sydney Rabbitohs (150 appearances, 1965–76)
	Manly Warringah Sea Eagles (51 appearances, 192–74)
	Also played for Gunnedah (1959–64)
Tests:	Australia (10 appearances, 1970–74)

Édouard Ponsinet (1923–2006)

Club:	AS Carcassonne (1944–1952)
Tests:	France (10 appearances, 1947–53)
Internationals:	France (9 appearances, 1949–53)

Alan Prescott (1927–1998)

Clubs:	Halifax (40 appearances, 1945–49)
	St Helens (404 appearances, 1949–60)
Tests:	Great Britain (28 appearances, 1951–58)
Internationals:	England (8 appearances, 1950–57)
	British Empire (1 appearance, 1952)
Honours:	St Helens Hall of Fame
	Lance Todd Trophy (1956)
	Medal for Man of Ashes series played in England named after him

Terry Randall (1951–)

Club:	Manly Warringah Sea Eagles (208 appearances, 1970–82)
Tests:	Australia (11 appearances, 1975–77)
Honours:	Manly Warringah Sea Eagles Dream Team

Tommy Raudonikis (1950–)

Clubs:	Western Suburbs Magpies (201 appearances, 1969–79)
	Newtown Jets (37 appearances, 1980–82)
	Also played for Wagga Kangaroos (1969) and
	Brisbane Brothers (1983)
Tests:	Australia (29 appearances, 1972–80)
Honours:	Australia's Test captain (1973)
	Western Suburbs Magpies Team of the Century

Mal Reilly (1948–)

Clubs:	Manly Warringah Sea Eagles
	(89 appearances, 1971–75)
	Castleford (316 appearances, 1968-85)
Tests:	Great Britain (9 appearances, 1970)
Internationals	England (3 appearances, 1977)
Honours:	Order of the British Empire
	Lance Todd Trophy (1969)
	Castleford Hall of Fame
	Manly Warringah Sea Eagles Dream Team

Kevin Ryan (1934–)

Clubs:	St George Dragons (106 appearances, 1960–66)
	Canterbury–Bankstown Bulldogs
	(52 appearances, 1967–69)
Tests:	Australia (2 appearances, 1964)
Honours:	Clive Churchill Medal (1965)

John Sattler (1942–)

Clubs:	South Sydney Rabbitohs (195 appearances, 1963–72)
	Also played for Kurri-Kurri (1961–62),
	Brisbane Wests (1973–74) and Brisbane Norths (1975)
Tests:	Australia (4 appearances, 1969–71)
Honours:	Australia's Test captain (1969–70)

Ray Stehr (1913–1983)

Clubs:	Eastern Suburbs (174 appearances, 1929–46)
	Also played for Mudgee (1934)
Tests:	Australia (11 appearances, 1933–38)

Brent Tate (1982–)

Clubs:	Brisbane Broncos (164 appearances, 2001–07)
	New Zealand Warriors (48 appearances, 2008–10)
	North Queensland Cowboys (9 appearances, 2011)
Tests:	Australia (23 appearances, 2002–10)

Sam Thaiday (1985–)

Club:	Brisbane Broncos (147 appearances, 2003–2011)
Tests:	Australia (16 appearances, 2006–11)

Joe Thompson (1902–1983)

Club:	Leeds (390 appearances, 1923–33)
Tests:	Great Britain (12 appearances, 1924–32)
Internationals:	Wales (8 appearances, 1923–32)
	Other Nationalities (5 appearances, 1924–33)

Derek Turner (1933–)

Clubs: Oldham (140 appearances, 1950–55)
Hull Kingston Rovers (135 appearances, 1955–59)
Wakefield Trinity (213 appearances, 1959–66)

Tests: Great Britain (24 appearances, 1956–1962)

Internationals: England (1 appearance, 1962)

Honours: Great Britain's Test captain (1962)
Oldham Hall of Fame
Hull Kingston Rovers Hall of Fame
Wakefield Trinity Hall of Fame

Jack Watkins (1894–1974)

Clubs: Eastern Suburbs Roosters (112 appearances, 1913–26)
Also played for Tumut (1925)

Tests: Australia (7 appearances, 1914–24)

Shane Webcke (1974–)

Clubs: Brisbane Broncos (254 appearances, 1995–2006)
Also played for Brisbane Brothers (1993)

Tests: Australia, Super League (1 appearance, 1997)
Australia, Australian Rugby League
(25 appearances, 1998–2004)

Billy Wilson (1927–1993)

Clubs: St George Dragons (174 appearances, 1948–62)
North Sydney Bears (54 appearances, 1963–67)
Also played for Picton (1950), Barrradine (1951)
and Wagga Magpies (1957)

Tests: Australia (7 appearances, 1959–63)

Honours: Australia's Test captain (1963)
North Sydney Team of the Century

Sources: photographs and illustrations

Pages 12, 15 & 17 Gronow family private collection; Page 23 Newtown
RLFC; Page 25 League Publications; Pages 26 & 27 Newtown RLFC;
Page 29 Pete Player; Page 31 League Publications; Page 39 Eastern
Suburbs RLFC; Page 44 Pete Player; Pages 49, 56 & 58 Newtown
RLFC; Page 68 Pete Player; Page 75 League Publications; Page 78
Louis Bonnery; Page 81 Ray Fletcher; Page 104 League Publications;
Page 109 Wal Sneddon; Page 127 Ulf Kaiser; Page 133 Rank
Organisation Publicity; Page 136 League Publications; Pages 139 &
157 Pete Player; Page 176 Ulf Kaiser; Pages 181 & 186 Pete Player;
Page 189 Louis Bonnery; Page 192 Eric Carney; Page 217 League
Publications; Page 250 Pete Player; Page 253 Wikipedia (author:
Djackmanson); Page 257 League Publications; Page 266 The Gillette
Company; Pages 277 & 301 Pete Player; Page 303 League Publications;
Page 321 Action Photographics. All others from Malcolm Andrews'
private collection.

The publishers would be grateful to hear from any copyright holder
who has not been acknowledged, so that the omission can be rectified
in future editions.